Ginny Dougary was born in Kuwait in 1956 and moved to England at the age of ten. After graduating from Bristol University in 1978 with a BA Hons. degree in English, she landed her first job in journalism the following year, as assistant to Nicholas Bagnall, literary editor of the *Sunday Telegraph*. She later worked in magazine production at the *Radio Times* and *Tatler*, under Tina Brown as editor. From 1981 to 1987 she lived in New York and Sydney, working as arts editor of the *Sydney Morning Herald* and staff writer on the *SMH*'s colour supplement.

In 1988 Ginny Dougary returned to England and was hired by Vicki Woods as staff writer on the *Daily Mail*'s short-lived colour supplement, *Male and Femail*, and became a regular contributor to the *Independent*, among other newspapers and magazines. Since 1992 she has worked for *The Times Magazine*, writing the major monthly interview.

The Executive Tart & Other Myths, an exploration of women in the media, and how they are treated, is her first book. In January 1994, as *The Times* wrote, 'Her interview with Norman Lamont in this magazine created the political brouhaha known as "Lunchgate". After spending two years examining media myth-making for her book, she now has personal experience of how they come about.'

Ginny Dougary and her husband, who is also a journalist, live with their two young sons in London.

The EXECUTIVE TART and Other Myths

Media Women Talk Back

GINNY DOUGARY

Published by VIRAGO PRESS Limited September 1994
42–43 Gloucester Crescent, Camden Town, London NW1 7PD

A CIP catalogue record for this book is available from the British
Library

Typeset by Florencetype Ltd, Kewstoke, Avon
Printed in Britain by Cox and Wyman Ltd, Reading, Berks.

TO MY MOTHER

Contents

Acknowledgements   ix
Introduction   xi

I SCREENED OUT   1
The Television Industry

VERITY LAMBERT, THE DRAMA QUEEN   23
BEEBAN KIDRON, 'I DON'T JUST WANT A
   SLICE OF IT. I WANT THE WHOLE THING'   39
PHILLIPPA GILES, 'I WANT MORE'   49
ANTONIA BIRD, CHALLENGING THE
   STEREOTYPES   57
LIZ FORGAN, 'NOBODY TOLD ME TO RUN
   OFF AND DO EMBROIDERY. EVER'   65
LINDA AGRAN, FUNNY GIRL   73
JANET STREET-PORTER, MADAM YOUTH   83

II ALWAYS THE DEPUTY   95
The Newspaper Industry

LYNN BARBER, 'AIM FOR THE TOP'   121
SUE DOUGLAS, 'WHEN YOU WIN, NOTHING
   HURTS'   131
EVE POLLARD, 'THEY DON'T THINK "GOOD
   BUSINESS BRAIN". THEY THINK "38-D CUP"'   141

III WHO'S GUILTY?   151
The Magazine Industry

LINDA KELSEY, SHE-WOMAN   157

IV WHAT WOULD THEY DO WITH A TAMPON? 167
The Advertising Industry

MARILYN BAXTER, OUTRAGED OF CHARLOTTE
  STREET 191
JENNIFER LAING, 'I'VE NEVER GONE AROUND
  BANGING MY DRUM FOR WOMEN' 201
M.T. RAINEY, 'AWAY FROM ADVERTISING, I'M
  VERY SHY' 211
CHRISTINE WALKER, SHE WHO MUST BE
  OBEYED 221
BARBARA NOKES, CREATIVE GENIUS 231

CONCLUSION 241
EPILOGUE 245
INDEX 251

ACKNOWLEDGEMENTS

I would like to thank all the women, and the handful of men, who agreed to be interviewed by me. They are all extremely busy people but made time to see me; without their co-operation, there would have been no book. I would particularly like to thank Verity Lambert and Linda Agran, who talked to me over many hours and were helpful and supportive throughout. I must also thank Janet Street-Porter for allowing me to sit in on numerous meetings at the BBC in London and Manchester. Thank you to Dragana Hartley for her guidance and for reading and commenting on the advertising section, although I must stress that she bears no responsibility for anything that appears within it. And thank you to Tessa Gooding of the Institute of Practitioners in Advertising for attempting to keep me up-to-date on a fast-changing industry. Thank you to Lawrence Charles of The Computer Centre for coming to my rescue so often, and at such short notice. Thank you, also, to Sara Menguc of Murray Pollinger, who convinced me that I should write this book. As well as being my agent she has been a friend, a therapist and a midwife who has cajoled, coaxed and badgered this book into being. Thank you to Ursula Owen, who took a risk on an unknown quantity when she commissioned this book for Virago, and to Lennie Goodings, my editor, who inherited the project and stuck with it. I must reserve my biggest thanks to the members of my extended family – to Elizabeth and Susan, without whose unstinting helpfulness and rock-solid reliability I would never have been able to do my own work, and latterly to Christine; to my mother, and most of all to my husband, Bruce, whose loving support has kept me going through the long haul. Thank you.

With thanks for permission to use the following: quote by Antonia Bird, *In Sync*, winter 1992, vol 2, no. 4; quote from Shona Martyn and Fenella Souter, *HQ*; quote from *Sex and Sexuality in Broadcasting*, BBC, 1992; speech by Brenda Reid; quote from *Private Eye*; quote from Matthew Parris, *The Times*, 26 October 1993; quote from Sue Phipps, Advertising Association, 1991; and to the *Guardian* for permission to quote from David Mellor's column.

INTRODUCTION

At the turn of the 1990s, when this book was conceived, there was much trumpeting in the media that we were about to enter 'The Decade of Women'. The demographics indicated that, because of a dearth of school leavers, companies would be needing to entice substantial numbers of women back into the workforce.

Media bosses and organisations responded to the rigours of this new climate by commissioning reports and holding conferences on 'The Female Factor'. In 1990, the advertising industry published no less than three major documents on the position of women within the business of advertising, and on the image of women in advertisements themselves.

In 1991, the BBC hosted Spot the Difference, a conference on the future of women in British television. John Birt, the corporation's chief, recommended a six-point-plan for achieving equal opportunity at all levels. Greg Dyke, then managing director of London Weekend Television, announced that 'Change has to come from the top.' Many a brave word was said and laudable commitment made to herald the new decade.

In the same year, Opportunity 2000 was launched to help women reach the upper echelons of corporate life, with the aim of shattering the glass ceiling by the end of the millennium.

And what of the media itself? For the first time three women were editing national newspapers, and a female trio were running their own major-league advertising agencies. London Weekend Television had a female Head of Drama; so did Anglia Television. Verity Lambert's production company, Cinema Verity, was one of the most successful independents, and Janet Street-Porter had just been promoted to an even more senior position at the BBC. This book would clearly be informed by a spirit of optimism.

But as the recession started to make its indelible imprint on the 1990s, the celebration seemed in danger of turning into a wake.

New stereotypes were invented for successful women, in a sort of pre-emptive put-down before women, in any significant numbers, had managed to gain a power base. And, on the odd occasion when a woman did reach the pinnacle of her profession – the first female head of MI5, the first woman Director of Public Prosecutions – reporters seemed to multiply their achievement, seeing serried ranks of prominent women wherever they looked – a picture which is hardly borne out by the facts.

As we drew further into the 1990s, certain sections of the media seemed to reflect, or perhaps to express – which is somewhat more sinister – a creeping ambivalence about whether high-flying females were a good thing. Advertising agencies coined a new title for the successful career woman: The Executive Tart. Advertisements, as the practitioners tend to say, must reflect patterns in society, and women could no longer be restricted to the roles of vacant beauties or homely housewives. The Gold Blend, single-minded, single career woman from the famous advertising soap opera; the Kenco boardroom bully, played by Cherie Lunghi; the Rank Xerox shrewish boss with clever secretary – the ET was as unreal, in her limitations, as the other female creations with whom she continues to share the small screen, 'Two C's in a K' (or, to spell it out, Two Cunts in a Kitchen) – a term which the ad industry came up with in the 1960s.

A BBC producer made a film about the first three women newspaper editors, and called it *Killer Bimbos On Fleet Street*. The shorthand has stuck, and set the trivialising tone for subsequent articles on Eve Pollard. When she moved from the *Sunday Mirror* to become the first female editor of a mid-market newspaper, the *Sunday Express*, the *Observer's* interviewer described her as 'A "Killer Bimbo" who knows how to use her bosom as a cosh'.

Media insiders may justify their choice of subjects, and the way in which they present them, with a range of caveats: we must give the public what it wants; it is our job to reflect the real world; we must entertain as well as inform. But, at the very least, the media has the power to reinforce attitudes and prejudices. And the shorthand it uses to define a particular type of story – 'sexy' or 'unsexy', or a particular type of person, the Executive Tart or the Killer Bimbo – is dangerous because it is diminishing. It creates a mythology of its own which leaks out of the confines of the workplace in which it was created and takes root in current thought. Powerful woman? Must be a tart or a bimbo. What a convenient put-down for any woman brazen enough to rise to the top in a man's world.

The media is a particularly interesting industry to explore because the images it offers impinge on our consciousness whether we like it or not. It is virtually impossible not to form opinions based on what is delivered to us through its various channels.

This book is a collection of interviews with women who *have* risen to the top of their areas of the media: in advertising, newspapers, magazines, film and television. My intention was to explore whether they have any real influence. Do they seek to make any impact as women on the environment in which they work, and are they interested in, or able to shape, the product?

Before I embarked on this book, I certainly had the sense, as a consumer, that the range of female stereotypes in advertisements, and on the large and small screen of cinema and television, was curiously restrictive: babe or bullygirl, victim or vixen. When I started to interview my subjects, I discovered that many of the women felt the same way.

While I do not believe that there is a single 'woman's point of view' or a unique 'feminine sensibility', nor that it is possible to take an advertisement or a television programme and say, 'Look! See! A woman was behind it. Can't you tell?', what is clear is that in the areas of the media where women do have an input, they can make a difference. It will take several generations of equal numbers of women and men in senior positions in these industries (as in others), to gauge more precisely what difference gender can make to the product, as well as to the working environment.

I wanted to look at other issues, too. Given that the media is such an image-conscious business, what sort of image of themselves do these women choose to present? Were their own role models male or female? Are they interested in advancing the careers of other women? How much power do they feel they wield? How do they deal with male prejudice? Or are they insulated from it because of their high-ranking positions? How important is it to achieve a balance between home life and work life? Do they believe it is possible to be successful mothers and successful career women? Do they see their roles as pioneers of change, or are they more concerned with their own success or, indeed, survival? And I wanted to establish whether women are making any significant progress in these industries.

I made the decision to focus on women in television, advertising and newspapers (not radio or publishing) because my perception was that these industries are imbued with a particularly male ethos (although I did speak to people in magazine publishing as an addendum to the newspaper section). For the same reason I wished to investigate the Garrick Club end of the media – the BBC and the more up-market newspapers – because it is here that the glass ceiling seems at its most impenetrable.

How did I select the women? The advertising chapters have an innate symmetry because some of the most obvious female subjects to interview – Marilyn Baxter, Jennifer Laing, Barbara Nokes, M.T. Rainey and Christine Walker – each happen to represent a different function of the industry.

Elsewhere the route to selection was less obvious. I wanted to speak to the decision makers and the power brokers in the mainstream media rather than to 'the talent', which is why there are no presenters or camerawomen or writers or, indeed, no black women. (The key decision makers are white; the non-white executive – male or female – is rarely to be seen.) I made an exception in the case of Lynn Barber, formerly the star interviewer of the *Independent on Sunday*, for a variety of reasons: I admired her writing; her critics – and even some of her fans – tended to call her interviews 'bitchy', and I was curious to know her response to this. She had once told me that at the *Independent* there was a more chauvinist culture than at *Penthouse*, the soft-porn men's magazine where she had worked in her twenties. This comment alone seemed worthy of examination.

I also extended the book to include some of the men who run the media since, for the time being at any rate, it is their attitudes towards women, both as employees and as consumers, which dictate working conditions within the media and women's place in the world it projects.

This book is not intended to be a definitive portrait, but I hope that the sixteen major interviews, and many micro-interviews with less well-known women, give some sense of the flavour of the different media industries and the personalities of some of its key female players.

Two distinctive themes emerged: power, or the lack of it, and the desire of many women to extend the definition of 'success' beyond the purely professional. Verity Lambert, the independent drama producer, seemed to speak for many women when she told me, 'It's not to do with having power over people; it's to do with having a wider influence over the programme-making.' So did Beeban Kidron, the film director, when she said, 'I think people are very unsophisticated about their definition of success. They don't get that it's important to have a whole life.'

A major preoccupation of the younger women was how they were going to combine a career with motherhood. As a working mother myself, this issue is of particular interest to me as well. Most of the women I spoke to in their forties and older felt that such an option was neither possible nor advisable.

Surprisingly, perhaps, the younger women said their male bosses – TV heads or newspaper editors – had expressed the view, with a sort of weary resignation about its inevitability, that their successors are likely to be female. The thirtysomethings are impatient for that moment to arrive. Twenty years from now, maybe there will have been a female Controller at the BBC. Perhaps a woman will be editing *The Times* or the *Independent* or the *Guardian* or the *Daily Telegraph*. The creative departments of advertising agencies might employ more than a handful of women. Then this book will seem like a quaint relic from the bad old days. Let's say fifty years, just to be on the safe side.

Ginny Dougary, 1994

SCREENED OUT

The Television Industry

'Why isn't there an organisation for Men in Film? There is. It's called the British Film Industry'

(BRENDA REID, HEAD OF DRAMA AT ANGLIA, AND CHAIRWOMAN OF WOMEN IN FILM AND TELEVISION)

Television executives have a distinctive form of communicating with one another. Across a crowded room, members of the TV tribe greet one another by clasping one hand over an ear, followed by an energetic fluttering of the lashes and twisting of the head. This curious, Masonic gesture means 'Phone me' or 'I'll phone you', depending on their relative status.

This is an environment in which people refer to 'windows' in their slimline Filofaxes, and expect you to know what they mean. (*Translation*: 'I have a small gap in my hectic schedule and could possibly fit you in for a pre-breakfast meeting.') Deals are set up or cemented with a flourish of personal business cards. Pity the poor soul who does not possess one.

Like most media insiders, television people are consumed with the machinations of their own industry. For an outsider attending television conferences or festivals, the details of quotas, of funding and staffing levels and redistribution of money, have an eye-glazing effect. But they are instructive for other reasons. One may observe, for instance, the truism that there is no clear female orthodoxy among the women who work in television.

At one such conference, hosted by a panel of television women, the atmosphere prickles with tension. A woman director says, 'I enjoy working with female production teams because women don't have problems with their egos . . .' and is stopped short by a woman in the audience yelling 'BOLLOCKS!' At another session, on the future of women in comedy, Jaci Stephens, the novelist and television critic, roundly upbraided the female creator of a comedy series, *Birds of a Feather*. The jokes, she complained, operate on the premise that innuendoes about bananas are side-splittingly funny. 'Is this your idea of what is supposed to appeal to women?' she challenged.

Where there *is* consensus among the women who work in film and television is that they feel they are not getting their fair share of the action. They are still excluded from the top jobs, and their views and interests are still not shaping the product.

- In any medium, the reporting of news is by its very nature an edited, partial and selected view of what happens in the world; as one woman said, 'You cannot separate the issue of the employment of women in senior positions from the effect that has on what is screened. Television news, on the whole, is run by men. Women and women's concerns largely disappeared from the screen during the general election.'

- A female drama producer at the BBC says that she repeatedly has to pitch her ideas to a male, who then decides whether to commission a project or not. Women's ideas, she says, tend to rely on atmosphere over narrative thrust, which makes them harder to sell. 'So quite often the ideas that are brought to me by women writers don't even get on to the page.'

- Why are the images of women in comedy, on both sides of the camera, so stereotypical? ask the women who work in television. And why are so many comedies apparently designed for less than half the audience? They already know the answer.

Juliet Blake, an independent producer in television comedy, says, 'If you look at comedy programmes in which funny women are not portrayed as silly, simpering pea-brains, you will find that women have been at the helm of the production.

'Ruby Wax's series *The Full Wax* had an almost entirely female production team and was overseen and produced by Janet Street-Porter. French and Saunders write and perform all their own material, and are in control of what they do and when they do it.

'Until there are at least a few more women writers and producers working in comedy, knicker-twiddling and cleavage-waving will always be part of comedy sketch shows.'

Television events are a useful conduit for meeting women who have no power at all in the business. They offer a different perspective on their industry, and on the more established women whom I interviewed for this book. For it is one thing to hear about the loneliness of being at the top from executive women; it is quite another to listen to the stories of women who are on the way up there, or on the way to nowhere.

Some of these women do not aspire to mainstream success. They make art videos or films for local health authorities or documentaries on the rave culture. Those who are intent on more conventional career paths are in the lower or middle ranks of the BBC: researchers, assistant producers, editors.

They say that the women who have made it have risen by adapting themselves to the male culture, and have lost something of themselves in the process. Time and again, they point out that many of the well-known power-women do not have children. And this seems to concern them. One young woman, in her mid-twenties and recently married, also told me that her male bosses at the BBC had indicated that she was over-ambitious to expect to have a successful marriage and a glittering career.

Suzanne, a documentary-maker who has won awards in her native Australia, is struggling to make films in Britain. She is astounded that I intend to devote my book to the likes of Verity Lambert and Linda Agran. 'But they're not role models for women like me,' she says. 'Women are allowed to be producers, since they are glorified nannies. Men are much more hostile to women who want to direct. The response is, "Well, she can be in charge of the piggy bank, but we don't want her playing with the train set."' It is the director who is closest to the product; the producer is usually several steps removed from it.

It is not always spelt out, but when I speak to the younger women the sub-text is clear: women in this generation are not prepared to sacrifice their personal goals for professional success. They believe, or want to believe, that they can have it all.

Spot the Difference, a BBC-sponsored conference held in 1991 on the future of women in television, underlined just how far off their goal was then.

Janet Street-Porter, formerly the BBC's head of youth and entertainment features and head of the BBC's Independent Production Entertainment Group since early 1994, is the most outspoken critic of the male orthodoxy. She has accused the BBC of resembling a 'Masonic league full of ritualistic men in grey suits'. At a London conference on advertising trends, she said, 'Prime time on Saturday night still transmits programming hosted by unattractive, sexist, middle-aged men. One could argue that this reflects the type of people that run television as a whole.'

But at the Spot the Difference conference, Street-Porter's distinctive voice was almost drowned in the clamour from her female peers. Anna Ford, one of the BBC's original heavyweight women newsreaders, who joined the Six o'clock News team in 1989, said, 'The board of governors and the board of management don't mix in the women's network. They don't know who we are, they don't know our frustrations. We want to influence policy . . . It's time for us to say what we want and demand it.'

Jenni Russell, a producer on Channel 4 news and former BBC employee, accused the corporation's news and current affairs division of blatant discrimination. 'I found in news meetings that women who speak out and make a name for themselves and challenge are penalised by being ignored, demoted, or not sent out on jobs.'

Francine Stock, then a presenter of BBC's *Newsnight* and now a BBC news and current affairs reporter, said that the gender problem was as relevant today as it was two decades ago. 'When I left school in the mid-seventies, I thought this battle was over and it would be a meritocracy regardless of gender. I went to university and realised that something was wrong. After that it got worse.'

Carol Haslam, an independent producer, referred to the broadcasting union's early 1980s report on the bias against women in the media. She had used the report as the basis for a programme she made for the BBC. Ten years on, she believes, the equality issue has come full circle.

There was considerable discussion at the conference about the structure of the corporation, which was seen to favour what was regarded as the traditional 'male' approach to work (strictly hierarchical and inflexible, with little or no allowance for the demands of family life) versus the 'female' way (a co-operative and collaborative approach to dealing with power; an acknowledgement that there is a life outside work).

One paper that was delivered at the conference was the result of an attempt to sample whether men and women really do work in different ways. A group of researchers from London's City University (1991) watched the complete production cycle of *Crimewatch* (which still has a predominantly female team, including a woman producer, Liz Mills) and dipped into other production teams which were made up of men and women. The researchers found that Nikki Cheetham, who was then the *Crimewatch* producer and who is now a director of Bazal Productions, a company which produces independent factual entertainment programmes for television, was a model boss for women – a consensual decision-maker, 'aware of individual career aspirations', 'providing career guidance and advice', supportive of her staff, and 'consciously using her power to empower others'. They were particularly impressed by her organisational skills, which enabled her staff to plan their lives outside work.

Although the researchers naturally could not claim that the obverse was true (that male boss equals bad boss), they did find that in mixed teams headed by men, women were challenged and interrupted more. Decisions were frequently taken, not during team meetings, but before or after, to the exclusion of the women in the team.

The researchers' report, *Watching the Crimewatchers: Women, Gender and 'Difference' in the BBC*, includes a list of comments from women which suggests that the BBC could not be described as a female-friendly environment:

- A camerawoman says she was accepted by the male crew when they discovered that she wasn't odd because she was a woman – 'Once they've got to know that you're good at your job . . . and that you don't feel you have anything to prove – you know, being a woman – then it's fine.' ('Are men judged in this way?' the researchers ask.

'As a man first, as a professional second?')
- Sue Cook commented that women presenters are often seen as a sort of sidekick to a male presenter. ('How many instances can you think of where this situation is reversed?' ask the researchers.)
- An actress had to deal with male directors seeking 'dinner and whatever', with the inference that directors often seek to sexualise a professional working relationship. (The researchers ask: 'Do male actors have to deal with women directors seeking "dinner"?')

The corporation has set 1996, when its charter comes up for renewal, as the target date for a more female-friendly look. Thirty per cent of its senior management and 40 per cent of its middle management are to be women. But as one commentator suggested, why not be really adventurous and set the target at 50 per cent throughout?

It was impossible to pinpoint to what extent, if any, the system would be modified or shaped if there were more women in senior positions, particularly since the female presence at this level was felt to be so negligible. Janet Street-Porter quoted a figure of five women and 43 men at top-level meetings, and said, 'I don't feel I fit into the system, nor will I in the future.'

And what of the future? What has happened to Anna Ford's brave words: 'It's time for us to say what we want and demand it'? Has there been any tangible improvement for women in broadcasting since they aired their grievances *en masse* in 1991? John Birt told the Spot the Difference delegates: 'Every time I am confronted by a roomful of men I am struck by the thought that half of those men are standing in the way of more talented people.'

The statistics I was given by the BBC's Corporate Human Resource Planning Department in March 1994 suggested that the director-general has applied himself somewhat vigorously to redistributing that talent. In Network Television, for instance, at the top AMP band (the most senior level at the BBC below Board of Management; includes heads of departments, heads of groups and controllers), the percentage of women has risen from 15 per cent in July 1992 to 31 per cent at 31 December 1993. In Band 4, middle management in Network Television (which includes deputy heads and special assistants), the percentage of women has risen from 20 per cent in July 1992 to 47.8 per cent at 31 December 1993. So the BBC has already exceeded its 1996 target for television at least, three years before its deadline.

The phenomenal increase of women in the workforce in this area of the BBC, however, may be partly accounted for by the fact that in April 1993 the craft and operational side of Network Television – studio technicians, designers etc., jobs which are predominantly filled by men – was transferred to the new Resources Directorate.

In early 1994, I asked Chris Whiley, senior assistant to the chief personnel officer, whether the statistics were also distorted by the number of women on short-term contracts. 'Analysis shows that the difference between men and women on short-term contracts is negligible,' he said.

And how do the independent companies compare? Greg Dyke, then group chief executive of London Weekend Television, told the conference that even though LWT had brought in equal opportunity initiatives years ago, there were still only three women among 40 top executives in 1990. Three years on, Dyke collected the 1993 Women in Business Award on behalf of Helen Auty Black, who had masterminded the Equality programme at LWT. This award, sponsored by the London Business School, is to reward companies for their commitment to promoting and developing woman managers. In March 1994, a quarter of LWT's top 40 executives were women.

In July 1992, Christopher Stoddart, managing director of GMTV, wrote in a letter to *The Times*: 'as we build our staffing towards our launch on 1 January 1993, we find that men in our company are an increasingly endangered species. At the last count our staff comprised 42 women and 21 men, and in our programming department we have 13 women in senior positions (producer/editor/correspondent and above) compared with only five men.'

By 1994, GMTV's staff count was 80 women and 54 men; in the programming department there were 54 women and 40 men. But in February 1993 GMTV's ten-person board shed its only female member, when the station's director of programmes, Liz Howell, was sacked after the breakfast programme failed to perform in the ratings game. Howell's critics found her guilty of the sort of stereotyping of which her male peers are usually accused, when she over-glamorised the image of the presenter, Fiona Armstrong, the former ITN newscaster, in order to enhance the show's so-called F-Factor (the F stood for Fanciability). When I asked Christopher Stoddart about Liz Howell's dismissal, he said, 'As a man fired in the heat of women's lib, I have to say that whoever had been director of programmes at that time, with the viewing figures that we had in the breakfast audience, could have been at risk.'

When I phoned the BBC in the spring of 1993 to find out whether the corporation was planning another Spot the Difference conference, I was passed on and on from person to person – none of whom could help me. Even some of the press officers seemed barely to have heard of the last one. The best I could hope for was, 'Oh yes . . . Gosh, that was a long time ago.' The increasingly fluid nature of employment at the corporation meant that it was hard to track down the original organisers. Eventually I did, and they were most helpful. But it seems clear that, for all the media interest at the time, the impact of the conference was depressingly short-lived.

By 1993, of course, the employees of the BBC and elsewhere were more concerned with keeping their jobs than addressing equal opportunity issues.

*

Sex and Sensibility

*'Broadcasting is frankly male-dominated
– the imagination of television is
dominated by male attitudes and male
fantasies. It is not that we need just more
women, we need many, many more'*

When Lord Rees-Mogg, then chairman of the Broadcasting Standards Council, made this statement in July 1992, it was leapt on by both the tabloid and the quality press. While the former responded with its customary relish for sex and violence (the *Daily Mirror* filled its front page with a huge headline – TOO VIOLENT – and illustrations of smashed TV screens), the qualities' coverage was lively in other ways.

This was partly because Lord Rees-Mogg seemed such an unlikely feminist champion, and partly because some of the programmes which he (or the tabloids) had targeted as unacceptable for female viewers because of the raunchy sex scenes had, in fact, been made by women. Small wonder then that while female commentators applauded the chairman's assertion that 'many, many more women' should be in key positions in broadcasting, they queried his assumption that more women behind the screen would equal less sex on it.

Janet Barron was the co-writer of the television adaptation of *Clarissa* – Samuel Richardson's eighteenth-century novel – and made the decision, early on, to include a rape scene, which 'should be frightening and disturbing'.

'When women do have more representation at the highest level, it should not be with the aim of turning Auntie into Nanny,' Barron wrote in an industry publication. And in the *Guardian*: 'I agree that there should be more women appointed to senior jobs in television, but I do not believe this would result, as the Mary Whitehouse brigade believes, in less sex on television. In fact I believe it would result in more sex.

'Women's concerns are not in some kind of cosy portrayal of sex: we're interested in issues about fear, degradation and danger in sexuality and the relationship between men and women . . .

'Lord Rees-Mogg thinks women want to clean up television, when they actually want issues to be more explicitly dealt with.'

A number of female broadcasters say that the dearth of women at the top does not impede women from making a significant mark on programme-making. Janet Barron, again: 'the content of programmes is deeply influenced by women'.

Sophie Balhetchet, producer of the TV adaptation of Mary Wesley's far from unsexy *The Camomile Lawn*: 'He [Rees-Mogg] says that if there were more female television executives this would have a profound influence on the programmes. I actually think that women do have quite considerable influence on much of the drama on British television.'

The Men's Room was one of the BBC dramas that same year to attract a high number of complaints (20) about its sexual content (the other was Melvyn Bragg's *A Time to Dance*). The key players behind the scenes were women. The drama series was based on a novel by Ann Oakley, adapted by Laura Lamson and directed by Antonia Bird. The focus was on female sexuality and relationships.

While Verity Lambert said she could not tell whether a drama was made by men or women, Bird disagreed: 'I feel that women are frequently treated stereotypically and I believe strongly that *The Men's Room* could have been different if it had not been a largely all-women production. It could have been horrific – the female character [played by Harriet Walter] could so easily have been exploited. It's all to do with how you present images . . .'

The Spot the Difference conference concentrated on the position of women in broadcasting rather than on their image on the screen, but one of the papers did touch on the subject. The researchers who produced the document *Gender and Difference at the BBC* wrote that, during their time at the corporation, they found the prevailing opinion at the BBC was that 'women have distinctive views and distinctive ways of working which seldom, if ever, surface on the television screen. Television continues to portray women in very narrow ways; women working in television have great difficulty in influencing, let alone changing, either the process or the product of programme-making.'

Antonia Bird, whose less controversial television credits include *South of the Border*, *Casualty* and *Inspector Morse*, has written a number of swingeing attacks on the industry. Her particular bugbear is the stereotyping of women, both behind and in front of the camera. Part of the problem would be solved, she argues, if there were more women – not just at senior levels, but at every level of production. This is an extract from an article Bird wrote for *In Sync*, the journal of Women in Film and Television (Winter 1992, vol.2, no.4).

The words come first of course, and that's where, all too often, the rot starts. Always John, never Janet. As a drama director I can manoeuvre the sound, pictures and performances, but film bears the biological imprint of its production team.

Because directors are expected to be male by both the male hierarchy and the public, very few women pursue it as a job option. This must be the key. Fifty per cent women directors would mean we weren't peculiar and I wouldn't feel so incredibly lonely and out on a limb . . .

Why should it be thought peculiar for me to have a female first assistant director [AD] or that two women working together might not be 'a good thing'? Who questions the fact that 90 per cent of the rest of the crew is male and nearly always is? . . .

A woman's perspective within a production can make a big difference to the content of a programme. I fight daily to avoid stereotypical images of women.

It is frightening how many times I still encounter male desires to patronise and stereotype female characters.

The need for greater representation of women is not vitiated by improved attitudes among men. Even the best-intentioned men are inadvertently sexist. The unconscious conspiracy of male writers, directors, crew and actors can only be broken by a strong female presence and solidarity . . .

We must . . . educate and encourage more young women to take up jobs previously considered male preserves. Where are the women operators, sound recordists, sparks, chippies, standby props, drivers, ADs? . . .

The reality of TV and film production is that we are engaged in co-operative enterprise, but the rationale and ethos of our activity reflect values unsympathetic to women, both as workers in the industry and as consumers of its product.

It is less and less about the opportunity to express and address new ideas and issues or challenge old ones, and more and more about appealing to male bosses' ideas of what the audience wants. *How on earth can a predominantly male hierarchy know what a predominantly female audience wants?* (My italics)

Certainly, many of the more controversial dramas of the early 1990s reflect the statement that 'the imagination of television is dominated by male attitudes and male fantasies'. Take *Blackeyes*, for example, Dennis Potter's four-part film about the sexual and literary manipulation of a beautiful, passive model. Or Melvyn Bragg's *A Time to Dance*, the story of a middle-aged man lusting after and possessing a young girl.

Blackeyes did have some unlikely female supporters, Kathy Acker and Germaine Greer among them. 'People always think that artists should write about what should be, rather than what is. I don't expect him [Potter] to be politically correct or to write about liberated women – because they don't exist,' Greer told me.

'What he's doing is writing in a bitter and tragic way about the female icon. Men are trying to pursue it and women are trying to be it, so they're both victims. If I see an outrageous female mask – of tragic passivity and gross sensuality – I don't think it's a reflection of me. Fellini gets the same abuse when he gives shape to male fantasies of women. They are not saying this is how it is, they are saying this is how *we* see you.'

But how often do we see the shape of female fantasies of men – on either the small screen or the large screen? I cannot readily think of a female director or writer who would be given the same licence as Dennis Potter to explore her sexual and emotional psyche on television.

Part of the problem is that the sexual triggers for female audiences are less known or predictable than those of men. When an Australian magazine, *HQ*, attempted to investigate what turned women on in the early 1990s, the results were uniformly un-uniform. Women from the ages of 18 to 80 were asked what they found erotic. The answers were often visual rather than tactile, and were also not always politically correct.

The editors, Shona Martyn and Fenella Souter, explained their reasons for the survey:

> No prizes for guessing what men find erotic. That territory is about as uncharted as downtown Manhattan. It's also not very big. A curve of breast, a flash of leg, a glimpse of genitals . . . and there you have the basic lie of the land. A small but reliable catalogue of visual triggers that work, as any ad man or pornographer will tell you, time and again.
>
> But what do women find erotic? Georgia O'Keefe paintings? Figs? A bunch of violets with the dew still on them? (Give us a break!) A smiling bit of beefcake wearing crutchless lederhosen? Two men in lingerie tongue kissing? Two women in lingerie kissing? . . . Who knows? Given that we're confronted at every turn by

imagery created by men for men, it's rather like trying to imagine what television might be like when you've only heard radio . . .

The mainstream media have been largely silent on the subject of women's erotica, but perhaps that's because it's easier to describe how to prolong orgasm (now that we've all learnt to have one) than to tackle the nebulous area of what arouses women in the first place . . . The novelist Jeanette Winterson, whose books many would find erotic, may be hitting the nail on the head when she says that 'women, unlike men, do not appear to agree on the broadstream of what is sexy'. While men seem to have a sort of erotic esperanto, women seem to speak in many tongues . . .

Oranges Are Not the Only Fruit, Jeanette Winterson's first foray into television, may be offered as an example of an explicitly female sexuality invading the small screen, but since it is about women loving one another it is a special case. Sandi Toksvig, the comic performer and writer, addressed this issue when she wrote for the BSC's 1992 annual review, *Sex and Sexuality in Broadcasting*:

There are strange moral codes about what is acceptable. With *Oranges Are Not the Only Fruit* and *Portrait of a Marriage* there were positive steps towards accepting lesbian love scenes on television. In the latter story, how-ever, of the marriage of Vita and Harold Nicolson, he too had homosexual experiences which were pivotal to their relationship. I do not remember seeing those. We heard about them but there was none of the softly-lit lace-draped panting that was shown with the women. Are images of women making love more acceptable than a male image of the same thing? Or is it that male television executives merely find the one titillating and the other disturbing? If there is a moral code for broadcasting standards shouldn't we make sure it is the same for everyone?

Some women filmmakers (and, to be fair, some male film-makers too) feel that simply by focusing on the naked male they are offering a different – even radical – perspective. The television writer Andrew Davies (*Mother Love*, *The Old Devils*, *House of Cards*, and its sequel, *To Play the King*, *Middlemarch*) told me that his wife always nagged him to put more naked men in his scripts, on the basis that 'fair's fair' and 'Women do like to see male bodies more than is generally thought'. And yet, as he says, 'Men are nearly always shot from behind. So all you see are the buttocks, and some rather flabby ones at that, I'm sorry to say.'

Phillippa Giles – who produced *Oranges Are Not the Only Fruit* (adapted by Jeanette Winterson from her own novel; directed by Beeban Kidron) as well as *Fatal Inversion* and several other Barbara Vine thrillers – has particularly strong feelings about the presentation of women on televi-sion. In the first episode of *Fatal Inversion*, for instance, it was the male bodies which were on display. The two male leads strutted around in the sort of 'posing pouches' favoured by body-builders. The woman, in contrast, was compara-tively decorously dressed in a man's baggy shirt.

'You actually see the men's willies when they come out of the lake,' Giles told me, with some satisfaction. 'I'm offended by the number of gratuitous shots you see of women in the nude: women getting out of the bath, women's breasts floating in the water.'

She believes that women and men have a completely different sense of the erotic. 'For women, eroticism is all to do with context,' she told me. 'In *Fatal Inversion*, we wanted to create a very strong sexual atmosphere which was laced with a homosexual element. Narrative thrust is a very male idea. There was no narrative thrust in *Oranges Are Not the Only Fruit*. It was meandering and atmospheric and slow-moving. All the things that women like. My feeling is that if you have to resort to showing everything, you've probably gone wrong.'

In her BSC essay, Sandi Toksvig wrote that it would be interesting to see if there was a statistical difference between male and female viewers' attitudes to watching sexual activity on the small screen: 'If book sales are anything to go by, then my guess would be that women are more interested in watching romance than actual shagging. It is the moments leading up to intimacy rather than intimacy which attracts . . .

'If that is true, then it is a worrying thought that sexual images presented on television may be those which are in general acceptable to men.'

Lord Rees-Mogg may well be right when he says, 'Women in general see TV as an alien force coming into their living room with standards, values and interests they do not share.' But, it would seem, for the wrong reasons.

*

To the Women in Film and Television awards, sponsored by London Weekend Television, held at the Dorchester Hotel in London. This is a swanky occasion: champagne, celebrities and right-on sentiment. The speeches – serious and funny – are by Anna Ford, Maureen Lipman and Brenda Reid, the WIF chairwoman.

The last time that I saw Reid was at the Edinburgh Television Festival. She had asked Michael Grade, Channel 4's chief executive, how the small independent film companies, which are struggling for support, would be viewed by the station in its more commercially dictated future. Grade ignored her question, and turned to chat to one of his co-panellists.

My neighbour, a struggling independent filmmaker, was stunned. As a regular attender of Women in Film functions, she was used to seeing Brenda Reid in her omnipotent role as chairwoman. If a woman of Reid's stature could be treated in such a way by her male colleagues, she whispered, what hope was there for less-established women like herself?

Brenda Reid's performance today is both spirited and regal. I understood at once why the filmmaker had been amazed to see her chairwoman treated in such a cavalier way by Michael Grade.

Here is Reid's speech in full:

I'd really like to welcome all the gentlemen here today – and it is to them that I address my remarks. It's really great to look around the room and see so many good-looking blokes here. We're delighted to prise you away from your beloved boardrooms where we know you potter happily away all day playing boys' games and making big grown-up decisions. All those things we know nothing about – or do we?

Luckily all you chaps here are totally committed to equality. Of course you are, it said so in your franchise applications and in your charters. We should know: we helped to type them. And all your job descriptions state quite clearly, 'we are an equal opportunities employer'.

So what's going wrong?

Come with me, then, while I walk into any of the 20 terrestrial broadcasting organisations in this country.

The first person I see is a woman – the receptionist. Perhaps I've come to discuss a programme proposal.

Then the second person I see will be a woman – that's the secretary or PA to the senior executive who might commission my idea. *In only nine out of 100 such meetings that senior executive will be a woman.*

Perhaps, however, my appointment is with the technical department. I'll walk past 15 or 20 men before I see a single female face. And if, God forbid, my appointment is with a DG or a chief executive, *there is not one chance that person will be a woman.*

Let me risk boring you for a moment more with some facts: *Sixty per cent* of women in our industry are in poorly paid secretarial or clerical jobs. *Still only 5 per cent of technical jobs are filled by women.* Jobs which are traditionally dominated by women – for example make-up and wardrobe – are considerably less well paid than jobs in which men predominate – electricians, scene painters, etc. etc.

The average man in our industry (and there are some)

is 15 times more likely than a woman to find his way into senior management. [My italics.] Although, funnily enough, female senior managers tend to have higher educational qualifications than their male counterparts. Strange, isn't it?

These statistics may bore you but they sure as hell don't bore me and they don't bore my fellow members of Women in Film and Television.

It's not that we don't trust what you promise in your franchise applications and the like. It's not that we don't believe you really do want to fill your studios with female crews and cram your boardrooms with equal opportunity women.

But . . . just to help you all we can and, incidentally, to help ourselves as well, we started this organisation 18 months ago.

And, believe me, we are here, not just to stay, but to make sure that the balance really does start to swing in our favour. And to recognise that – as 50 per cent of our audience is female – so too should women be represented backstage.

Applause.

I spoke to Brenda Reid in early 1994, and asked her whether the statistics were more encouraging now. 'Not at all,' she said. 'As long as all the decision-making roles are held by men, the status quo will continue. For example, of the 15 ITV boards across the country, there are 102 men in executive directorships. And there are four women. This has to change.'

BBC TELEVISION
Board of Governors: Men – 9; Women – 4
Board of Management: Men – 9; Women – 4
Senior Staff: Men– 23; Women – 4
Senior Staff, Regions: Men – 28; Women – 6
* Top Executives: Men – 199; Women – 21

CHANNEL 4
Executives on Board: Men – 6; Women – 0

S4C
Executives on Board: Men – 3; Women – 2

ANGLIA TELEVISION
Executives on Board: Men – 3; Women – 0

BORDER TELEVISION
Executives on Board: Men – 2; Women – 0

CARLTON TELEVISION
Executives on Board: Men – 6; Women – 0

CENTRAL TELEVISION
Executives on Board: Men – 5; Women – 1

CHANNEL TELEVISION
Executives on Board: Men – 5; Women – 0

GMTV
Executives on Board: Men – 9; Women – 1

GRAMPIAN TELEVISION
Executives on Board: Men – 5; Women – 0

GRANADA TELEVISION
Executives on Board: Men – 5; Women – 0

HTV WALES
Executives on Board: Men – 7; Women – 0

ITN
Executives on Board: Men – 5; Women – 0

LWT
Executives on Board: Men – 12; Women – 1

MERIDIAN BROADCASTING
Executives on Board : Men – 11; Women – 0

SCOTTISH TELEVISION
Executives on Board: Men – 8; Women – 1

TYNE TEES TELEVISION
Executives on Board: Men – 5; Women – 0

ULSTER TELEVISION
Executives on Board: Men – 3; Women – 0

WESTCOUNTRY TELEVISION
Executives on Board: Men – 3; Women – 0

YORKSHIRE TELEVISION
Executives on Board: Men – 8; Women – 0

Independent Television Companies: Overall Statistics[*]

	Total	Men	Women	% Men	% Women
Executives on board	106	102	4	96	4
Board of directors	207	184	23	89	11

[*]This does not include the BBC, Channel 4 or S4C. All statistics were compiled with the assistance of Women in Film and Television in February 1993, partly with reference to the Arthur Andersen Corporate Register in September 1992.

VERITY LAMBERT
THE DRAMA QUEEN

Verity Lambert set up her own production company, Cinema Verity, in 1985. She is one of our most successful independent producers of small-screen drama. Her first job in television was in the early days of Granada, one of Britain's first commercial television stations. At the BBC, Lambert was responsible for introducing the Daleks to *Dr Who*. Her long list of credits since then include *The Naked Civil Servant*, *Rock Follies*, *Minder*, *Rumpole of the Bailey*, *Edward and Mrs Simpson*, *GBH* and the somewhat less acclaimed *Eldorado*.

Verity Lambert and Arthur Daley arrive at the office each day at 10 a.m. And everywhere that Lambert goes, Daley is sure to go. Which is not against the rules, as it happens, because it is Verity Lambert who makes them.

Arthur Daley is a huge, lolloping and extremely soppy Great Dane. His owner is the small, neat and extremely savvy television producer. She named him after Arthur Daley (played by George Cole) who is the star, of course, of *Minder* – one of the peaks in a long range of excellent television series which Lambert has originated over the years.

The office is a converted flour mill in Shepherd's Bush, west London, not far from the BBC offices at White City, in convenient proximity to the corporation which has bought more than half of Lambert's 11 productions since she went independent in 1985. Cinema Verity is one of the most successful independent production companies, but in these straitened times even Lambert has to fight to stay on top.

The days are punctuated with visits from industry insiders and outsiders who want to draw on the expertise of the elder stateswoman of television. Lambert is probably closer to 60 than 50, but tells those who are impertinent enough to ask that she is simply over 50. Whatever her age, she looks good in her black and white sneakers, her dark hair tied back in a black satin bow.

Lambert does not sit, omniscient, behind her big black desk with its backdrop of awards – a Prix Italia for *The Naked Civil Servant* in 1975, the Australian Film Institute's Best Film in 1989 for *Evil Angels* (known in England as *A Cry in the Dark*; Lambert's first and only film under her own company, starring Meryl Streep as Lindy Chamberlain, and Sam Neill as her husband, and directed by Fred Schepsi), a nomination for Outstanding Achievement in the 1990 British Academy Awards, and many more. This being an informal discussion, we sit on sofas at the other end of her office. And this being an informal office, Arthur Daley wanders in and out at will. His first appearance elicits a startled yelp from a producer who is seeking her advice, when he turns round to see what's breathing down his neck. Daley, one senses, could be a useful decoy.

The big excitement of the day for me – but clearly not for Lambert, who remains unruffled throughout – is the drama behind *GBH*. She receives a phone call from the director. The chiefs at Channel 4 don't like the ending of the last episode. They want it changed. Pronto. This conversation takes place at midday on Wednesday. *GBH* goes out the next night. Lambert has yet to see the finished version. The director arrives, video in hand, to await Lambert's decision. He knows that if she's happy with it, she'll fight to preserve it the way it is. She's not.

GBH ends with its schoolmaster hero (played by Michael Palin) driving over a bridge. In this earlier version the final image is suffused in a tangerine glow which gives it a surreal, slightly mystifying edge. 'I don't like it,' Lambert says matter-of-factly. 'It's too complicated.' The director coughs, 'It's very straightforward compared with what a certain person wanted.'

The certain person is the writer, Alan Bleasdale. He has a reputation for clinging tenaciously to his work; he is said to be intolerant of interference. Lambert picks up the phone. 'Hello Alan . . . a slight problem with the ending . . . let's have a little play with it and we'll report back.' I have been holding my breath, expecting (to be truthful, half-hoping for) verbal fireworks. This is, after all, the dramatic finale to his major work. But no such luck. A location is booked. The crew is reassembled (even though many of its members are now working on other projects) and they will work through the night.

This incident is illuminating for several reasons. First, it underlines the extent to which creative decisions are circumscribed by financial considerations – even on *GBH*, which is one of Channel 4's most expensive series. For dramatic reasons, the last scene should have been shot at night. But it would have cost too much to light up the bridge. Hence the non-naturalistic tinting.

More importantly, I see how Verity Lambert operates under stress. She must find the situation aggravating, but shows no indication of it. When she talks to Bleasdale her manner is pacifying and soothing – almost maternal. With the Channel 4 bigwigs, she is calmly efficient. And she is chummy but firm with the director. Chameleon-like, she offers a slightly different version of herself to each man; her personality seems to undergo a subtle fine-tuning.

But there is one constant. You know that Verity Lambert will get exactly what she wants.

Her female peers identify this adaptability as one of Lambert's strengths. Liz Forgan says, 'She is sensational at exploiting her female skills and brilliant at handling corporate men.' And Linda Agran says, 'Verity is a bit like Margaret Thatcher. She knows how to be extremely cross and she knows how to be skittish and like a 12-year-old girl. She knows how to perform and she knows how to get rip-snortingly drunk and threaten to punch you on the nose. She has the ability to go either way.'

But what I find weirdly liberating about Lambert's performance – perhaps because it still seems so implausible – is that she is 100 per cent in control. I am not sure that I have ever seen a woman treated with such respect by so many senior men. And although I know, since she told me so herself, that she can scream and shout and carry on like a banshee, what I see is a woman who handles each meeting or disaster with a sort of demure restraint.

At the end of the day, we zoom off to location in Lambert's 1981 Mercedes Benz. Half-way across London, she realises that she's left Arthur Daley behind. Omygod. She is mortified. 'This is like your forgetting your baby!' she exclaims, and picks up her mobile phone to talk to her PA.

Home

The next time we meet, it is at Lambert's flat in Holland Park. We are sitting in the living-room, which is like a miniature version of Biba's Rainbow Room. There are Lalique vases among a collection of art deco and art nouveau glass in a cabinet along one wall. The colours are beige and rose. The furniture is large and elegant. Arthur Daley sprawls at Lambert's feet.

In the kitchen is a display of cardboard boxes bearing the name Nutri-system. Lambert is on a diet, having gained weight after giving up smoking. For years, every interview with Lambert was an inadvertent advertisement for Silk Cut. In an article on health in the *Observer* magazine, in the eighties, there is a hint that Lambert has been seriously ill: 'She has not seen her doctor for a year and describes her health as "excellent, but when I'm sick it's for major illnesses". She says she has spent many nights in hospital.' But it is a friend who reveals that Lambert has had cancer. 'At one point,' I am told, 'she said that she found the idea of death seductive.' She makes no reference to it herself.

Lambert's strongest childhood memories are of sirens and air-raid shelters, playing games with pieces of shrapnel, and her mother boiling crimson stubs of lipstick to make it go further.

At the age of 12, she was sent to Roedean, which strengthened her independent spirit. Particularly as she didn't fit in. 'If you are an individual who doesn't fit the mould, you become a difficult person. Which is not the same as being naughty,' Lambert says. 'I couldn't knuckle under. My housemistress thought I was wilful. And so did my teachers.'

Stanley Lambert had wanted a son, but transferred his ambitions to his daughter. His wife wanted their daughter to marry a suitable boy and have babies. He wanted their daughter to have a brilliant career, and was dismayed when Roedean's headmistress said she did not consider that Verity Lambert was university material. (I am surprised, given her chequered history there, by how often the grown-up Lambert tells me that Roedean did not invite her to its centenary celebrations. She is very clearly wounded by the oversight. She tells me that she even used to send Roedean regular bulletins of her career highlights. This is unexpected, and also rather touching.)

At 16, Lambert left school and went to the Sorbonne. During the day there were lectures in literature, art and politics, and once a week an evening class in philosophy. It was an emboldening experience for a young woman – as beneficial for developing her social skills, she says, as broadening her education. On her return to England, her father was adamant that she should study for a degree. But Verity refused. For a while, it looked as if she was in danger of turning into her mother's daughter. At 19, she had completed a secretarial course and was engaged to be married to Laurence Blonstein, a hard-working medical student.

Lambert's first job was for Sidney Bernstein – referred to by his staff as Mr Sidney – who ran Granada, one of Britain's first commercial television stations. But her inexperience was matched only by her incompetence, and she was fired. 'Whenever the internal phones lit up for Mr Sidney I would resolutely ignore them, thinking that I would cut them off if I picked them up.'

The six months at Granada – job or no job – convinced Lambert that she wanted to have something to do with this 'new-fangled industry'. In some way, it also convinced her that she didn't want to settle down and become a doctor's wife. With her usual determination – brooking no opposition from her parents – she broke off the engagement and left England to pursue her career in America.

The Start of it All

In her twenties, Verity Lambert was living in Los Angeles with her boss, a director called Ted Kotcheff. I am amazed that Lambert is so open about this relationship, since most high-flying women would consider such an admission to be damaging, tempting the public to speculate about the precise nature of subsequent career promotions.

But Lambert is unusual. I notice this, in a different context, when I ask why she doesn't hire women directors. (Cinema Verity, at this point, had only used a female director once: Jane Howell on *Boys From The Bush*,) I level the same implicit criticism at some of her powerful peers, and they make small, panicky noises – 'not enough experience . . . not right for the film . . . they didn't exist, at the time'. Lambert, in contrast, takes it on the chin. She says thoughtfully, 'Yes, we may talk about helping women but we don't do it as much as we'd like to. If you're an independent, you have to present to a broadcaster and – it sounds like an excuse and perhaps it is – but even as a successful independent producer, you have to work very hard to make ends meet.

'I don't feel totally ashamed of my record with women. My company is run by them and I do promote them. But I have some sympathy for women who are freelance directors, who are out of the system, and don't feel we do enough for them.' So – will you do something about it? I ask. 'I'll try,' is her reply. (Jane Howell directed three of the seven episodes of the comedy series *Class Act*, starring Joanna Lumley, in 1994; Sylvia Bowden directed the third series of the BBC sit-com *So Haunt Me*.)

With hindsight, Lambert continues, her involvement with Kotcheff was the turning point in her life. He was the first person to make her really see that it would be a smart move to exercise her brain. 'It is quite extraordinary,' she says. 'I had had a good education and I wasn't stupid. But I had led quite a trivial life. I didn't feel the need to apply myself in any way. Of course,' she adds wryly, 'as soon as I started to do so, that's when the relationship went wrong.'

Lambert returned to England determined to become a director. She applied for directing jobs but never got an interview and, disheartened, returned to her old position as a production assistant, giving herself a year for her career to shape up. If it didn't, she told herself, she would quit television.

'There is luck,' Lambert has said. 'For any woman there has to be luck, and after that it is what you do with it.' Lambert's luck came in the shape of her former lover's former boss. Sydney Newman had moved from America to head the drama department of Thames Television. He moved to the BBC, where his name became synonymous with some of the best television drama Britain has produced.

It was Sydney Newman who created the concept of 'The Wednesday Play', and persuaded James MacTaggart to produce it. He hired Tony Garnett, who directed *Cathy Come Home*. Garnett recommended Kennith Trood, who went on to produce Dennis Potter's most notable work for the BBC.

It was Newman who produced one of Harold Pinter's first television plays. And it was Newman who gave Lambert her big break. 'My genius,' he tells me, 'is that I make fewer mistakes hiring people than other people do.'

Lambert's track record goes back so far that it is difficult to imagine her as a very young woman. At the ABC in the late fifties, Newman remembers her as 'a very sassy lady. She talked back. She was never foolish. She was very electric and a bloody good person to have around.' (Lambert tells me that she was always pestering: 'Let me do it. I can direct. I can do it. Go on.' It was one break she never got.) Newman, who now lives in Canada, adds 'Verity is still a handsome woman, but she was a gorgeous kid. And the fact that she was pretty certainly helped.'

At the BBC, he offered Lambert the job of producing an outlandish new children's series called *Dr Who*. It was, as Newman says, 'a terrific promotion . . . jumping light years. In the first two or three months people imagined she must be my mistress – which she wasn't.'

Lambert's transition from producer's assistant to producer did not go smoothly. There were casting rows with the director. Male, of course: 'I could hear him thinking, "Here's a young girl I can walk all over."' The director resigned. A BBC bureaucrat told Lambert, 'I don't know why we're employing you when we have people with much better qualifications.' Lambert just asked for a rise. Most of her moves paid off handsomely. Newman tells me a story. 'There is a science fiction shorthand – the BEM, which stands for Bug-Eyed Monsters. I told Verity, "Whatever you do. I don't want any BEMs. OK?" I'm watching the second episode of *Dr Who* and there's this Dalek. I bawled the shit out of her. "But Sydney," she keeps saying, "but Sydney . . . They're not monsters. Inside the metal are the brains of people who've been atrophied. So, you see, they're human, really."' We both laugh at Lambert's audacity. But, as Newman has the grace to admit, the Daleks were the secret of the show's success.

After 18 months, *Dr Who* had broken the ITV entertainment monopoly and entered the ratings. Lambert was 27. She was the youngest, and the only woman, producer at the BBC.

Her Brilliant Career

Lambert stayed with the BBC for seven years. She listened to a colleague's advice: 'The BBC has the best back-up resources in the world. But you have to get them working for you, rather than you working for them.' After *Dr Who*, she went on to produce a series for adults. Some successful: *Somerset Maugham Short Stories*, which won a BAFTA Award in 1969. Some less so: *Adam Adamant Lives* – 'A lot of people thought it was terrific; my sorrow was that it wasn't as good as it should have been,' Lambert says. 'It needed more wit. I could see the writers I wanted but I couldn't persuade them to write for me. As the producer, I can only blame myself. I think it taught me that everything wouldn't get handed to me on a plate.'

In 1970, even worse, the work dried up. Verity Lambert had eight traumatic weeks of worrying that she'd never get another job. Her fears, as we know, proved groundless.

For the next 12 years, Lambert worked for commercial television stations. At London Weekend, when Stella Richman was director of programmes – the first woman to rise to such a high level in television – Lambert produced *Budgie*, the comedy drama written by Keith Waterhouse and starring Adam Faith, and *Between the Wars*: six one-hour adaptations of stories written in the 1930s. In 1973, she co-created and produced a series about the suffragettes, *Shoulder to Shoulder*, for the BBC.

By 1974 Lambert had risen to Sydney Newman's old job at Thames Television – controller of drama. In previous interviews she has said, somewhat disingenuously, that she does not consider herself ambitious. Perhaps, as Suzie MacKenzie suggested in the *Guardian* in October 1990, the adjective instantly summons images of the Faye Dunaway career-woman prototype in the film *Network*: 'The shattered fragments of her personal life present a pitiful contrast to the linear and single-minded thrust of her brilliant career. There are no children. Marriages either do not happen or, if they do, are unhappily resolved. Such women, maintains one TV man, are a particular breed. In some ways a media image.'

At any rate, the story Lambert tells me suggests that there was nothing haphazard about her ascent. 'London Weekend had offered me a carte-blanche contract, when I heard that Thames was looking for a new head of drama. I was impressed by Jeremy Isaacs [who was then director of programmes at Thames]; I'd seen his documentaries; I'd attended his seminars. I was interested in working with him.' I ask her whether she liked the idea of power. 'It would be a nerve to say I didn't. But it's not to do with having power over people; it's to do with having a wider influence over the programme-making.'

Lambert asked her agent to phone Isaacs to arrange a meeting at the Café Royale. 'He said, "We'd like you to produce something for us." I said, "I'd like to be your head of drama." My contract at LWT came up in a week's time, so I couldn't beat around the bush.' The meeting ended in a job offer. The one Lambert wanted, of course.

In the two years that she was at Thames, she generated an astonishing number of high-quality series and films. Among them were *Rock Follies* (BAFTA Best Drama Series, 1977) written by Howard Schuman; *Rumpole of the Bailey* (now in its seventh series) written by John Mortimer; *Edward and Mrs Simpson* by Simon Raven (starring Edward Fox, who won an Emmy Award); *The Knowledge*, by Jack Rosenthal; and *The Naked Civil Servant*, starring John Hurt as Quentin Crisp, which won the Prix Italia, an International Emmy and the Broadcasting Press Guild Television Award for 1975. It had been turned down, twice, by the BBC.

Lambert tells me the story she told the audience at the 1990 Edinburgh television festival.

'When I joined Thames in 1974 . . . I was determined to make innovative contemporary drama. As luck would have it, I was presented with two ideas which seemed to fall into that category. One, from Stella Richman, was a series about a radical Labour MP written by Trevor Griffiths. The other, from Andrew Brown and Howard Schuman, was a non-naturalistic and highly original drama series about a female rock group. Feeling very pleased with myself, I took these ideas to Jeremy and told him that these were the first two new series I wanted to put into production. Jeremy's face fell – "Don't you realise," he said, "the two most difficult things to sell to the network are dramas about politics and show-biz?" However, he did sell them to the network, and because of his trust and support, *Bill Brand* and *Rock Follies* were made – two series of which I'm very proud.'

It is an important story because of what it suggests but does not spell out. It was not just the programmes that found their way on to the screen; Verity Lambert was also able to make her mark on television because she had the full support and confidence of her male boss.

In 1976 she moved sideways and upwards to become chief executive at Euston Films, a wholly owned subsidiary of Thames Television. She was executive producer on *Minder*, *Fox*, the first series of *Widows* and *Reilly: Ace of Spies*, among others. In 1982 she moved into film, as the director of production and executive producer of Thorn EMI Screen Entertainment. It turned out to be the one false move of Lambert's career.

Up to this point, Lambert had been fortunate enough to be protected by her male champions: Sydney Newman at the BBC, Jeremy Isaacs at Thames, Bryan Cowgill at Euston (who endorsed Lambert's decision to make the second series of *Minder*, despite the first series's low ratings). At Thorn EMI, Lambert had no protectors. She had been hired with a specific brief to make British films. Her contract dictated that she had her own budget and that she was, more or less, autonomous. But, for the first time in her life, she found herself making decisions against her instinct. One of which was a forgettable thriller called *Slayground* based on a novel by Richard Slater. 'I wasn't very keen,' she told a journalist, 'but I thought, "Well,

I'm starting off and this is definitely different to television and maybe I have to go by somebody else's judgement.'"

Lambert didn't like the screenplay, and it was the director's first film. 'I knew it wouldn't work,' Lambert says, but the distributors were convinced it would be a commercial hit. It was a flop, and a flop which coincided with a restructuring of the company. Lambert lost her budget and had to go to her new bosses with a begging bowl. She says she did make some reasonable films: *Comfort and Joy*, written and directed by Bill Forsyth, *Clockwise* by Michael Frayn, starring John Cleese, and *Dreamchild* – Dennis Potter's own fantastical version of *Alice in Wonderland*, starring Coral Browne. She is not even ashamed of *Morons from Outer Space*, starring Mel Smith and Griff Rhys Jones.

She had a salary of £100,000. Her name was mentioned in the same breath as Hollywood's Sherry Lansing at 20th Century Fox. And she was miserable. After the first year, she wanted to leave. But Lambert endured and honoured her three-year contract, emerging bruised but wiser. 'I made mistakes. But I learned that contracts can't protect you. I learned how to handle difficult situations. I learned the difference between television and feature films. Unfortunately, I still don't know how to make a successful feature film. If I did, I would be a very rich woman.' In 1985 she set up her own company, Cinema Verity Ltd.

The low points in Verity Lambert's life appear to have been few and far between. There was, it is true, a nervous breakdown early on in her career, around the same time that she ran out of work at the BBC. There was some unpleasant news coverage in 1984, when Lambert was acquitted on a drunk-driving charge after lunching with *Minder* stars George Cole and Dennis Waterman. 'I must admit the publicity was quite horrible,' she says. 'All I can say is I made page three of the *Sun* without having to take my clothes off.' There was the breakdown of her marriage to the director Colin Bucksey in 1987. After 12 years, she told a journalist, he 'eventually' left her for somebody else. And there is her period of ill-health which we do not discuss.

Sydney Newman, who clearly adores Lambert, told me, 'It's murder being freelance. You have to kick ass and wheedle. It's a hurly-burly world. Verity's driven too much for personal success. It worries me. She's burning herself up, and I don't quite understand why.'

Independent by Name

I spend hours and hours watching and talking to Verity Lambert. But I don't feel that I get to know her at all. There is something so essentially reserved about her character that, without being chilling or intimidating (although I am sure she can be both when it suits), her inner self is kept firmly behind a locked door. When I ask her about this, she says, very readily, that her weakness, if you can call it that, is self-sufficiency. Something, she supposes, to do with boarding-school and being an only child.

She told a journalist why her marriage foundered: 'Perhaps, I was just too resilient and didn't make Colin realise how much I need him.' I wonder whether it may also have had something to do with their power dynamic. When the couple met, Lambert was already a successful producer. Colin Bucksey was a cameraman and ten years younger than Lambert. Just before her wedding, she tells me, Lambert discovered that her mother, who had died in Lambert's early twenties, had also been ten years older than her husband. She had destroyed her passport in case anyone found out.

Lambert says that when a woman tells people what to do in the office ten hours a day, it is extremely difficult to adjust to not being in charge at home – 'And I think that's probably emasculating for men.' She may have done the washing up – as a sort of Pavlovian response – but she was hardly an ordinary wife.

In her twenties, Lambert wanted to have children. But her relationships were all wrong. In her thirties, she had lost interest. And, anyway, her husband didn't want them. She says that she doesn't mind being on her own. 'Except that people tend not to invite you to dinner parties unless you're in a couple. And, sometimes, it would be nice to share my experiences with someone.' But, but, but . . . there are consolations. She has her lovely flat in Holland Park. And another one in Antibes. Working holidays in Australia. Christmas in the Caribbean. There is Arthur Daley. And there is always her work. And – make no mistake – work can be a lot of fun, when you are the boss.

*

There are eight people in Verity Lambert's office. Six women and two men. We are all glued to the television set. Lambert has five full-time employees, in finance, creative development, and production. Only one is a man. 'I'd like to say that I went out of my way to go in for positive discrimination, but I didn't. At least, not consciously. But when women reach a certain position, they're just so good,' Lambert says. She is aware that a lot of men don't like working for women, particularly divorcees: 'They think that you never want to go home because you don't have any life of your own outside work.'

Someone opens a bottle of wine. There is a lot of laughter, and a few groans. We are watching the tapes of five actors auditioning for the lead role in a new series. Number Two starts ad-libbing and putting his own spin on the lines. Lambert is not impressed: 'He's been watching too much *Columbo*.' Number Three comes on. It's no good: he hasn't learned his lines. 'I don't like him. Yes, he's good-looking . . . in a sub-Hollywood sort of way.'

One of the men present is the controller of drama, who has commissioned the series. The other is the director. They are both gunning for Number Three. 'He did the most intelligent reading, Verity. He's definitely the most experienced. He's worked at the National . . .' But the women are unanimous. Number Five is sooooo cute. 'I don't know about his acting,' Lambert says, 'but I do know that he's got the potential to be a big star.' Number Five gives a lazy, heavy-lidded look to camera, which is greeted with a swoon from more than half the room. This is followed by a series of ribald remarks, from the boss and co., about his dating potential and marital status. The two men look distinctly uncomfortable. The controller, a large, affable type, sits there with a cheesy grin on his face. The director turns a pinkish colour: 'This isn't on. I can't believe what I'm hearing. Don't you know how sexist this sounds.' He leaves shortly after. We open another bottle of wine. It is Number Five, in case there were any doubts, who gets the job.

BEEBAN KIDRON

'I DON'T JUST WANT A SLICE OF IT.
I WANT THE WHOLE THING'

Beeban Kidron made her first film, *Carry Greenham Home*, a fly-on-the-wall documentary about the anti-nuclear women's camp, when she was a student at the National Film School in the early eighties. In 1990 she directed Jeanette Winterson's adaptation of her own novel, *Oranges Are Not the Only Fruit*, for the BBC; this went on to win many international awards. In 1993 she directed her first Hollywood big-budget film, *Used People*, starring Shirley MacLaine and Marcello Mastroianni. At the end of the year she returned to documentary-making, with a film on the New York sex industry – *Hookers, Hustlers, Pimps and Their Johns* – which was screened on Channel 4.

When Beeban Kidron was 11 years old, she had an operation to correct a cleft palate which left her speechless for a year. She had to relearn how to speak. She also learned how to use a camera and discovered that you don't need words to tell a story eloquently.

Her own story started in 1974, when she was on holiday with her family in Portugal; the year of the revolution which overthrew Caetano's dictatorship. Kidron took photographs, sold them for publication and was offered a job – on the spot – by Eve Arnold, the distinguished American-born photographer whom Kidron still describes as her heroine. 'She roared with laughter when l told her I was going to be 14 the next day,' Kidron recalls. At 16, Kidron left Camden School for Girls in London with eight O levels to become Arnold's assistant.

It was Arnold who persuaded her protégée to abandon still photography for the moving picture. Film, said the veteran of photographic realism, was the future. In 1982 she helped Kidron secure a place at the National Film and Television School. One of Kidron's earliest projects was *Carry Greenham Home*. She and a film-school friend, Amanda Richardson, camped at Greenham Common for seven months and captured the minutiae of the protesters' lives. The same team complained to the ACTT about the lack of women on their course – there were five. 'The equality officer spoke to the school, we spoke to the school, and it was responded to,' Kidron recalls. 'The year after us the numbers were equal, which shows that it's worth being political.'

(In recent years there have been more female than male students at the school. despite the fact that there are many more applications from men than women. In 1992, for instance, there were 455 male applicants and 182 female applicants. A first interview was offered to 87 men and 56 women; a final interview was offered to 45 men and 33 women; places were offered and accepted by 19 women and 17 men. The previous year, there were 16 female students and 14 male students accepted into the school.)

In 1988 Kidron made her first feature film, *Vroom*, written by Jim Cartwright, with Clive Owen as a likely lad escaping from a Northern town in a pink Chevrolet. She directed *Antonia and Jane* for the BBC in 1989 – a larky and telling film about female friendship starring Imelda Staunton and Saskia Reeves and written by Marcy Kahan, which went on to have a successful theatrical release in the United States. In 1990 *Oranges Are Not the Only Fruit*, directed by Kidron, was screened on the BBC and on cable television in America. (Jeanette Winterson adapted her novel which has been somewhat reductively, but somewhat truthfully, described as a story about lesbians and evangelists, and chose Kidron to direct it in 1987.)

Oranges was a resounding success, winning a brace of international awards, and cementing Kidron's reputation. She was 28, and Hollywood beckoned. In 1993 she directed *Used People* for 20th Century Fox (with a budget of £10 million, starring Shirley MacLaine, Marcello Mastroianni and Kathy Bates. The plot: a wrinkly love story; critical response: the best and worst reviews of her work to date.)

When we speak, she is working on another Hollywood project – *Payment in Full*, a film about blacks and Jews in New York, and her own highly idiosyncratic version of *Alice in Wonderland*: 'My Alice teaches the parents that there isn't only one way of being. I like to give power to people in my films who don't necessarily get it in the real world.' And there is more low-budget filmmaking with *Great Moments in Aviation* (£1.8 million, mostly put up by the BBC) which centres on a young black woman *en route* for 1950s London from the Caribbean. In 1993 she also returned to documentary making, with a film on the New York sex industry, *Hookers, Hustlers, Pimps and Their Johns* which was shown on Channel 4 at Christmas, and drew four million viewers despite being screened after 11 p.m.

Kidron describes her films quite unselfconsciously as 'personal journeys'. And for some reason, when I'm in her presence the statement doesn't sound the least pretentious. 'Because I'm a woman, a lot of the things that interest me interest other women, and a lot of the stories that I'm attracted to have women in central roles. Four of my last five projects have been centred on women, and it's a great source of pride for me to have given good roles to female actors. But it's not exclusive. As far as my work is concerned, the world is my oyster. I don't just want a slice of it; I want the whole thing.'

In Hollywood, she was struck by how many women directors had a body of work which defied categorisation. 'That's a victory because it's not just, "Oh, we have a woman's film here." Look at Penny Marshall who's made *Big, Awakenings, League of Her Own* – all mainstream movie motion pictures [affecting an American twang]. And then there's Kathyrn Bigelow who makes the sort of films that I don't make [violent macho movies, *Blue Steel* and *Point Break*]. There's loads of them doing it.'

It may be tempting to see Kidron's early setback as the making of her. And indeed some of her closest colleagues take this line. 'She's had to fight to make the world better for herself, and because of that, wants to make the world better for other people,' says Phillippa Giles, Kidron's producer on *Oranges Are Not the Only Fruit* and *Great Moments in Aviation* (also written by Winterson). 'When you're a girl and you've had something nasty done to your face, it's hard, because you want to be a pretty girl. It takes a lot of striving to realise that life isn't all about being a pretty girl' (*Independent* magazine, 27 March 1993).

When you meet Beeban Kidron, however, she is so forthright, so much her own woman that, adversity or no, it is hard to imagine her not succeeding at whatever she sets her heart on. There is a certain in-your-face bravado about her manner and dress. She seems more at ease telling stories that illustrate her toughness (of which there are quite a few) than being drawn into areas that expose her vulnerability.

She is small and sturdily built and thumbs her nose at the convention that only the willowy should wear short skirts. For our interview – a rushed lunch of canteen sandwiches on adjacent desks in a BBC office – she is in a black miniskirted suit, outsize gold earrings, Doc Marten lace-ups and a hair-do which juts out at odd angles. She has a deep, husky voice which sounds strangely vampy when it is disembodied on tape. This may be a legacy of the surgery or, perhaps, her (reduced) nicotine habit. Her favoured mode of expression is New York Jewish – 'Miss/Mrs/Ms? Please. Give me a break. I'm Beeban [pronounced Beeeeebaaahn]. It's enough already.'

Phillippa Giles told me admiringly about Kidron's technique for dealing with obnoxious behaviour on the set. 'Beeban will pick up on a sexist comment and broadcast it to the rest of the crew. It's rather good, the way that she does it, and it's certainly effective.' Kidron is more than happy to supply her own don't-mess-with-me-Buster stories. 'On my first film I had a male assistant director who clearly had a problem with my gender. He called me "the little lady", he didn't wait for me to finish a shot or call a lunch break . . . silly things. On the third day, I sacked him. I did it in front of everybody because he was very rude to me in front of everybody. I sat there and I said, "You know what – everybody on this unit has a day to be surprised about my age or the fact that I'm a woman, whatever. Everyone then has a day to get over it. But on the third day, if you're not making my film then you can go make someone else's film."'

She tells me that on another film – a documentary – the cameraman persisted in placing the camera 18 inches away from the position Kidron requested – 'So either I didn't get what I wanted or I was the nagging bitch because I kept on asking.' Kidron opted to give him a taste of his own medicine. She let him shoot the shot from his chosen position. Then she asked him to shoot it again 18 inches away. 'He had to do every shot twice. By lunchtime he was really fed up and he never did it again.'

There is more. 'I have taken people aside and said, "You can assume one of two things. You can either say, 'She's young, she's a woman and she doesn't know what she's doing', or you can say, 'In this world, if she's young and she's a woman, she must really know what she's doing – otherwise she wouldn't be here.' And I would assume the latter until proven otherwise."'

I ask Kidron whether she enjoys confrontation. She says

she tries to avoid it wherever possible by having long discussions with the members of her team before filming. Her rule is that they can say whatever they like to her in private, but they absolutely cannot bawl her out in public. 'And most of the time, the crews are phenomenally generous,' she says. 'A lot of the men have come up to me and told me how much they've enjoyed working for a woman. I think a lot of women are guilty of not taking the space. I want to be liked, too, but first and foremost I see my role as the guardian of the script.'

When I mention that some female directors have complained to me about cameramen setting up voyeuristic shots of the female stars, she leans forward and says emphatically, 'That would *never ever* happen to me. *Nobody* on my crew ever frames a shot any other way than I had it in my head. I decide what the shot is going to be and that's where the camera is. My film is my world.' Beeban Kidron, it is clear, is the unassailable mistress of her workplace. There are other areas in her life which are less certain.

'Caught between the Camera and the Cradle' was the headline of an article in the *Independent* (July 1992), in which five female directors spoke about their difficulties combining a successful career with any sort of private life. They blamed the break-up of their marriages on their work; they blamed their work for their lack of love life; they said it was impossible to have children and be a successful director. (Sarah Hellings, one of the five, with a long list of prime-time drama credits, also said she had twice been turned down for jobs because a member of the cast objected to working with a woman director!)

Molly Dineen, a leading documentary-maker (the BBC series on London Zoo; women who spend their nights cleaning the London underground) recalled working with a sound recordist who was a mother: 'I was trying to get her to stay in the station all night and get drunk with me and the ticket collectors [and] she basically really wanted to be with her babies, and that's when you realise that there is something a little bit out of the ordinary about making films like this and trying to have your own life. A boyfriend once said, "I think I'll make films now and have babies when I'm about 46" – I wish I could say that.'

Sharon Miller (director of *A Woman Alone*, starring Lynn Redgrave) believes that women have to choose: 'The demands of the business made the choice for me, which was that I neglected my private life while my professional life benefited hugely. You are permanently under attack in this business, your confidence, your energy and your validity, and it's difficult for any partner to understand the complexity of what you're going through.

'It's very hard when you're in your mid-thirties and you've got to make some sort of decision. I want both – I want a family and I want to make a wonderful film, and that's the dilemma.'

It's a dilemma that Beeban Kidron knows all about. She points out herself, with some consternation, that she keeps on referring to her films as her children. Her closest relationships suffered when she went to Hollywood. 'The toughest thing of all is this conflict between the personal and the professional. It is phenomenally difficult for women directors to sustain a personal life. First of all there is the geographical thing: you go wherever the work is, and the work is anywhere. Then there are the hours: we work from dawn to dusk, for months on end. Then there is the intensity of the relationships [actors phoning up with their problems in the early hours and so on]: you are everyone to everybody for that period. That inevitably affects your most personal relationships.

'The other thing is that there is a limit to the marriages and births and funerals you can miss and still be part of people's lives in a significant way. If you miss all the key moments of your friends' and family's lives, you cease to be part of the community. It is the details of people's lives that matter, and yet you are absent again and again and again.'

And so to the children issue. When Kidron was 22 she went to the Berlin Film Festival with *Carry Greenham Home* and met a group of women filmmakers. 'Most of them were in their late forties and had kids and then started to work. They said, "If only we'd started filming when we were your age." Amanda and I said, "Well, when do we start having families?"

'Everyone says, "Don't worry about it, it'll happen when it happens", but I'm here to tell you there's no right time. There's always another film or you're nervous that the last one didn't work or it did so well that you've got to keep building on that . . .

'If you talk to a lot of women directors they'll say it's hard enough making room for a lover, let alone a child. It's hard making room for their parents let alone the nanny of their child.

'I would love to have a child and I'm ambitious to get to the point where I can take some time off to do that. Another ambition is to share my life with someone who understands the level at which I work.' This is a key point, since Kidron believes men find it hard being involved with women who earn more and are more successful than they are. But people in general tend to be self-conscious in the presence of the famous, which is why at parties she sometimes pretends that she is an editorial assistant in a publishing company. 'Ultimately,' Kidron says, 'I'd like to give up directing and become a teacher.'

Given the hallowed way in which she talks about her films ('my children', 'personal journeys'), this last goal may seem surprising. But if there has been a constant in Kidron's life, it is her desire, as Phillippa Giles observed, 'to make the world better for other people'. And where better than to start with children? It was her teachers, Kidron says, who first gave her a sense of herself and of what her life could be. And she feels an obligation to repay the debt.

The other day, she tells me with some pride, she was contacted by a young woman who had joined the film industry after hearing one of Kidron's talks at a girls' school ten years ago. Her sense of owing something to the community may be partly inherited from her parents – north London Jewish intellectuals who ran Pluto Press, a left-wing publishing company – but if so, it is an inheritance which is underpinned by feminism.

'I go to schools and I stand in front of girls of 14 or 16 who are deciding what to do with their lives and I say, "You know what, I've been a camerawoman and a sound recordist, I've done this, I've done that. You can be what you want to be. Look at me. I'm not so much older than you."'

In a standard Hollywood movie (the sort Kidron doesn't make), it would be tempting to end here: a bright, hopeful note for the future, resonant with attitude and the chutzpah for which Kidron is known. But, in truth, the conclusion of our interview is more solemn. Because what really seems to bother Beeban Kidron is not the big picture in which she is cast as the superstar, but the small domestic drama: those tiny details she keeps missing out on.

As she says, 'You could be an Oscar-winning director. You could break the final barrier. You could be considered to be the top amongst your peers. And you could still be the victim. I think people are very unsophisticated about their definition of success. They don't get that it's important to have a whole life.'

PHILLIPPA GILES

'I WANT MORE'

Phillippa Giles is an executive BBC drama producer. She joined the corporation in the early 1980s. Her first big success was producing *Oranges Are Not the Only Fruit*. Since then, she has produced a trilogy of dramas by Barbara Vine (aka Ruth Rendell).

Phillippa Giles has a brisk, efficient manner and a brisk, efficient work schedule which, when we speak, has been rerouted by a major event: her wedding. Weddings, births and funerals tend to focus the mind on the larger human questions, pushing the pressing details of workaday life into the background.

This may explain why Giles is more than usually reflective about personal matters. Within minutes of starting our conversation, she talks about her desire to have a family. 'I spend about 50 per cent of my time thinking about it; it's a real preoccupation. I have worked for ten years to get to this point in my career. Suddenly I have more choices and more clout and I'm actually listened to . . . so it's quite a big thing to give up. But I will give it up to have children because, in the end, television is ephemeral. If you looked back on your life and asked yourself what you've done, just having made television programmes, however good they were, wouldn't be enough.'

These were not her sentiments, of course, when she first entered her profession. Phillippa Giles graduated from London University in 1981 with a first-class degree in English. She wrote to the independent producer Verity Lambert and asked for a job. Lambert wrote back with the best advice she could offer: become a secretary at the BBC. It worked for her; it worked for Giles. Now Phillippa Giles is a role model herself for the next generation of women.

The secretarial years were useful for Giles in that they enabled her to get around the different departments of the BBC without committing herself to one particular area. She worked on everything from *Miss Great Britain* to *The Best of Brass*, with a stint in the newsroom. She made good use of the corporation's traineeships, learning how to make promotional trailers; directing Victoria Wood for *Jackanory*; interviewing Michael Aspel for *Did You See* and other useful but less than dazzling tasks.

It was when she moved to the drama department – first as a script editor (*Vanity Fair, The Diary of Anne Frank, The Franchise Affair*) but then, more significantly, as a producer – that her career began to take off. Her first production was *Oranges Are Not the Only Fruit* which went on to win Best Drama Serial award both at the British Academy of Film and Television Awards, and at the Royal Television Society. Since that success she has produced a series of six plays by new writers, called Debut on Two (three directed by women), a trio of dramas by Ruth Rendell writing as Barbara Vine (*A Fatal Inversion, Gallowglass* and *A Dark-Adapted Eye*), and a film, *Great Moments in Aviation*, with the same trio who made *Oranges*.

But it is not just her curriculum vitae which is impressive.

Giles is a plucky and outspoken critic of the male orthodoxy at the BBC and a risk-taker. (She makes a point of hiring young women directors whenever possible – even though they are invariably less experienced than their male counterparts – and pushes to work with female writers.) She also admits to being fiercely ambitious. So why, I wonder, does she keep hammering her bosses? The answer is in part because she wants to make a different sort of drama from the ones her male colleagues have in mind.

When we speak there is not one single woman who has full commissioning power in the drama department of the BBC*. As she says, 'There may be more female producers [just over a third of the producers in her department are women] but are we doing our ideas? No, and that's the important thing. I'm sure that Michael Wearing and Alan [Yentob] see me as a shrill troublemaker. But my frustration is that I am always having to pitch my ideas to a man, who then decides whether to commission my project or not. It means that quite often the ideas that are brought to me by women writers don't even get on to the page.' *Two Golden Balls*, a series about the women's erotica industry, was an exception. But, because of the subject matter, it is unlikely to be made. (One of Margaret Matheson's first commissions on her appointment as head of Screen One, four years later, was to give the green light to *Two Golden Balls*.)

Giles is a firm believer that women and men tell stories differently, and that her senior male colleagues are not sufficiently aware of this. 'It makes it very difficult when you're doing a pitch because you have to describe the idea in a couple of sentences – a woman's story may sound less attractive because it may be discursive, it may be to do with nuance, it may be to do with characterisation. In the same way that a woman's novel may have less plot than, say, a Melvyn Bragg novel.'

In telling me about herself, Giles does not cast herself as the feminist heroine of a corporate saga. It is simply, one feels, that she is too bright to keep her mouth shut when the inequities are so blindingly clear. For example, Michael Wearing (head of drama, series and serials) was reading out the list of dramas that he was recommending for production in 1993–94. 'As he was reading them out, it became obvious that not only were the stories all male-dominated [she offers the examples of action thrillers, stories about public figures] but that out of the 12 writers there wasn't one woman. So Caroline [Oulton, the other most senior female producer] and I kept taking it in turns to point this out.'

At first glance, it seems encouraging that at least there are more women producers in the drama department than there were when Giles first joined the BBC (and certainly since Verity Lambert's day – when she was the *only* female producer at the corporation). 'Not really,' Giles says crisply. 'It doesn't matter what proportion of women are in the room. It all comes down to seniority. All that matters is who is at the head of the table; who is the commissioning editor; who is the head of department.' And, ultimately, who is the controller.

The other day, Giles tells me, her head of department said, 'I don't know why you're worrying. The next generation of television executives will all be women.' 'They do feel very under threat by us,' she says, 'because we are the most vociferous people in their department and we're probably the ones with the most challenging ideas. So what they're doing is holding us down. There'll come a time when they'll roll over and take retirement, and then we'll move in. But that might take another 15 or 20 years.'

I interviewed Giles on the eve of her wedding, when she was 33. She had her future as mapped out as her past. At the age of 35, she would get pregnant. Then she would abandon her career for seven years to bring up her family. After this period, she would return to television, if she still felt like it. Her friends, she told me, were appalled. 'They think I'm selling out,' she says, with a sigh. 'They tend to be writers, actresses or directors, like Beeban, who work freelance. And I'm the one with the most stable job, so they think I'm the one who should be able to make it work. We're all preoccupied by the thirtysomething obsession – how do you have children and keep your career going?'

Giles is a perfectionist. She is not willing to subject herself to the push-me-pull-you tensions which are fundamental to working motherhood. She does have colleagues who combine the two, and they cope, 'but that's all they do. Cope. I want more.'

When I next spoke to her, it was – quite by chance – her 35th birthday. So, I asked, rather flippantly, was she pregnant? She told me to ring next week and find out. By the time this book comes out, if all goes according to plan, Giles will have had her first baby. She has every right to pursue her personal happiness, and she will have got what she wants. But, sadly, we will have lost a champion when we need all the shrill troublemakers we can get.

*

This it transpires is not quite true. In April 1992 Ruth Caleb was appointed head of drama, BBC Wales. She is somewhat miffed that no one appears to be aware of her existence. This one can understand, since so many award-winning and/or controversial series have come out of her department: *The Lost Language of Cranes*, adapted from the novel by the young American novelist David Leavitt, starring Brian Cox and featuring the most explicit homosexual scenes yet seen on the small screen; *Black and Blue*, the series about racism in the police force; *Sweet As You Are*, starring Liam Neeson and Miranda Richardson, a four-part drama about male sexuality within a marriage (directed by Angela Pope); *The Old Devils* (adapted from Kingsley Amis's novel by Andrew Davies); *Civvies* by Lynda La Plante. The list goes on and on . . .

Caleb is 51. She became pregnant with the first of her two children when she was 38, and describes herself as 'a weekend mother', since her home is in London, her office is in Cardiff and her job entails regular trips abroad. When she was an associate producer on *Oppenheimer*, she took her family with her to the States. The experiment did not work. Her husband gave up his job in advertising to look after the children. I ask Caleb how she copes with the dilemma of sustaining her career and her family life.

'I'm all right because I was never wildly maternal,' she says. 'At 5.30 when I knew that I should be going home to change nappies, I thought, "No, I'll go to the pub and have a drink." I'd much rather do that. It was easy for me because I had no pull to go back home. Quite the opposite. My pull was to go back to work.'

She says that her experience of motherhood has meant she is tough with working mothers. When she was a script editor she was assigned to work with the former journalist Marjorie Wallace who was writing her script of *The Silent Twins*. 'One day Marjorie said, "I think something's happening" [She was nine months pregnant at the time]. I said, "No, no, it's probably just Braxton Hicks. Let's get on with the script." Three hours later her baby was delivered. If it had been a male script editor, I'm sure he would have stopped work. I had no such qualms.'

She tries to use female directors whenever possible – 'because I was a director briefly, and I know how hard it is to get on' – and she deliberately assigns women to macho subject matter to prove they can do it. For example she offered *Night on the Tyne*, a drama about a group of shipyard workers who are faced with redundancy, to Corin Campbell-Hill, a first-time director.

Caleb does not believe that there is such a thing as a 'feminine sensibility', or that women do things differently from men (although she does think that women are less sentimental than men). 'I suspect that it makes no difference whether the head of a department is male or female, in terms of the work. As a commissioning editor, I'm interested in looking at society and defining it through drama – especially in human terms. And as a human being, I'm interested in people on the margins of society: ordinary people who get embroiled in extraordinary experiences. And sometimes the two overlap.'

Recent senior appointments and promotions of women in BBC drama and film

- *Andrea Calderwood* replaced Bill Bryden as Head of Drama, Television, BBC Scotland in 1994.
- *Margaret Matheson* replaced Richard Broke as Head of Screen One in October 1993.
- *Tessa Ross* was appointed Independent Commissioning Executive, Drama.
- *Phillippa Giles* was promoted to Executive Producer, Series and Serials in November 1993.
- *Caroline Oulton* was promoted to Executive Producer, Series and Serials in November 1993.

ANTONIA BIRD

CHALLENGING THE STEREOTYPES

Antonia Bird moved from directing theatre at the Royal Court to directing drama for television, where her début was with *Play for Today*. She went on to learn her craft on *EastEnders* and *Casualty*. Credits include *Inspector Morse*, *The Men's Room* and *Safe*, an award-winning television film about the homeless.

'First' and 'only' are the two words that crop up most frequently in an interview with Antonia Bird. She was the first person to receive formal training as a director at the BBC, and get paid. She was the only female in a team of 13 directors to direct the 'blood and guts' ITV series *Saracen*. She was the first and only female director on *Inspector Morse* (28 episodes; 18 male directors; one female director).

She is neither the first nor the only woman to rail against the inequities of her industry, but she is certainly one of the most vociferous. From her work and articles, I had formed an impression of a woman who was ballsy, active, angry, funny, and most definitely not coy. So it is a surprise to discover that Antonia Bird is reluctant to quote her age. 'Mid-thirties?' I suggest helpfully. 'Yes, you could say that,' is her ambiguous reply.

The reason for this lack of precision, it transpires, is the same old problem – male prejudice. 'I work in an industry which is run by men; it's OK to have a young attractive female around,' Bird says, 'but not a middle-aged frumpy one. They like to think I'm younger than I am.' My face must be registering a certain amount of scepticism (could this be mere vanity masquerading as politics?), so Bird continues: 'When I first started directing I was 23. I was a cute little thing, like a puppy dog. I was fun to have around, and I was patronised like crazy. But now it's different because I've attained a certain position and I get offered a lot of work, and I do get the sense that they're ever so slightly frightened of what I'm going to say to them or do to them.'

Her favourite frightening tactic is a mixture of humour and humiliation. One of her first big BBC drama series was *Thin Air*, starring Kate Hardie as a young reporter investigating corrupt developers in London's Docklands. 'We had set up the shot, with Kate walking out of this building. She was wearing a little grey suit, slightly above the knee, black Doc Martens and white socks. The three men around the camera started saying [animal grunts], "Coooahhhh. *I like that*. Coooahh, 'ere she comes." I said, "What the *fuck* are you going on about?" And they said, "Coooeeehugh, schoolgirls in white socks, love it . . ."

'I was absolutely horrified. Kate was only 18 at the time. I told her about it and we decided to have a laugh. When we resumed filming, I started to say, "Coooooeerrr, look at Barry's blue socks, Kate," and then we got on to the Y-fronts. "I bet he's got a lovely pair of purple Y-fronts under those jeans. *Worrrr*orrr." I have never seen so many embarrassed guys in all my life. It was done very jokily, and they *hated* it.'

Bird is a battler from way back. She started working in the theatre when she was 17, and made a rapid progression from general dogsbody to stage manager. When she was 20, she told a male colleague that she wanted to direct – 'He laughed in my face and I remember thinking, "Right, you bastard, I'm going to show you."' She went on to direct new plays at the Bush Theatre in west London, worked as an assistant director to Michael Bogdanov at the Leicester, and directed at the Royal Court for six years, which led to her break into television.

Her first champion was the late Innes Lloyd, who produced most of Alan Bennett's plays for television. He was sufficiently impressed by Bird's Theatre Upstairs production of *Submariners*, an anti-nuclear play set on board a nuclear submarine, to fight for her to direct it at the BBC. Thus Antonia Bird's directorial début in televison was with *Play for Today*. It was, as she points out, an unusual place to start.

She learned her craft on a new series, again on Lloyd's recommendation, produced by Julia Smith (who was more recently associated with *Eldorado*). The series was *East-Enders*. Antonia Bird directed 18 episodes in the first year, under Julia Smith's tutelage. 'She became a huge champion. She saw someone who wasn't trained, decided that she wanted me to direct *EastEnders*, and gave me a three-month apprenticeship – which was unprecedented – trailing other directors to watch how the programme was made,' Bird says.

She went on to direct the first series of *Casualty*, *Thin Air*, *South of the Border* (these two series were produced by Caroline Oulton), and then left the BBC to work on what she describes as 'boys' stuff' for ITV. *Saracen* was an action series about 'acceptable mercenaries', and very heavy on shooting and killing. Why did she take the job? 'I thought I *had* to do it, because women never get asked to do this sort of thing. I was the only woman out of 13 directors. And it was good training. If I ever want to use those sort of activities for whatever reason, I've got the experience.' (In *Safe*, her boldest film yet, screened on the BBC in late 1993, Bird drew on this early 'action' experience to film the street-fighting scenes between the homeless and the police.)

When we talk, Bird is working on a drama series for

Meridian, a new post-franchise company, called *Full Stretch*. The writers are Dick Clement and Ian La Frenais, whose long list of credits include *The Likely Lads*, *Porridge*, *Aufwiedersehen Pet* and the screenplay for *The Commitments*. 'They've chosen me for a very good reason,' she says. 'They're men in their fifties, they write for men, their stories are about men and their characters tend to be men. This time they have got female characters, and they're clever enough to know that in the wrong hands [that is, sexist male hands], some of the material could be well dodgy.'

The story, in brief, hinges on a man who runs a limousine company. His wife, Tanya from Essex, was runner-up for Miss TV Times in 1974. The limo man's best friend has a wife who is obsessed with bottom tucks and bosom implants, and a mistress who is a 19-year-old model. As Bird points out, somewhat redundantly, the three women are, potentially, perfect sexist stereotypes.

One of Bird's strengths, she believes, is her ability both to subvert and to improve on the original material. In an article for the *Independent on Sunday*, she wrote that every day of her working life is a struggle to cast women unstereotypically and to avoid the usual restricting clichés.

'Are drama directors hauled over the coals for panning the camera up a pair of female, generally stockinged, legs, or for starting a shot close up on her bottom as she walks away from the camera? No. It is my refusal to follow such formulae that creates the problem.

'I struggle to depict women realistically – [but] I find some of my male bosses insisting on their own standards of attractiveness. They seem obsessed with dressing women straight out of fashion magazines.'

She presented an example. 'I offer a leading role to a well-known, highly acclaimed and beautiful young actress. The following day, she appears on television in a character part wearing no make-up and severe, "unsexy" clothes. I am impressed by her performance, her ability to change her personality, her aura – her acting, in fact. The following morning one of my male bosses telephones a male colleague and insists that the job offer to this actress should be withdrawn; she is not "crumpet".'

When we talk Bird tells me, several times, 'We've got to keep challenging the stereotypes. The more you do it, the more confident you get, and the more people feel that they can follow you. I do consider, as one of the few female directors around, that I lead the way a bit.'

One of her mini-victories, or so she thought, was to intervene over *Full Stretch*'s opening credits, which featured a limo and a customer's legs which were attached to – surprise, surprise – a female in a miniskirt, stockings and high heels. 'We were looking at the storyboard and I waited for someone else to say something about this particular picture, and of course no one did. Eventually I said, "I couldn't put my name to a film with an image like that. I think that's deeply sexist." So one of the production team went, "Hohoho. All right then, we'll put her in a pair of trousers."'

We ruminate on why these tired old images are still in circulation in the nineties. One can just about understand a generation of middle-aged males resorting to such formulae, but the men who are responsible for this dubious shorthand are often in their thirties or younger. As Bird says, 'What I found completely gob-smacking [about the meeting] was that these guys were the same age as me, and yet they're completely unwitting about what is acceptable in the 1990s to over half the population.'

You don't have to be a right-on feminist to be aware that there is something woefully inadequate, not to mention unrealistic, about this lazy recirculation of 1950s stereotypes. You just have to be a woman. But in the boardrooms, as on the film sets, it isn't the women who make the decisions, and this is what frightens Antonia Bird. 'There are probably eight or nine men who are making the final decision about this particular bit of film – and one woman, who happens to be me. If I hadn't put a stop to it, that image would still be there.' Quite often this sort of decision is being taken without a single woman being consulted, so it's totally unbalanced. (When the series went out, however, the legs may have disappeared but were replaced by a shot of a female bottom encased in a lycra miniskirt. No trousers. Bird had not been consulted.)

Antonia Bird is still probably best known, certainly outside the film industry, for *The Men's Room*. She has said that it was one of her most enjoyable working experiences, partly because it was unusually top-heavy with women. Bird spent days building up the trust of the actors – both Harriet Walter and Bill Nighy – who were equally nervous about the famous nude scenes. 'We were all terrified about it. Wouldn't you be?' Bird asks rhetorically. 'What we tried to do, was never to show a bit of Harriet's body without showing a bit of Bill's body. So if you saw Harriet's bottom, you also saw Bill's bottom. The thing that really irked me was that I wasn't allowed to show men's genitals but I would have been allowed to show women's genitals, which I refused to do.' (She is delighted that Phillippa Giles got male genitals into *Fatal Inversion*.)

In 1993 Bird won the Chaplin Award for Best First Feature Film at the Edinburgh International Film Festival. The film, *Safe*, is a harrowing drama about the plight of the homeless in London, starring Kate Hardie and Aidan Gillen. The jury praised Bird for her 'courageous' direction; the critics wrote shell-shocked reviews. Who knows – despite its uncompromising subject – *Safe* may prove to be the breakthrough Bird needs, since her sights are set firmly on Hollywood.

As her career has prospered, Bird has made the tough decision not to have children. 'It became clear to me that if I was going to have a family it would happen just as my career was taking off. There's always the next step of the career and if you stop and have children, then you're going to miss out on that next step. I'm very, very sad about it. But it is not a very good world to bring people into and . . . well, that's how I make myself feel better about it.'

In her twenties, Bird was married to an actor who resented her success. She gave up working in the theatre and found a job in a wine bar in a bid to save the marriage. But she failed. Ten years ago she joined the Labour Party and got involved in local politics, partly as an antidote to work. She met her present partner, as she puts it, 'across a crowded Labour Party meeting'. The relationship works, she firmly believes, because he is as obsessive about his job (which is not in television) as she is about hers. As a consequence, she says there is no cosy home to come back to each night. 'But that leads us back to what we are led to believe we should have, which gets you back to stereotyping, which gets you back to what are you putting on television. Does everyone have to go back to a nice, cosy home? I don't know.'

What she does know is that, almost without exception, the women with whom she works don't have children and the men do. 'When you're filming, you're leaving the house at six in the morning and coming home at eight or nine at night. The guys go home to a meal, to clean clothes for tomorrow, to lovely, cuddly children. And you go home to a dark house.

'It was something Harriet Walter and I used to get very uptight about. One night, we were sitting together and getting drunk in the pub [after filming *The Men's Room*], and Bill had gone home to put his kid to bed . . . and we both went – [big sigh] "Look at us."

'It is odd, because they all talk about their kids. And they still all go and play golf on Saturday.' Antonia Bird concludes our interview with a great wolloping shriek, 'What I want to know is: *Who is doing the shopping?*'

LIZ FORGAN

'NOBODY TOLD ME TO RUN OFF AND DO EMBROIDERY. EVER'

Liz Forgan was the chief leader writer of the *Evening Standard* at the age of 27. In the late-seventies she was women's editor of the *Guardian*. In 1981 she was appointed Channel 4's head of news and current affairs. She was offered the job, famously, after interviewing the station's first chief, Jeremy Isaacs, for the *Guardian*. In 1993, since this interview, Forgan moved to the BBC to become managing director, Network Radio.

Liz Forgan, the most influential woman in British broadcasting, is wearing a conservative suit and talking, as she is wont to do, much solid common sense. Suddenly she pauses, gives me a straightforward look, and says: 'Just because I speak quietly and dress like a bank manager doesn't make any difference to my views. I'm still as radical as I ever was.'

We have been trawling through an earlier stage in her

career, the late-1970s, when Forgan was women's editor of the *Guardian* and commissioned Jill Tweedie, Polly Toynbee, Linda Blanford and Posy Simmonds. It was this appointment, in fact, which radicalised Forgan. 'I had not even read books like *The Female Eunuch*,' she has said. 'Working at the *Guardian* opened my eyes to the political, social and sexual experiences of women. I realised what a closed life I had led. Women like me, who really had never experienced discrimination, had suffered least.'

She was born in 1944 in Calcutta, where her father, the son of a Presbyterian minister, was serving with the Gordon Highlanders. After the war her parents were posted to California, Iran, Kuwait and Venezuela, by her father's new employer, Shell Oil. She was educated in England – holidaying with her grandparents – attending 21 schools before she was nine, then Benenden and Oxford.

It was a cloistered upbringing which gave her no reason to doubt – despite the evidence of the wider world – that women could be achievers. She is the older sister, with no brothers; she went to girls' boarding-schools and a women's college at Oxford. All her role models were women; all the structures were run by women. 'Nobody told me to run off and do embroidery while my male counterpart runs the world,' she tells me. 'Ever.'

So achieve she did. Forgan's career path – first in newspapers, then in television, now in radio – has moved unwaveringly upward. In 1970, after a stint in Iran on an English-language paper, Forgan went to the *Hampstead and Highgate Express* and became the paper's first woman news editor. She joined a new London magazine, *Inside London*, as political editor. It folded and the *Evening Standard* offered her a job as a reporter. At the age of 27, Liz Forgan was promoted to chief leader writer. 'When I went to parties, people would ask me, "What do you do, dear?" and I'd say, "I'm the chief leader writer of the London *Evening Standard*." I'd watch their mental picture of an omniscient, godlike, anonymous, authority figure crumble,' she recalls, with obvious relish. 'Instead of this old man with the white beard that they'd imagined, it was this flibbertigibbet of a girl. It's the only real service I've rendered to democracy in all my years of journalism.'

I wonder, since she cut her teeth on the boys' own jobs of journalism – news, politics and leaders – why Forgan ended up editing the women's page. Was she pushed there or was it her own choice? Forgan says it is an illustration of how 'dim' she was about women's issues then, that it didn't even occur to her that she might be being sidelined into a female ghetto. 'I just thought, "Heavens, how interesting. It's a subject that I know nothing about at all." But if I'd been asked to be the badminton correspondent, I probably would have said "Yes" to that too, for the same reason.'

When I push her on this, she says, slightly too breezily, 'Of course I said, "I don't want to be the women's editor. Can't you give me another job?" But what they needed was someone to do the woollies and the jellies. And the *Guardian*, being as ambiguous as it always is, didn't want a womanly women's editor. They wanted to demonstrate that they'd got a serious political journalist.'

It is years, she says, since she last heard a male colleague make a sexist remark. I presume that this may have something to do with the fact that she is the boss. And a pretty formidable one, I would guess. She is the sort of person of whom people say, 'She doesn't suffer fools gladly.' But her businesslike manner, precise way of talking and a particularly rigorous brand of intelligence can make even the reasonably bright feel like fluff-heads in her presence.

Her manner is often distinctly prefectorial. (Although, when I phoned Benenden to check whether Forgan had been head girl, I was surprised to discover that she hadn't even been made a prefect.) Her favourite derisory comment is 'pathetic', and one can easily imagine her ticking off a colleague for being 'wet'. She is also immensely jolly. She has invented a new word for her style of jogging (running downhill and *slowly*) – 'rumbling'. She sings in a choir. She spends her holidays on Orkney with the man with whom she has been involved since she was a cub reporter. They have no children. Her explanation for this is that 'the women of my generation didn't believe that we could have it all'. But in her case the family issue must have been dictated or, at least, overshadowed by the fact that her partner had three children of his own, and lived with his wife.

Ostensibly, she says, newspapers took women seriously more promptly than the other media. 'But the macho, heavy-drinking, show-off male culture is also very strong in news-papers. The daily banter was much more openly and crudely sexist than it was in television.' But surely not at the *Guardian*? Not, at least, in the immediate vicinity of the women's page? 'Guardian Women was a formidable force – a daily reminder – against all that, but it didn't stop some of the men – with enormous daring' – she grins, 'deliberately uttering sexist jokes in our hearing, and expecting us to fall off our chairs.'

Forgan is committed to positive discrimination but wishes there were another phrase for it. 'The label makes every-one's hair stand on end, so you mustn't call it that, it's too frightening for people. You must just quietly do it, I think.' She changes her mind. 'No, no, that's not enough. In a small organisation like Channel 4, as long as you keep appointing women and they keep appointing women, you can just do it. But in a big organisation, you have got to be systematic. I have a great admiration for what the BBC is doing. They're hopeless at taking the big leap and just appointing good women [with some exceptions, most notably Forgan herself]. But they have dug the asparagus trench. They have started the long haul of putting in the training schemes, the system of ladders which will ensure that they will have a whole cohort of good women to choose from.'

One of the few generalisations she is prepared to make is that women – including herself, I assume – tend to feel happier working in a non-hierarchical environment. This is the reason, she says, why there are so many female producers in the independent sector; they have had enough of clawing their way up the corporate ladder and being blocked by senior men.

Channel 4 started up with women in key positions, and they were instrumental in moulding the culture. It is, she says, run in a more collegiate and devolutionary way than other television stations. So I attempted to ask her, a year or so after her defection from the channel she helped to set up, how she has adapted to the byzantine bureaucracy of the BBC. But she was always too busy to return my calls.

When Jeremy Isaacs appointed Liz Forgan as Channel 4's head of news and current affairs in 1981, he was probably not aware that his appointee didn't watch television. It hardly seemed to matter. One of Forgan's first innovations was *Video Box*: 'I thought it would give people a chance to air their views without the excruciating experience of being interviewed.'

And her initial, remarkable experiment was to give women complete responsibility for the current affairs slots. The result was *Broadside* and *20/20 Vision* (the name of both the series – each strand comprising between 20 and 30 programmes – and the companies, which were run by women). The programmes covered a broad range of issues and were specifically not geared to 'women's' stories.

(One of the most controversial programmes was called *MI5's Official Secrets*, which involved the participation of Cathy Massiter, a former MI5 officer. The IBA banned the programme because it was in clear breach of the Official Secrets Act. Claudia Milne, who co-produced the programme, tells me that it was largely due to Forgan's efforts that it finally went to air. According to Milne – whose company, 20/20 Television, continues to make documentaries for Channel 4 and other television stations – the experiment proved that the editorial judgement of the women involved was affected by many other factors apart from their gender.)

Right to Reply, in which the Channel 4 viewer confronts the individual whose programme he or she disagrees with, was also Forgan's. As a profile writer observed, '[It] reflects Forgan's thinking that ordinary people, not just specialists, should be enabled to have their voices heard in the media.'

By the mid-eighties, of course, Forgan herself was becoming less and less ordinary, and more and more heard in the media. She was promoted to controller of programmes, and in 1987, when Isaacs's successor, Michael Grade, made her his number two as director of programmes, she became – incontrovertibly un-ordinary – the Most Powerful Woman in Television.

Forgan's byline reappeared in newspapers in the early 1990s. She was writing about censorship – which is the one issue on which she remains clearly political. (She was a Tory in her teens, left-wing Labour in her thirties, and has moved to the centre-left in her forties.) In 1990, in a series of spirited attacks, she condemned the new proposals of the Broadcasting Bill to introduce a more restrictive code of practice for programme-makers. In 1992 she defended Channel 4's refusal to identify their anonymous source in the *Dispatches* programme about the alleged collusion between security forces and paramilitaries in Northern Ireland (for which both the channel and the production company were found guilty of contempt of court). But when we talk, Forgan reserves her ire for Lord Rees-Mogg.

I ask her what she thinks of his 'crusade' to get more women into television, and she looks as though she has swallowed something singularly unpleasant. 'Oh, *don't*. I really cannot stomach listening to Lord Rees-Mogg going on about women. He's a *sexist pig*.' She has spat it out, but she hasn't finished. 'He ran *The Times* like a gentlemen's club. He thinks like a gentleman in a gentlemen's club. And to hear him justify censorship, i.e. the Broadcasting Standards Council, in the name of protecting women just turns my stomach.'

Forgan once interviewed Rees-Mogg for the *Guardian*. It was not, she says, her proudest moment in journalism. The editor of the women's page was so incensed by the editor of *The Times* constantly referring to his paper as 'she' that she was quite unable to write a balanced piece. 'For the editor of a national newspaper to do that in 1980 revealed such a complete absence of knowledge or interest or consciousness of the revolution that had been happening in attitudes to women in the last 15 years that I was just outraged.'

I have to confess that I find it rather beguiling that such a public figure is willing to be so indiscreet, since many people in power are co-opted by the organisations they head into becoming bland mouthpieces. But then, as she says, Channel 4 is an unusual organisation; one of its original aims was to subvert and destabilise the notion of the broadcaster as the authority. 'Some people would say that we went far too far, but I might say that the great danger of the next age of television is that it's going to be so fragmented that there will be no solid ground from which people can jump off.'

Liz Forgan likes to deal with the concrete, the known, the verifiable. She does not like to be coaxed into making generalisations. Since much of our conversation hinges on the uncodable, highly speculative area of the differences between men and women, 'wishy-washy stuff', as she puts it, there are times when she is clearly impatient with my line of enquiry. 'I don't really like talking about women in organisations or women in television,' she says, 'because I feel very unable to rely on any observation I make. It's always unscientific.

'I'm also wary of the two-edged sword. If you write about women in that sort of way it is important, and it makes people understand things they hadn't thought of before – but, on the other hand, it does brand you together as a kind of collective phenomenon. Which we're not.' (This was one of the reasons why it took several overtures on my part before she would agree to be interviewed for this book.)

My 'window' in her schedule is rapidly closing. Her male colleagues have been kept waiting outside her door for long enough. 'If you can make anything out of this,' she concludes, just a little wearily, 'then all I can say is, you're a better man than me.' And at this, she laughs hugely.

Channel 4

- Controllers: one male and one female
- Heads of department: men – 9; women – 5

- Commissioning editors: men – 13; women – 2 (one of whom is in film acquisition)
- There is not one woman who has full commissioning power in the drama department at Channel 4.

When I spoke to a senior woman in Channel 4 after Forgan's defection to the BBC, she told me that Forgan had not been supportive of the station's decision to give its female employees a special allowance for childcare – on the grounds that women should not be treated as a special case. Not being a mother herself, it was felt by her critics, meant that Forgan had not taken on board the reality that it is mothers, not fathers, who generally stay at home to look after the sick child or who are the first back-up if the nanny or childminder is suddenly not available.

*

'Radio 5 gives way to a news and sports channel; 400 hours a year of children's programmes is to be reduced to 75.'

In October 1993, Forgan made the decision to abandon children's programming on Radio 5. Maggie Brown, media editor of the *Independent*, expressed her dismay in an open letter: 'Dear Liz Forgan . . . Uncharitable thoughts surface. Perhaps you don't value children's programmes because you have no children? Certainly your former colleagues at Channel 4 regard you as unsympathetic to family issues. And have we not been here before? When you were programme director of Channel 4 you seemed to prefer buy-ins such as *Little House on the Prairie*: it is only on your departure that your successor has started to commission new children's programming.

'But, of course, Liz, you are not a free woman, you had to make space for more news, while satisfying sports-mad executives. So Radio 5 is being recast as Radio for Blokes. And children, sad to say, are an easy target.'

LINDA AGRAN
FUNNY GIRL

Linda Agran started in film production as a story executive at Warner Brothers. In 1976 she became head of development at Euston Films when Verity Lambert was the Thames Television subsidiary's chief executive. The two women developed and nurtured the successful *Minder* series, and launched Lynda La Plante's writing career by commissioning the former actress's first script, *Widows*. Agran went on to become deputy controller at London Weekend. In 1988 she left LWT to head the French-run company Paravision UK, which she bought from L'Oréal-Nestlé in 1994. It is now called Agran Barton Television.

Linda Agran's name is stamped on some of the most successful television series of the past two decades: *Minder*, *Widows* and *London's Burning*. She persuaded Lynda La Plante to write *Widows*; it was La Plante's first script. Agran's ascent of the ladder has not cramped her flamboyant style; nor has it muzzled her outspokenness. She can always be relied on for a pithy quote on the plight of women in general, and in television in particular: 'Women are handed out opportunities like children are given sweets. They're given certain bits and bobs and are supposed to be satisfied'; 'High-flying women are like pet gerbils. There's only ever one high-placed woman in an organisation at any time.' 'It's a fallacy that this industry has a good record on employment opportunities for women. The successful ones are invariably single.' She describes herself as 'lippy', her best friends call her 'Mouth', and newspaper headline-writers have labelled her 'Angry Agran'.

At television festivals she berates her male colleagues for not doing more for women. Her view on positive discrimination is that it already exists for men, so why shouldn't it be legislated for women? In 1986 she confronted a panel of men which included John Birt (her boss at the time), Michael Grade and Greg Dyke. 'I am very angry to hear what the men have said,' she told them. 'You have the power, you have the authority. Change is within your capabilities.' In 1988, in front of a live audience, she embarrassed Michael Grade by asking him for a job when the BBC's top male executives were answering accusations about the representation of women in television. Grade said that the corporation would love to employ more women but they had to come forward. So Agran did: 'Well, Michael, you've got a couple of jobs coming up, haven't you? Controllers of BBC1 and BBC2? Where do I get my application form?'

But the other, non-lippy, side of Linda Agran is very much in evidence when we speak in the early nineties. This one makes the world of television sound so ruthless and revolting that one cannot imagine why any woman would want to join it – let alone stay there to be humiliated. To hear Agran speak so bitterly is slightly shocking; it is like watching the private, sad face of a public clown. After we speak for the last time, I am left with a series of mental tableaux in which smartarse young men in braces sit behind their giant desks enjoying the sight of this ballsy veteran producer pitching her projects – only to turn her down.

It was not always thus. The story of her brilliant career may have its dark moments – the firings as well as the hirings – but it is essentially a story of triumph. It started 30-odd years ago, when Agran became secretary to an agent, then PA to glamorous David Niven Jnr at the William Morris Agency, then story editor at Paramount, story executive at Warner Brothers, head of development and board director at Euston Films, deputy controller at London Weekend and now, as she would put it, Le Grand Fromage at Paravision UK.

Women, I have noticed, often like to attribute their success to chance – right time, right place, random events, an encouraging mentor. Linda Agran is different. She only made it, she says, because she was a thick, fat, unhappy teenager. 'If you're in a body and you're treated negatively wherever you go,' she tells me, 'you either sit back and say, "You're right." Or you say, "I'm going to prove you wrong."'

She developed her big personality as a defence mechanism in a school where the headmistress informed her, 'We've got another of your people coming here.' It took a while for her to realise that she meant Jewish. 'I thought, "Instead of drifting like a blob, I'm going to be the first one to make the jokes and then I'll be popular." It was almost a conscious decision to become the class clown.'

The class clown got fatter and fatter. She became so ashamed of her body that she kept her coat on whenever possible. She was sent home from school for bad behaviour; at home she would feign illness to avoid going to school. She was a disappointment to her mother and father. 'I was fat. I wasn't bright. Their lovely little girl had turned into this . . . creature. And they were arguing with each other about me.'

When Agran was 14, her headmistress suggested that the class clown's salvation might lie in a typing pool. 'My parents were the sort of people who believed in authority,' Agran says. So she was dispatched to a college in Finchley, with no O levels on the horizon. There was Helen Shapiro on the gramophone, and nights at the Whisky-A-Go-Go in Soho, where Linda would hold the handbags while her friend, pretty Helen Mitkoff, the kosher butcher's daughter, danced with the boys.

It was only when Agran started working that she began to develop some self-confidence. Her first taste of show-business was when a friend tipped her off that G.A.C. Redway, the theatrical agents, needed a secretary – 'Go on. You'll love it. You'll meet all these actors.'

Of course, in those days all Agran's supporters were men. There were no female mentors; powerful women hardly seemed to exist. 'It wasn't possible to say, "I want to be like Verity Lambert",' Agran recalls. 'There were no role models.' Does she think that life would have been easier for her if they had existed? 'It would definitely have been nicer. Maybe I would have had more advice and support. I would have known that I had rights and that I could be assertive and that it was important to be clear about what I wanted and to get answers quickly.'

As it was, she found herself stuck behind a typewriter; but at least her boss was fabulous. She worked for David Niven Jnr for seven years, and moved with him from William Morris to Columbia Pictures and on to Paramount. 'Someone once asked David, "Is it true that you and Linda are having an affair?" And he said, "Please. Do me a favour. Look at her",' Agran recalls, without rancour. (He instantly sounds distinctly less fabulous to me.)

Her first job as a story executive in her own right was at Warner Brothers, where Agran had her first and only experience of sexual harassment. One of the company executives came to her hotel room, when they were shooting a film abroad, and suggested they go to bed. When she turned him down, he said, 'How do you think you got this job? We could have hired a man.'

It was around this time that Linda Agran and Verity Lambert met. Their first sighting sounds like something out of a science-fiction movie – Wow! So female life does exist on Planet Television. Better still, they liked one another and became close friends. In 1976 they also became colleagues when Agran joined Euston Films as head of development;

Verity Lambert was chief executive. These were Linda Agran's golden years in television.

She is telling me her life story in Paravision's Chelsea Harbour offices which, whenever I visit, seem strangely empty and devoid of action. The glass-fronted rooms opposite Agran's are usually unoccupied. Business, I would guess, is slow. There are meetings with writers and lunches with directors in smart restaurants, but not a lot in actual production. Welcome to the 1990s.

Agran describes the seventies – in contrast – as 'the headiest, most glorious days in television'. She goes on, 'If you had any imagination, if you knew any interesting writers, you could get something on to television. And, in those days, you had the right to fail.' This is an important point: programme-makers were prepared to take risks. *Minder*, for instance, was a bold decision to do something out of the mainstream. And the first time it was screened, amazing as it seems now, it bombed. In the present climate, it is inconceivable that a second series would have been commissioned, as it was then.

Lynda La Plante, an old friend of Agran's from her days at Columbia, was known, even then, for her impressive network of friends in the police force and the criminal fraternity. What she wanted to write about, however, was a criminal sorority. She had a great idea for a story about the wives of jailbirds who get up to their own highly illegal and highly profitable activities. But . . . she'd never written a script. Agran took one of her calculated risks. 'I said, "I'll commission the first part, and if I like it I'll commission another." The script came in and it was all over the place. But I was impressed by her energy and obvious talent.'

The first-time writer ended up completing a six-part film serial – *Widows* – which Agran was so excited by that she abandoned her producing role on *Reilly: Ace of Spies* to switch sets. 'Everything about *Widows* was pushing back walls,' she still enthuses. 'It was a woman writing women's roles and that had rarely been seen before.' There was one tiny problem: in La Plante's script, the women get away with their heist. The Independent Broadcasting Authority's regulations dictate that television cannot show that crime pays. '"Bollocks to that!" I thought,' Agran recalls. 'So I contacted Clare Mullholland at the IBA [now director of programmes at the ITC] and said, "I'll send you the script and if it's your decision that the women must be caught and punished, then so be it." She phoned me up as soon as she'd read it and said, "They *have* to get away with it."' Agran murmurs approvingly, 'Hmmm. Another woman, of course.'

The best part of working at Euston Films for Agran was her relationship with Lambert. She says they were like Sid and Doris Bonkers. They holidayed together in Barbados. They went to one another's houses for dinner. They rowed and yelled and slammed doors and generally terrified the men. 'It was a spectacularly good relationship. Whenever we fell out over a project, it never occurred to me that our friendship was in jeopardy. To be in a company with a woman whose opinion you respect is wonderful.'

But it was not to last. In 1984 Verity Lambert left to be director of production at EMI Films. Two years later, Agran was sacked from Euston. Talking to her five years on, she exudes the feeling that her best work is behind her – back in the good old days of Sid and Doris Bonkers. 'Well, Verity and me, we're all grown up now,' Agran says wistfully, 'but I do think that the sum of two is better than one. And no one's doing it better than we did it.'

At Home

Linda Agran comes to the door of her home in Newbury. She is wearing what she calls her Babygro ('I wouldn't be seen dead in this at work') and what most of us call a tracksuit. It is in purple velour. Her high-heeled shoes have been replaced by leather slippers. Her busby of thickly textured, grey-streaked hair now looks seriously at odds with the rest of her appearance. At Paravision – where her hair and clothes match – we spent some time discussing executive uniforms. Before setting off to interview Agran each day, I would feel the urgent need to glam-up-to-the-max – lipstick, make-up, the smartest clothes in my wardrobe. For the Chief was always pristine in a succession of pale suits and pearls.

In the 1970s, she told me, if you were a 'character' you could dress as eccentrically as you liked and get away with it. She speaks with the warm glow of nostalgia about long-discarded frocks, 'a quilted dressing-gown thing' and a multi-coloured silk tent-dress from Thea Porter which she called 'Gadaffi's House'.

But now she says, sounding not unlike a 'Dress For Success' handout, the important thing is to look neat, remember that you are representing your company and, above all, ensure that your clothes make you look as authoritative as your male peers. Her suit is a sort of camouflage. When she puts it on in the morning, she breathes a sigh of relief. 'If people don't like me, they dislike what I represent, not who I am.'

Linda Agran in mufti looks as though she is in fancy dress. She looks so unlike herself, the one, at least, that I am used to seeing, and so like a housewife from an affluent suburb, that it is quite some time before I can take her seriously. Which just goes to prove her point.

We sit in an attractive room, a glowing log fire, cushions made out of kelims, lots of paintings and a lot of photographs of Linda Agran (but no children – 'I don't really like them. And in my day, you couldn't do both. Maybe you can now . . .'), a huge bunch of pink and white amaryllis, windows overlooking the garden and the fields beyond.

It was here that the marriage of Sandy Scott, the chairman of a marketing agency, and Linda Agran was celebrated in 1991. (The entertainment was free: Salman Rushdie sang 'Tutti Frutti'; soul sisters Verity, Janet and Lynne Franks backed the bride on 'Stop in the Name of Love'.) Scott appeared at a time in Agran's life when she'd long since abandoned the notion that a man could make her happy.

It has been in the nature of Agran's jobs to work long hours, involving heavy-duty, semi-compulsory socialising with people in the same industry. Most of her relationships had been with writers, which presented the odd problem. She remembers one occasion when a writer took her out to dinner: 'I thought he was absolutely fabbo. Towards the end of the evening, it became clear that what he wanted was for me to see his script. And there was I thinking he'd only been after me for my body.'

In 1986 Agran told an interviewer, 'I think I'll always be single. I've got over the panic of the twenties and thirties. I like the independence. I don't really envisage a life of "Have you had a nice day at the office, dear?"'

There was no one to ask her that question when she was fired from Euston in 1986. She only began to notice the hostility towards her from certain men at the company after Lambert went to EMI, leaving Agran as the only woman on the board. 'There are so few of us at the top,' she says, 'that we're very easy to pick off.'

There were no leaving presents and no leaving party from the management. Agran could not bring herself to go out of her house for days on end. 'Work, you see, had been everything,' she tells me. There were some compensations. John Birt offered Agran the position of deputy controller at London Weekend. And Jack Rosenthal, the writer, took *London's Burning* away from Euston to LWT because he wanted to continue working with Agran.

London's Burning, Piece of Cake (a six-part drama about a group of young pilots in the first year of the Second World War) and Agatha Christie's Hercule Poirot series starring David Suchet – this was the sum of her work at London Weekend. In 1988 Sean Day-Lewis wrote a cheeky item in *Broadcast*: 'Combative Linda Agran is deputy controller at London Weekend. Far be it from me to use the word "sinecure" . . . Let it just be delicately suggested that she probably does have a little time left over for other things.'

Agran herself says that she didn't commission nearly as much as she would have liked to have done at LWT. Why not? 'The stuff that I like to make becomes increasingly difficult to justify because it's so expensive.' She was also frustrated by the different style of management: 'I was used to pumping it out, and at LWT Nick [Elliott, her boss; now managing director of productions at LWT] would say, "Well, we'll have to get this approved at board level." That was OK, but I wasn't used to it.'

In 1988 Agran replaced Gus Macdonald as presenter of Channel 4's *Right to Reply*. And the same year, she left London Weekend to head Paravision. When I push her to explain why she didn't stick it out for longer at LWT, she comes out with all the usual reasons that women cite for becoming independent producers: glass ceilings, lack of encouragement, and so on. 'I suppose I felt a bit resentful because no one ever told me, "You are part of the major plan; you are an important part of this organisation." I am so tired of hearing – even at my level of success – that "Women lack the experience", "Women lack the skills". Why don't they teach us them?'

It is the end of a long day. Linda Agran has been tapping into too many unpleasant memories. But the present is not that great either. She has lost out on the franchise bid for Anglia, which makes her feel bitter. Commissioning editors and heads of department don't return her phone calls, which makes her feel even more bitter.

'I'm so depressed. I try and put out of my brain all the things that I'm waiting to hear, waiting to hear, waiting to hear . . . I've been waiting to hear from the BBC on the Pepys diaries (Kenneth Branagh to star and direct). Fourteen months later, the answer comes back: "No. It's too much money."

'I really resent pitching to people who've had less success than I've had. It sounds arrogant, but it's true. I see indifferent men making decisions, and I don't want to do it any more. I don't want the fight.'

I ask her: if I had interviewed her at any other time in her career, would I have found her so disillusioned with the television and film industry?

She says: 'If you'd interviewed me in the early days of Euston, I would have said: "I'm too busy having such a wonderful time here. Can't talk. Bye."

'At London Weekend, I would have said, "I feel really

delighted and pleased that London Weekend has accepted me and that everyone's been so nice to me. And I'm pleased that I've been able to deliver them *London's Burning.*"

'At Paravision [in 1988] I would have said, "International co-productions are the future and, God knows, I want to be at the forefront of all of that."

'And today, I'm saying, "If anyone can think of a really good way for me to earn a living and get out of this game – I'll get out right now."'

In the two years since we last spoke, Agran produced *Bye Bye Baby* written by Jack Rosenthal, screened on Channel 4. It won the 1992 Prix Europa and the WGGB best screenplay in 1993; *Boswell and Johnson's Tour of the Western Isles* for BBC's Screen 2 slot, written by John Byrne, starring Robbie Coltrane and John Sessions; and *Moving Story* for Carlton TV, written by Jack Rosenthal and others.

JANET STREET-PORTER

MADAM YOUTH

Janet Street-Porter started training as an architect, but went on to become a design writer, a national newspaper columnist and, in the mid-1970s, a television presenter on a variety of current affairs series' and magazine shows. In 1980 she became a producer. Her greatest hit was *Network 7*, the BAFTA award-winning, innovative weekly current affairs programme which she devised for Channel 4 in 1986. In 1988, she was appointed the BBC's first Head of Youth Programmes, and introduced the early evening *Def II* slots. Her flagship programmes in this role are the award-winning *Reportage* and the *Rough Guide* travel series. In 1991, Street-Porter was designated head of Youth and Entertainment Features. In January 1994, she was appointed Head of Independent Productions for the Entertainment Group within the corporation.

'Yo, yo, YO, yes this is really happening. Dance Energy – itsbackinfulleffect with a slamming new series and a ramjamfirst show . . .'

The lights are on full glare. The set is a huge barn of a room in Manchester, white with Mondrian blocks of colour in the background. Normski is doing his presenting thing. He is sweating. He can't get the words out fast enough. He keeps fluffing his lines: 'And now people, time to find out what's happening out there in the record club and gig scene. Kicking off with two hot releases the first from Ce Ce Penniston, a track called "Finally" . . . Jazzy Jeff and the Fresh Prince return to the seventies with a version of "Ring My . . ." oh shit.'

Standing next to me is a woman who appears to be at least six foot tall. She is looking on impassively. She has beacon-red hair. She is wearing spectacles, black tights, flat shoes, a very short pleated skirt, and a canary yellow jacket with big black buttons. Her shoulders are hunched around a plastic bag which is full of papers and magazines. She is over 45, but looks like a bolshy gangly schoolgirl. She is, of course, Janet Street-Porter, the one blast of colour in the monochrome Corporation of British Broadcasting.

The very first time I meet Street-Porter, for a preliminary chat, I have not done my homework. She mentions Normski, I look puzzled, and her mouth falls open like the gangway to a P & O ferry. It goes without saying that I *should* have read the cuttings file. But Street-Porter's reaction was an early warning of the BBC head of youth's myopia; her tendency to inflate her own impact on society; her absolute assumption that her interviewer would be familiar with the club scene highlighted in one of her programmes. I *mean* . . . how could one *not* have heard of Normski?

Street-Porter wants to be written about and talked about, but through her own lens. It matters to her that she is known. And I have doubly transgressed since Normski, it transpires, is not only Janet Street-Porter's star; he is also her – um – well, whatever the hip word is for boyfriend.

My subject is one of a handful of senior women at the BBC. Her London office is a penthouse suite, she controls an annual budget of £28 million and a staff of 250. Her department has an annual turnover of £30 million, and rising. She wields a considerable amount of power, and she wants more. Janet Street-Porter wants to be the BBC's first female controller. Is this such a ludicrous ambition?

Her television career started in 1975. She was a presenter on a current affairs series, and various early evening magazine shows: *The London Weekend Show*, *The Six O'Clock Show*, *Saturday Night People*. For five years the cockney motor-mouth and fluorescent hair-dos regularly appeared on the screen. Then in 1980 she turned producer, creating youth and children's programmes for ITV and Channel 4. *Network 7*, devised in 1986 for Channel 4, was her greatest hit – a two-hour weekly current affairs programme, with factual stories, live events and what Street-Porter's curriculum vitae describes as 'innovative use of graphics', and what her detractors tended to describe as mind-numbing infotainment for the pea-brained. Jibes be damned. The series won its creator a BAFTA award for originality in 1988, an audience of one-third of those aged between 16 and 24, and a job with the BBC.

In 1988 Janet Street-Porter was made the BBC's first commissioning editor for youth programmes, and the tabloids responded by dubbing her 'Miss Yoof'. She came up with the DEF II slot (DEF as in street-cred for 'happening'): Monday and Wednesday evenings on BBC2, it reaches an audience of 1–2 million viewers. Her flagship programmes are the speedy current affairs series *Reportage* and the 'electronic scrapbook' Rough Guide travel shows, with nocturnal Magenta de Vine hiding behind her black shades, and Sankha Guha as co-presenter (now Rajan Datar). Street-Porter discovered Antoine de Caunes and *Rapido* when she went to France to see Prince in concert. The BBC bought the series, and now De Caunes has his own show, *Eurotrash*, with the fashion designer Jean-Paul Gaultier, on Channel 4.

In 1991, in recognition of the fact that she was capable of attracting viewers who were older than 25, Street-Porter's title was beefed up to head of youth and entertainment features. The programmes she has commissioned and produced under her extended title, however, have not been found universally entertaining. *Ps and Qs*, a quiz show on what's U and non-U in 1990s social etiquette, has drawn audiences of 3 million. *The Look*, behind-the-scenes documentaries about the fashion world, was well received. *The Vampyr*, a five-part 'soap' adaptation of Heinrich Marschner's nineteenth-century opera, set in present-day London with lots of sex and drugs, picked up a Prix Italia Award in 1993. But *Style Trial*, a game show in which contestants made films about their lifestyles which were then dissected and pilloried by a panel of minor celebrities, was axed because of disappointing viewing figures.

At the time of our meetings, in the early 1990s, Janet Street-Porter's youth department is being moved to Manchester as part of John Birt's massive restructuring programme for the BBC. The press is divided in its response to the announcement. Upmarket papers report it as a promotion. The tabloids smirk that it signals her demise: 'Janet Street-Porter has become the victim of a savage reorganisation of power at the BBC2', and, 'Have the men in grey suits finally beaten Miss Yoof?'

The tabloid press has taunted her seemingly forever. As Zoe Heller observed in an interview with Street-Porter, 'The *Sun* – shortly after she was taken on as the BBC's first Commissioning Editor for Youth Programmes in 1988 – printed a picture of Street-Porter alongside one of a horse, with an invitation to readers to phone and nominate the less prepossessing.' But the tabloids alone are not to blame for Street-Porter's image. Nor is it simply the prejudice of the male mandarins who run the BBC which explains why JSP may rise no further than her senior position in the corporation. The truth of the matter, it strikes me, is that Janet Street-Porter is in some ways her own worst enemy.

Most of the time she carries on like a horrible, maladjusted teenager: swearing, scowling, slouching around in her suede trainers and designer leggings. She is always at least half an hour late for interviews, and seems to make a point of *not* apologising. I later discover that I am not alone in suffering this treatment. The *Evening Standard* quoted this comment from one of her 'underlings': 'She grossly overcommits herself, is hugely disorganised and unreliable about time if you're not important. She'll turn up late for meetings or not at all.' In fact, the only good thing one can say about her time-keeping is that it is not selective.

On one of the days when I trail around in her wake, JSP's secretary has a conversation by proxy with Nigel Finch, the editor of 'Arena', who is to direct *The Vampyr*. They are arranging a meeting. JSP: 'Tell him to eff off. I'll be there. Alan's [Yentob] promised me the money, so I don't want no grief.' Finch's reply is relayed: 'Just tell the old goat to be on time.' A week later, we are at her home and she is on the phone to Tony Elliott, the owner of *Time Out*, who is one of her ex-husbands. They are meeting for lunch – game pie at the Hilton. 'No, no,' she keeps saying. 'I won't be late.' I even witness a ticking-off from Jonathan Powell: 'The controller BBC1 and Jane Hewland have been waiting for the head of youth programmes, and she is late.'

Here is a riddle. Most times, when famous people unwittingly let down their guard, they reveal an unpleasant, hitherto unseen, aspect of their character. The curious thing about Janet Street-Porter is that it is only when her aged-brat mask slips – talking to an ex-husband or catching a few words with Normski [she calls him plain old Norman in private] or relaxing with her good friend Lynne Franks or sitting at a table surrounded by women who like her – that you catch a glimpse of someone quite congenial. This person smiles a lot and seems at ease with herself. You begin to understand why this person gets so incredibly hurt when she is lampooned in the press. And why she is romantic or vulnerable enough to get married so often. (There are three ex-husbands: Tim Street-Porter, a photographer; Tony Elliott, a publisher; and Frank Cvitanovich, a filmmaker.) So why, one has to wonder, does Janet Street-Porter take such pains to present her least attractive characteristics to the world at large? She clearly needs an image rethink.

And, funnily enough, in the months that follow our interviews this is precisely what she sets out to do. My first inkling that something is up is when Street-Porter phones my publisher and says that the nature of her work is quite different these days and she thinks this should be acknowledged and, by the way, she doesn't want her chapter to focus on her family.

A few months later Zoë Heller interviews her for the *Independent on Sunday*. The headline is TIME TO ADJUST HER SET. Street-Porter, according to Heller, was assiduous in her attempts to prevent a picture of herself as a highly serious 'professional person of consequence' who goes to the theatre, to the opera and goes walking. These days, gravitas was in, wackiness was out, and the big job of Controller at the BBC was very much on her mind. But as Heller observed, 'Many of the public "misconceptions" that she is now anxious to dispel are ideas that she has happily promoted about herself in the past.'

In 1993 I receive another phone call from Janet Street-Porter: 'A book's come out on producers – inaccurate – I've been misquoted – I'm doing different things now. And I don't want you writing about my family.'

What she did say about her family was either pretty innocuous or already in print. She had spoken mostly about a godmother, 'Auntie' Eileen, who took the young Janet Bull to the opera, to the ballet, or to art-house films every Saturday, and I wonder for one spooky moment whether JSP has made it all up, as part of her reinvention.

*

Manchester is a blur of corridors and lifts and empty rooms and endless discussions about money. JSP has a filthy cold and sucks lozenges all day long, but her stamina is impressive. By 5.20 we are on our nth meeting of the day and she's still raring to go. She tells me later that she is so exhausted by the end of each day that when she goes home she can't speak for at least an hour.

Street-Porter is familiar with every last detail of her productions: the look of the shows, the graphics for the opening credits, the presenters' clothes, the music. She talks knowledgeably about 'wipes' and 'whip-pans'. She is a hands-on producer. At one point she turns to one of her directors and says, 'People don't like working with me because I interfere too much.' He answers slightly toadily, 'I would use the word interventionist, rather than interfering.'

Lunch is in a Malaysian restaurant in central Manchester. JSP tucks into her noodles with gusto and proudly informs us that 'Neil Tennant [of the Pet Shop Boys] says I've got the biggest appetite of anyone he knows.' She produces a big notebook, like a doodle-pad, from her plastic bag, and writes MOST IMPORTANT THINGS TO DO in scrawly capitals.

High on the agenda is getting another black face on to the screen. JSP's fans, as one journalist observed, say that she has worked hard 'to promote talented blacks, Asians and females'. The young man in question looks great, but has he got the current affairs background? A female reporter is being difficult and JSP hates being messed around. Her usual response is: 'Well, if s/he has problems with the job, I'm sure there are plenty of other people around who would like it.' She tells her director, 'Look, it's no good being nice to them. They hate you.'

There is a long discussion about wardrobe and budgets and the questionable clothes sense of the reporting team. JSP reminisces about her presenting days: 'When I was on *Vox Pop*, they wouldn't let me wear my fur coat because they wanted me to look plebby.' Suddenly – eureka – she has a brainwave. T-shirts. They can all wear T-shirts. Black, of course. And maybe the star reporter can have a slightly different design. The name of the series will be emblazoned on their chests. It'll be cheap, effective and terrific product placement. She is well pleased with herself. 'A brilliant idea, even if I say so myself,' she tells me.

In another meeting, I am struck by how sharp she is about budgeting tricks. An investor has pulled out. No matter,

JSP says. Look at the books over the past three years, find the unused resources, make up the shortfall in the budget. She's asking for outside quotes from production companies before Producers' Choice (John Birt's cost-saving measure which forces all BBC units to compete in price and quality against commercial rivals) has even been introduced. 'Why?' someone asks. 'To force the internal prices down,' she replies.

It is the end of the day. Two hundred dancers have arrived. So have the six bands, with names like Zodiac Youth and Adeva. As they filter into the vast white space, one of Street-Porter's senior male colleagues starts talking to me. He tells me that I should be talking to other, less aggressive, women, and reels off a list of producers and directors who are so modest about their achievements, that, unfortunately, no one outside their industry has heard of them. 'The problem with Janet Street-Porter [and her famous peers],' he says, 'is that they're still fighting the battles they've won.'

Television Centre, White City

This is a turn-up for the book. The newspapers have been punctuated with references – anonymous, naturally – to strained relations between the controllers and Janet Street-Porter, and I am to sit in on meetings with Street-Porter and her bosses.

I had been quite candid to Street-Porter about my reasons for sitting in on these meetings. I had told her that I wanted to see how a powerful woman negotiates with her more powerful male colleagues. Janet Street-Porter, I am amazed to report, comes on like a pussy-cat. She wheedles, coaxes and flatters. Alan Yentob sits sleepily in his chair, looking like a koala who has overdosed on eucalyptus leaves. JSP complains that Yentob's partner is looking skinny. Yentob makes a joke about his own figure and JSP indulges him: 'Oh, it doesn't show, you wear baggy clothes.'

It is when she gets down to the nitty-gritty of pitching programmes or talking about the inappropriate wardrobe of a presenter that the encounter becomes mildly awkward. Partly because Yentob looks so bored; he really does not seem to want to be bothered with these details. It is oddly diminishing to see Street-Porter having to sing for her supper this way. It is also a useful reminder of the limits of her sphere of influence. Yentob sits up only when JSP informs him – with the most dazzling grin – that she would like a substantial sum of money, please, for her pet project, *The Vampyr*.

Someone in the next room (it turns out to be Jonathan Powell) makes a loud remark about Manchester. JSP pretends to be furious (she probably *is* furious). Her deferential manner suddenly evaporates, as she breaks into her characteristic vernacular. The controllers and JSP seem to be joshing together perfectly amicably, but Street-Porter – and her Mancunian exile – is the butt of the jokes. Afterwards, back in her own office, she looks drained and paler than ever.

At Home

Janet Street-Porter's house – home is really too cosy a word – is a futuristic folly in Clerkenwell. Entirely surrounded by building sites, it is a sort of fortress-cum-palace designed by one of her best friends, Piers Gough, who was a fellow student at the Architectural Association.

JSP comes to the door and takes me on an abbreviated tour. Everything is jokingly deconstructed or reversed or demolished. You get to one part of the house by climbing the outdoor fire escape. A giant colander masquerading as a chandelier dangles from a black plastic cord. Her bed is reportedly a British Rail parcel trolly.

We talk in her study. In the bookcase I see five Ruth Rendells in a row, Tama Janowitz, Richard Rayner, Peter York, Bret Easton Ellis, Norman Mailer's *Marilyn* and ... *The Wild Flowers of Great Britain*. One wall of the study is devoted to the history of Janet Street-Porter. Files upon files of old photographs and cuttings. It seems the right time to go back to the beginning.

Street-Porter was a natural school swot. She was in the Young Conservatives quiz team, she was in the Girl Guides, she was Charity Monitor in the sixth form, she was a member of the Spartan Ladies' Athletics Club, she was good at netball and rounders. She sounds like a model schoolgirl in her red and black striped blazer at the high-achieving Fulham grammar school Lady Margaret, where she took 10 O levels and 3 A levels and was told she should also take elocution lessons if she wanted to get anywhere in life. Can she laugh about this now that her teachers were proved so wrong? 'No, it made me feel fucking inferior,' she says feelingly.

In amongst all this wholesome 'Four Marys' activity, Street-Porter somehow found time to design her own clothes, dress up as a Mod, and discover boys and clubs and bands. It is when she talks about her first forays into the pop culture in which she was later to become a key player that she stops looking sulky, at last, and her eyes begin to shine.

She left home when she was 19. Years of arguing about not being at home by 10.30 had left their mark. 'By the time I went to college,' she says, 'there was a big distance between me and my family.' Her friends at the Architectural Association became her new family and, more than 20 years on, she still goes on holiday with them.

One of the highlights of her shortlived student years was being hand-picked by Antonioni – on account of her fab gear – to be an extra in *Blow-Up, the* cinematic expression of the Swinging Sixties. 'At that time, I was wearing silver plastic clothes at college. In the movie I wore red and yellow plastic trousers, a silver coat and I had silver hair. I was bloody brilliant, or I thought I was. This bloke came up to me and started going, "I ... am ... a ... Dalek" and everyone laughed at me.'

Street-Porter dropped out of college in her second year to pursue a career in journalism. She worked for and with Audrey Slaughter, Lynne Franks, Maggie Goodman, Frankie McGowan and Eve Pollard on *Petticoat*: 'It was a real laugh. I learnt about layout and design. I could commission who I wanted. I had people like Terry Gilliam and Michael Roberts working for me.' In the late 1960s and early 1970s, Tim and Janet Street-Porter's joint bylines appeared on pieces from Japan and America. Janet Street-Porter wrote a Saturday column and helped edit the fashion pages for Shirley Conran on the *Daily Mail*'s new *Femail* section; she wrote about design for *Queen* magazine and worked on the *Evening Standard*. She split up with her husband, took up with Tony Elliott and started working for *Time Out*. When he offered her the job as deputy editor of his magazine the staff went on strike, JSP recounts without emotion. So she resigned, escaped to America and came back to be a radio journalist with LBC before turning to television. Her first job as a TV presenter was on *The London Weekend Show* in 1975.

Janet Street-Porter's remarks about the grey men in grey suits who run television have been well documented. But – as I discover – this does not mean that she would necessarily prefer to see women running the show. It is always difficult to elicit a considered response from her, but what she does say is: 'The thing about me is that I think like a man. I suppose I'm a woman – I've got a pair of tits – but I don't believe in singling women out as a disabled group. I fight my own fights.'

On the floor in my study are three newspaper cuttings. The headlines tell a story: BBC ACCUSED OF REMAINING MALE DOMINATED (*Independent*, 10 April 1991); STREET-PORTER IN LINE FOR BBC1 JOB (*Independent*, 1993) – 'Janet Street-Porter, the BBC's head of youth and entertainment features, is emerging as the strongest inside candidate for the job of controller of BBC1 Television'; and RIVAL IN BID TO WOO JANET FROM THE BBC (*Evening Standard*, 30 September 1993) – 'Janet Street-Porter is reported to be holding "active" talks about leaving the BBC at the end of her contract, signalling the end of her ambitions to land one of the corporation's top jobs . . .'

Janet Street-Porter did not become controller of BBC1. Alan Yentob did. She did not become controller of BBC2. Michael Jackson did. When Michael Jackson vacated his role as head of Music and Arts, Kim Evans, his deputy, was appointed. And David Liddiment from Granada Television replaced James Moir as head of Light Entertainment the same year.

When we last speak, two years after our first meetings, I mention to JSP that I have decided to interview some women from the next generation. There is a slight pause, and she says, 'I don't know about the *next* generation. They don't seem to know what to do with *my* generation.' I had never heard Janet Street-Porter speak so quietly.

ALWAYS THE DEPUTY

The Newspaper Industry

The day that we have a woman editor on a broadsheet newspaper will be when women are taken seriously. But that day will take an aeon to arrive.

(SUE DOUGLAS, EXECUTIVE EDITOR, SUNDAY TIMES)

We will know that there is equality when there are as many second-rate women in newspapers as there are second-rate men.

(VERONICA WADLEY, ASSISTANT EDITOR, DAILY TELEGRAPH)

Women have never wielded so much influence and power in the media as they do today. This is how it may appear, at least to the outsider. Fleet Street is one of the most visible examples of the progress of women. Since the early 1990s there have been three women editors of national newspapers. The *News of the World* is edited by Patsy Chapman; the *People* by Bridget Rowe; the *Sunday Express* by Eve Pollard.

It was an outsider to the British establishment, the Australian-born Rupert Murdoch, who was the first newspaper proprietor in this country to appoint a woman editor. He placed Wendy Henry at the helm of the *News of the World* in 1987. She went on to edit the *People*, and earned the dubious reputation of being sacked by both Rupert Murdoch and Robert Maxwell for being too controversial.

The appointments were all the more remarkable in the light of the cut-throat nature of papers at the 'popular' end of the market. At the time, Pollard was the first female editor of the *Sunday Mirror*. The response of the late Jean Rook, 'the First Lady of Fleet Street', was astonishment. 'In my day it just didn't happen,' she said. 'You wouldn't even expect a woman to be a features editor.'

None of the women appears to have altered the tone of the papers they edit. Indeed, Wendy Henry's departures were attributed to her overstepping the mark on taste and decency. Pollard maintains that she highlighted the need for crèches and launched the seatbelts for children campaign in the *Sunday Mirror* – issues which she was sensitive about as a working mother, and which were aimed particularly at a female readership. Her critics claimed that the sleaze factor hardly altered under her editorship, referring to her front-page stories on the pay rates of Fiona 'Five-Times-a-Night' Wright, and other tawdry scoops.

It is only when you consider that there are 21 top editing positions on Fleet Street newspapers, 18 of which are occupied by men, that the dazzling figure of Three Women Editors loses its lustre. As a top-ranking woman at News Limited says, 'There should be ten women editors by the year 2000. But my guess is that there won't be.'

Women have been allowed to edit the downmarket tabloids – the so-called comics of Fleet Street – but they are still effectively barred from the heavyweight broadsheets. This is significant because it is the quality newspapers which have real influence; their editors are the opinion-makers of society. Which is why, when Eve Pollard became the first female editor of a mid-market paper, it was seen as such an important bridging step for women between the popular and quality press. As one commentator put it, 'The chair of the *Sunday Express* ... represents a slice of the British establishment, in a way her previous jobs on Fleet Street did not.'

In late 1993 I asked Amanda Platell, the young director of marketing of the Mirror Group, when she thought we might expect there to be a female editor of a quality broadsheet. 'I don't think that any of us will see it in our lifetime,' she said. This was at a meeting which was attended by at least 200 women, many of whom were in their late twenties.

Her comment was depressing but not entirely surprising, since I had focused my research and interviews on the quality press. I had spoken to Veronica Wadley, assistant editor and features supremo of the *Daily Telegraph*. Her editorial strengths, as she saw it, were in 'soft' features, but she had also edited the leader page for a year, giving the position up only when she had her first child. Max Hastings, editor of the *Daily Telegraph*, appeared to value her opinion. During the ERM crisis, for instance, she was asked to attend the news pages conference: 'Max asked me to stay because he thought that I might have a different insight to offer.'

After our first meeting, Wadley wrote me a letter. It suggests that Max Hastings's interest in the opinions of his female colleagues is not necessarily shared by other *Telegraph* males. 'On the subject of men v. women,' she wrote, 'perhaps I did not make enough of the fact that I do think that women can often bring a wider range of interests to a paper, and a different perspective on certain stories. Which perhaps explains why some men are so protective and patronising. They simply can't get used to the idea that just because you might be interested in the ideas of Christian Lacroix or Penelope Leach, this doesn't mean that you don't know anything about Major and the money markets.'

But if the fogey-ish *Times* and tweedy *Telegraph* do not wave the feminist banner in the workplace, what's the surprise in that? I shifted my attention to the liberal news-papers: the *Guardian*, the *Observer* (both owned by the same group) and the *Independent*. The readers of these three newspapers may assume that the men who run the papers are pro-women, because that is what their leader articles suggest. But what is the reality behind the mythology? Do the editorials reflect what the editors really think about women? My conversations with the women who work on these newspapers would suggest otherwise.

The *Independent* has a particular reputation among the liberal newspapers for being an Oxbridge, Boys' Own outfit. When its Sunday paper was launched, a film crew came in to record the event. Half-way through filming the daily news conference, one bright spark noticed that there were no women in the picture. Some juniors were hastily wheeled in to masquerade as senior editorial women. Even now the paper employs so few senior women that they are hesitant to speak to me for fear of being identified. One journalist says that I should sit in on conference; the numbers still say it all. Another woman makes the point that because the *Independent* was a new paper, 'The founders really had an opportunity to represent women properly. But they showed their hand. Didn't they?'

If, I have been warned, you ask Andreas Whittam Smith, the editor of the *Independent*, a tough question, he will make you feel uncouth. Actually, he makes you feel like an appalling yob. We are talking about general working pat-terns, how women and men differ, research from America, the importance of attracting more women readers, and so on. We are getting on well. Then I ask him why all the top jobs on his newspaper are filled by men. His sober, kindly face sags. He says that it is all a matter of time, but the expres-sion in his eyes – mournful, not angry – seems to say: how can you ask me something so indelicate? 'Women are now in the number two positions. And next time we look, they'll be in the number one positions. That's all. When I entered journalism in 1962, there weren't any women. Anywhere.' Ah.

The *Independent* is an excellent newspaper. But there is a discrepancy between its editorial line and its editorial practice, which is worth exploring.

At the beginning of the 1990s the *Independent* geared itself up to respond to Peter Sissons's assertion that it was difficult to find high-flying women for the BBC's *Question Time*: '"You must be joking," the *Independent* thought. So did many readers, who wrote in and said so: We threw down the gauntlet and asked you to nominate "intelligent, articulate and well-informed women" whose views would be trenchant and lively. You did. The final total fell a little short of 200 and came from almost every area of professional and vocational life.'

On consecutive days, the *Independent* devoted two full pages to a short-list of 72 women the newspaper considered were perfect candidates for *Question Time*. This was a shining example of how a newspaper can react effectively and dynamically to what is, essentially, a reader-led campaign.

What was particularly interesting was the paper's serious attempt to explore the issue of whether women operate on a different agenda to men. Women decline to appear on *Question Time* in far greater numbers than men. Is this because they dislike the format of the programme, which requires its participants to be combative and highly opinionated, not unlike a debating society at a boys' public school – or Parliament, for that matter? In short, is it *Question Time* itself which is at fault?

This is the *Independent* at its very best: tackling an issue head-on, assigning a member of staff, in this case Penny Jackson, to work on it full time, devoting whole pages to the debate, and, above all, recognising that a subject which is of primary concern to women is also of wider importance.

Elsewhere in the paper, there are signs that its editor

takes women seriously. The leading articles are invariably pro-women, which is significant since Whittam Smith tells me that his female staff cannot often be prevailed upon to write them. (*The Times*, in contrast, has three women leader writers.) 'Leader writing, I think, may be slightly foreign to the temperament of women,' he says. 'They don't think that it's very clever to set down an opinion, just like that. I can't quite put my finger on it, but I think that the form may be repugnant in some way to women.'

So, one may assume, the *Independent's* rousing leaders on the position of working women, with headlines such as A FAIR SHARE FOR WOMEN, have been written by men. And even if a woman has been roped in, a leader is different from a column. It does not allow for mavericks. The very point of its solemn anonymity is that it stands for the general attitudes of the newspaper; *ergo*, those of its editor.

But given that the *Independent's* women journalists are not getting their fair share of higher-paid positions, and given that Lynn Barber, when she was the star interviewer of the *Independent on Sunday*, told me that the paper was the most sexist place she'd ever worked (and she was at *Penthouse* before moving on to the *Sunday Express*), and since all the decisions about senior appointments on the newspaper are made by four men, and since Whittam Smith himself tells me that 'some wonderful women reporters have not been so effective after they have had children', one might be tempted to say that he should put his own house in order before making pronouncements about other people's.

I am not the first person, of course, to notice this anomaly. Nor is the *Independent* the only liberal newspaper to flourish the pro-women banner while conveniently overlooking the fact that its own track record on women journalists is not exactly impressive. In the early 1990s, this item found its way into *Private Eye*:

In its job ads, the holier-than-thou Grauniad proudly trails itself as an 'equal opportunities employer'. So the newspaper naturally gave a warm welcome to John Major's recent launch of Opportunity 2000, the mission to give women a better chance of promotion at work.

'Only one in five of the 45,000 people on public bodies – from the Bank of England to the Registry of Friendly Societies – is a woman,' the paper tut-tutted in a pious editorial. 'Local government is even worse, with only five female executives out of 400. Company board-rooms have 18 female directors among the 1,333 in the top 100 companies.'

And how many women are to be found in the upper-echelons at the Guardian itself?

The following key executives are men: editor, deputy editor, executive editor, managing editor, foreign editor, City editor, weekend magazine editor, home editor, news editor, sports editor, features editor, literary editor, chief sub-editor, pictures editor and the three principal leader-writers.

Women occupy the humbler posts of women's editor (surprise!), home affairs editor, assistant foreign editor, arts page editor, letters editor, and . . . er, that's it.

And what of the *Observer*, the third major liberal newspaper? Yvonne Roberts edited its Living pages from 1990 to 1992. She was often the only woman at conference, and certainly the only dissenting voice in the male orthodoxy. 'I was always pointing out the number of dead white males who appeared on the book pages; the number of cricketers who appeared in the big profile; the latest EC directive's implications for maternity leave. I got sick to death of having to remind the men that women exist.'

Roberts was operating from a position of strength. She wanted to write; the *Observer* persuaded her to stay on as an editor. She was doing them a favour, albeit a well-paid one. 'The problem is that if you are a career journalist, and you are the most senior female executive at conference, you are *not* going to open your mouth all the time,' she says. 'Too many women remain silent because they're fearful that if they speak out, they will lose the slender gains they've made. But what is journalism, if it's not a risk business?'

Nevertheless, Roberts is enormously optimistic about the prospects for women journalists. Why? 'Because we've got capitalism on our side.' She offers the American example, where newspapers, across the board, were losing women readers; editors were forced to recognise that in order to regain them, they must change the structures of their workforce: appoint more senior women, have a more evenly balanced gender split in 'hard' areas such as politics and foreign news, and reappraise the presentation of their 'soft' features.

Andreas Whittam Smith has been doing his own research to find out how to woo more women readers to the *Independent*. In an effort to find out What Women Want, Whittam Smith set up a series of internal conferences. Every week for two months, the newspaper's female journalists were invited to speak out. And this is what they told him: women need to see that they are visible in the newspaper.

Whittam Smith listened and learned. 'It sounds mechanical, but I now run three bits of analysis on this subject. I regularly show all the heads of department what proportion of the people in our pictures are men and women. The figures are running at about 75 per cent men; 25 per cent women. I am trying to raise it. I also run a count on the number of letters that are signed by women. Since we started the exercise, the number of letters published by women has risen from about 15 per cent to 30 per cent. And I count the number of women's bylines. We knew that we couldn't change that very quickly because your staff is given. We could only change it by the use of contributors. About 25 per cent of our bylines are female.'

I ask him whether he thinks that the proportion of women readers would also rise if there were a higher proportion of senior women on the paper. 'Yes,' Whittam Smith says. 'I'm fairly sure it would.' So – perhaps, it is absurdly simple – but why doesn't he just appoint them? Lynn Barber presented an equally straightforward solution at one of the famous meetings. '"Why not fill all your senior vacancies with women until you achieve parity?" They thought this was hilarious. But why not, for heaven's sake?'

'Decent' and 'honourable' are the first adjectives Whittam Smith's female staff use to describe him. Swiftly followed by the words 'traditional male' and 'of his generation'. (No one has yet been refused a job-share, he says. If a woman drops a day's work to spend more time with her family, however, Whittam Smith agrees that her career prospects are likely to suffer.)

I ask him whether he considers that the *Independent* is a sympathetic environment for women. 'I think the women here are subjected to . . .' He starts again: 'I think a number of my men colleagues unconsciously treat women in a patronising fashion, to a degree that irritates some of my women colleagues. They notice it all right.'

It is time for conference. This is the meeting at the end of the day when the department heads present their best stories for tomorrow's edition. It is like an auction. Andreas Whittam Smith, at the head of the table, peering over his spectacles, is the auctioneer. 'Maastricht around the world . . . 600 words from our correspondents . . . Anything from the business pages? 500 words? Fine. Home?' Whittam Smith turns to the picture editor. What's he got for page 1? The obvious photograph is Mona Bauwens coming out of court. A woman! 'And what does that make the score? Six men; two women.'

It is 6 p.m. It will be some hours yet before tomorrow's edition is put to bed. Whittam Smith has done his calculations; now I do mine. Sitting around the table are some of the most senior people on the *Independent*. And what is the score? Ten men. And two women – one of whom is me.

*

The Soft Spot

In the late 1980s, the chaps who run the *Guardian* decided it was time to update the paper. They wanted to attract a younger, hipper readership. Out with the old guard, bring in the new.

The *Guardian* women's page was the most potent symbol of what the Young Turks least liked about the *Guardian*'s image – worthy, right-on, low on style, heavy on consensus feminism. How old-fashioned. How pitifully out of tune with the racier tastes and aspirations of the readers the paper wanted to attract. It had become the butt of jokes. It featured in *The Singing Detective*, under Dennis Potter's long list of the most boring things known to man: a right turn-off. No further proof was needed. The *Guardian* women's page had clearly had its day.

When the rumours of its death sentence began to circulate, a meeting was held, attended by the mass ranks of the women's page contributors. The *Guardian* women's page, they pleaded, was a sanctuary. It was the last bastion of feminism. Fold the women's page at your peril, they cried, for the *Guardian* will lose its female readership. It was this last point which must have proved the most compelling.

Brenda Polan, who had edited the page for six years, was sacked, along with most of her contributors. The late Jill Tweedie, the feminist writer, journalist, and stalwart of the *Guardian* women's page was one of the last to go, in February 1991.

Louise Chunn was appointed editor of the woman's page. Her previous job was deputy editor of *Elle*, a magazine which is devoted largely to fashion spreads and celebrity interviews. She is in her early-thirties. A year or so after Chunn's appointment, in 1989, the journalist and author Kate Saunders sought her views on feminism for the *Sunday Times*. 'In the 1970s and 1980s, it was assumed that all women felt exactly the same about every single issue, and I don't believe that's true any more,' Chunn said. 'Idealism doesn't win anything. I'm not saying we have got to copy the boys, but we have to live in the real world. Our generation is likely to benefit from taking a more conventional route. That is grown-up feminism.'

In 1992, a new study of British attitudes was published which revealed a strong anti-feminist sentiment in young people. Five hundred male and 500 female students were asked their views on feminists and feminism. The co-authors of the study, Dr Gerda Siann of Glasgow University and Dr Halla Beloff, said: 'Half of the female students questioned made negative comments about feminists, such as, "campaigning busy-bodies; man-hater; lesbian sergeant-major type."' Even more men were negative – one, who said he was "slightly sympathetic towards feminists", used the following words to describe them: "short hair, dungarees, lesbian, parrot earrings, close-minded, bitch, loud mouth, sexist."'

And where does the youth of today get these funny ideas? Well, as it happens, from large sections of the media. The feminist and writer Joan Smith was reduced to writing an article in the *Guardian* to spell out that feminists can live in attractive homes, have long blonde hair, wear make-up and nice clothes, after she had been interviewed by a woman from the *Evening Standard* who, looking at her living-room, reeled in astonishment and said, 'You don't expect this degree of femininity from a feminist.'

The dictionary definition of feminism, *I* feel reduced to spelling out, is as unthreatening as this: 'a doctrine or movement that advocates equal rights for women'.

In 1991 Chunn had launched her own survey of contemporary attitudes. *Guardian* readers were asked to fill in a questionnaire covering points such as, 'Do you call yourself a feminist?' 'Treading on the heels of Tweedie's departure, the survey could be interpreted as a symbol of self-doubt at the dear old *Guardian*,' Kate Saunders wrote. 'Can they still afford to carry the unfashionable feminist label?'

The answer, according to the results of the *Guardian's*

survey, which drew an impressive 11,000 responses from the readers of the women's page, was a resounding *yes*. Nearly two-thirds of women under 35, whom the media has dubbed the 'post-feminists', reject the prefix. They continue to call themselves feminists, even though roughly the same proportion believe the feminist movement is viewed negatively.

Although 'the young women have not swept the gains of their mothers under a carpet of selfishness and personal greed ...' the *Guardian* surmised, 'they are not the same feminists their mothers were ... They no longer believe that all women need to unite behind a single banner. It was the schism of the women's movement in the seventies, after all, that contributed to the shrewish image of feminism that still lingers today.'

Louise Chunn tells me that *Everywoman* magazine's response to the survey was that 'it was appalling that the *Guardian* was excited by the fact that two-thirds of its women's page readers would call themselves feminists.' But, Chunn says, with some determination, 'I *was* excited and surprised by the results. "Feminist" is a frightening word for a lot of women for damn good reasons. It has been used as a stick to beat both women and men. It is used by the tabloids as a form of abuse for any woman who is powerful or opinionated.'

I ask Chunn why she thinks the *Guardian* men appointed her as the women's page editor. 'I think they liked it when I said that I didn't read anything on it,' she says semi-flippantly. 'My biggest card was sex,' she continues. 'We could have renamed it the Sex Page. The early nineties was the era of Madonna-feminism. I wanted the page to reflect that in-your-face, younger strand of feminism.' Anything else? 'It was said to me, by one of the people involved in my appointment, that they were very pleased that the job was going to a woman who was married and had children. I was a normal person, like the readers, and I wasn't particularly political, as anyone who has seen the pages under my tenure would realise. I was also more glamorous than my predecessors.'

The glamour factor, Chunn believes, makes it easier for her to get certain stories into the page. There were raised eyebrows at conference, for instance, when she announced that a man would be writing about his views on having sex with menstruating women. 'But it didn't get pulled,' she says. 'If I'd been the sort of person who doesn't wear lipstick and a velvet scarf, it might have been different.'

When I ask her how she fits in with the men who run the *Guardian*, Chunn starts quoting from a letter her father recently sent her. He has coined a new acronym: SNAG, which stands for Sensitive New Age Guy. (It is also Antipodean slang for sausage. Chunn was born and brought up in New Zealand.)

'People have this idea that the *Guardian* must be full of SNAGs,' she laughs. 'But while there may be some men like that further down the line, they're certainly not all like that. The guys at the top are Oxbridge types. I get on very well with them individually because they're amusing and entertaining. But *en masse*, I can feel excluded, particularly when they go on about football and cricket at conference. Usually, Georgina [Georgina Henry, the media editor and deputy features editor] and I will retaliate by talking about lipstick or periods. They usually get the point.'

In recent years, the liberal newspapers have been devoting an increasing amount of space to men sounding off about women. And about feminists, in particular. Editors, across the board, are clearly in tune with the conclusion of Glasgow University's survey of contemporary attitudes towards feminism: 'A theme apparently emerging is that in the wake of feminist victories it is men, rather than women, who are disadvantaged, if not economically, then emotionally and socially.'

In the early 1990s, the journalist Neil Lyndon attacked feminism in every newspaper – both liberal and conservative – that would give him space. Plenty did. And the *Guardian* has consistently devoted more space to men's opinions on women than vice versa – from Bryan Magee on 'Bad Feminist Arguments' to Philip Norman on men's sexual bewilderment.

The men get the prestigious cover stories, and three or four pages in which to develop their argument. The women's right to reply – when there is one – is printed towards the end of the paper or incorporated into the letters page.

G2, the tabloid section of the *Guardian*, had been running for a year when I spoke to Louise Chunn. 'Every day there's a front-page story [on G2], and it's well known on the paper that I'm disappointed that there haven't been any stories about women that aren't either anti-women or about fashion.' In a year!

Could it be, in newspaper speak, that women's voices are no longer 'sexy', whereas men's thoughts on intimacy, sexuality, emotions, women – you name it – could not be hotter?

I wonder, too, whether, in the present climate, younger women journalists are not encouraged to feel that it is actually quite smart to write knocking pieces about feminism. There is a whole school of sub-Julie Burchillian hackettes who seem to believe that a string of glib, half-clever phrases is a substitute for cogent thought. You expect to find it in the *Daily Mail*: 'Feminism – that immaculate deception – gave birth to a plethora of con tricks we would have been better off without . . .' et cetera, ad nauseam.

But you will find more sophisticated expression of the same sentiments in the quality press. Even in the *Guardian*. And why not? says Louise Chunn. 'I will simply not put up with this idea that there should be special pleading for women,' she says. 'It's part of the old feminist orthodoxy that "Thou must never criticise any feminist or any woman." We're all grown-ups now.'

This would all be fine if there really were some equity between the sexes; if women were written about in a balanced way. But the fact is that most newspapers are still all too willing to leap in and have a go at the female sex, as Matthew Parris noted in *The Times* in October 1993, in the wake of two big news stories:

Okay, so Austen Donnellan didn't rape her. Okay, so Labour's silly scheme to promote women to the shadow cabinet backfired. But to read the press commentaries, you could be forgiven for thinking that rape has now been shown to be a female plot against men, while the idea of trying to boost women in employment has been completely discredited . . .

It is at moments like these that the essentially male place that Fleet Street still is obtrudes . . . [But] some of the sourest anti-feminist sentiment comes from women. Those who have stayed at home, forsaking other ambitions for their family, can feel a special resentment for those who find a different life . . . Those who have done so, making their own way in the media or in politics, often against great odds, can feel that they did it the hard way, and why should others expect an easier ride?

I cannot be alone in detecting this, nor in feeling uneasy about it. So much that is good and right about women's liberation has still to anchor itself in popular thought. Last week's backlash showed how shallow that anchorage remains.

Louise Chunn herself tells me, 'The danger in doing a woman's page is that some of the most newsworthy, sexy features are anti-women. I looked at six months of my page, and counted the number of anti-women stories: female sex abusers, the female serial killer in America, a piece written by a man who had been falsely accused of committing rape. When we ran a piece on false memory syndrome [a condition in which women are allegedly encouraged by therapists to 'remember' rape or abuse by male members of their families] I knew that we would get lots of women writing in who would say, "You are denying me my pain." But it's all about balance. For every page that could be construed as anti-women, I could show you 20 or 30 that aren't.'

*

Andreas Whittam Smith told me of some interesting research into social trends which indicated a new convergence of tastes between different groups of people. One is gender convergence: 'the interests of men and women are much more similar than they used to be.' The success of men's magazines such as *Arena*, *Esquire* and *GQ* – with features on men's fashion, beauty, accessories, sexuality and emotions, all much the same terrain as women's magazines – is a symptom of the narrowing divide between men's and women's interests.

As newspapers seem to redesign or relaunch themselves every other week, in a future incarnation the *Guardian* may well rename its women's page to enable its editor to respond to a broader agenda. It would not be the first time, after all, that the *Guardian* has done so. When Linda Christmas was appointed women's page editor in 1973, she immediately changed the banner to Miscellany, and introduced some male voices to the page, including James Cameron as an alternating columnist with Jill Tweedie. In 1975, Christmas became a specialist writer on the newspaper and the women's page was reinstated with Suzanne Lowry as editor.

Louise Chunn would not be in favour of renaming the women's page in the 1990s. When she was offered the job, she knew that 'The men had seriously considered getting rid of it, but I thought it was wimpy to change the name. In an ideal world, if you were starting up a paper you wouldn't have a women's page. But it's not an ideal world. If you got rid of the title, you wouldn't be able to cover the same stories, in such depth, that are of broad interest to women.

'The first-person accounts about any old woman's life would go. We know that ordinary women do feel disenfranchised and that they don't have a voice, which is why it is important. Where would you run the pieces on rape or abortion or female circumcision, or facial hair, for that matter? I have never had anything pulled from my page, though I have been urged to reconsider covering such issues – which are often seen as being 'worthy'. And what about the pieces that make women laugh but don't make men laugh? They would go too.

'The *Guardian* has a greater percentage of women readers than any other broadsheet newspaper. And 10 per cent more than the *Independent*. Tell me why? I believe the women's page has got a lot to do with it.'

(The up-dated NRS figures from July–December 1993 show the figures of women readers as follows: *Guardian*: 45 per cent; *Daily Telegraph*: 45 per cent; *The Times*: 39 per cent; *Independent*: 39 per cent; *Financial Times*: 30 per cent. The *Daily Mail* continues to score highly with women readers: 50 per cent – the deputy editor of the newspaper is Christina Appleyard.)

It is not just men who dislike the idea of there being a woman's place in a newspaper. Just as it is not only women who turn to the soft features pages of their newspaper before reading the news.

Some of the women journalists I interviewed felt that a women's page – whatever its title – was subtly undermining to women. It allowed the men who run newspapers to make a ghetto of women's concerns, and encouraged an insidious form of tokenism. Yvonne Roberts felt that it was difficult to get the balance right when you only have one page, or two at the most, to cover the whole spectrum of women's issues. Lynn Barber hated the very idea of women's pages – 'You've got a 28-page newspaper and they say, "Ooh, here's a page that women can read!" They're always a downer, full of gynaecological problems and rape.' Far healthier, they say, to have women's issues spread evenly throughout the newspaper, given equal weight to what newspaper editors have traditionally considered to be the more 'important' news coverage or analysis.

There are signs that this is already starting to happen. Since the *Independent*'s relaunch in late 1993, three women columnists – Angela Lambert, Margaret Maxwell (Maggie Brown, who began writing the column under her real name in April 1994) and Beatrix Campbell – appear on the Comment pages, the heavyweight core of the newspaper which are also edited by two women: Mary Dejevsky and her deputy, Jane Taylor. Suzanne Moore, who is living proof that committed feminism does not make for dull copy, transferred her column from the Living pages of the *Independent* to her own page in the *Guardian* – 'Mooreover'. Joanna Coles has a column on the *Guardian*'s Comment page. And there is Janet Daley on *The Times*'s Opinion page, whose column also used to appear on the *Independent*'s Living page.

More radical still, critics of the woman's page argue, break down the barriers between 'soft' and 'hard' stories altogether. (The very choice of words is revealing: soft equals human interest, which for some reason is considered to be female, a suggestion of fuzziness, vulnerability, warmth, bordering on the sentimental; hard equals male, with inescapably phallic overtones, tough, gritty, unequivocal cold logic.) Lynn Barber again: 'Women are very specific; men like nothing better than to talk about demographics and draw graphs all over the place.' If you were to present a story on how the recession is affecting people in the north of England versus those in the south, a woman would illustrate the divide by talking to two families, she says, while most men would prefer to use a graph. 'I don't know why an interview with a real person is "softer" than a graph,' she adds. 'They seem to think that if the story is based on statistics, it is meaningful. But if it is based on an individual's experiences, it's not.'

The arguments in favour of shaking up the male/female, hard/soft format of newspapers are persuasive – particularly if the interests of men and women continue to converge. But since there is such an imbalance of women to men in the higher echelons of newspaper organisations, isn't there a danger that a woman's perspective, as Louise Chunn seems to fear, may be lost altogether? Would it not mean that the few women who do have some editorial clout would face even more battles to get certain stories in the paper? The only way that we can hope to achieve a more satisfying menu of stories for male and female readers (and this goes beyond the straightforward category of subject matter; it has to do with tone, presentation and emphasis), surely, is when there is an even number of male and female journalists at every level of the newspaper. And, most particularly, at the top.

There is something else. The stories I heard from women who have edited or contributed to the women's pages, surrogate or otherwise, suggest that their senior male colleagues can be curiously prescriptive about what they like to see on the page. Yvonne Roberts talks about 'a secret door' which slams in the face of an awful lot of subjects – 'and not always the obvious ones too'. Scarlett MccGwire wanted to write about children's sexuality for the *Guardian*. Slam. (This was several years before the Family Planning Association advocated that schools should be teaching four-year-olds about sex in order to prevent teenage pregnancies.)

Roberts had only one article removed from her pages at the *Observer*. It was on testicles. Slam. What she noticed was that the stories that got the best response from her female readers were the ones that went down least well with the men in her office. They were nearly always to do with a different spin on female sexuality: country-and-western singing lesbians and the S & M scene; a debate about bisexuality; a 1990s sex club; the case of a well-educated woman who had fallen for a latter-day Casanova swindler – 'She only fell prey to him because he was such a good lover; the *Observer* men thought it was all a bit disgusting.' Roberts had noticed that women were particularly interested in articles on female sexuality in 1988, when she wrote for the *Independent* a piece on the lack of erotica for women, and received hundreds of letters.

At the *Observer*, she interviewed a prostitute who had a thalidomide child. This was not well received at the office. The combination of sin, motherhood and brutal honesty in the face of adversity proved too unnerving. The taboo subjects seem to be those in which women are cast unstereotypically. 'It is all right if women are treated as victims,' Roberts concludes, 'but they're not comfortable with battling women. Really, they don't like women behaving in any other way than is safe or nice, and if they do, they must get their come-uppance.'

Roberts started her career in journalism in the 1970s. In her twenties, she tried to ape the behaviour of her male colleagues. And since male journalists are often, in her opinion, caricatures of men, there was something particularly ludicrous about her attempts. Twenty years on, she no longer feels the need to dissemble. 'I don't have to prove myself. Staying at the office till all hours is buying into the male culture. At the *Observer*, I would leave at seven o'clock. And if I burst into tears, it didn't strike me as inappropriate behaviour.'

What she is saying, in effect, is that she no longer has to pretend that she isn't a woman. Yvonne Roberts has age, experience and confidence on her side. What is interesting is that her younger female colleagues are often unwilling to take the Boys' Own route to get to the top.

When Simon Jenkins was editor of *The Times*, he told me that he had offered promotion to two women on the paper. They had turned it down because of the hours and the nature of the work. No male journalist, he said, would turn his back on promotion. More recently, a friend of mine was offered a deputy editorship on the home news desk of another newspaper: more money, more prestige; longer hours and a macho environment. She said 'No, thank you.' And so large sections of the newspaper remain male preserves. It would be in the editors' interests, one might think, to investigate this problem further.

One can understand why some women feel apprehensive about these appointments. It takes a particular sort of focused ambition to take on the position of the only woman in a team of men: to boldly go where no woman has gone before. A female sports journalist once told me that she didn't know what was worse – the blatant sexism of her younger male colleagues or the paternalistic chivalry of the older men. (She was, of course, the only woman.) Surveys show that 94 per cent of sports writing is about men and 100 per cent of national sports editors are male. Once again, the statistics tell the story.

But attitudes count for something, too. In the early nineties I read an interview with Fiona Pitt-Kethley by Lynn Barber. Barber had asked a respected literary editor for his views on Pitt-Kethley's poetry. His considered response was, 'Well, of course she's got amazingly bad teeth.' Have we got a long way to go?

*

Top Positions on National Newspapers

While researching this book, I tried to find out whether there was any organisation which was monitoring women's progress in newspapers. To no avail. The National Union of Journalists has an equality council, but has not collated any figures relating to seniority for about ten years. Women journalists themselves are not keeping tabs on their employers: at this point, they are the only female media professionals who have not established their own networking or lobbying group.

In the end, I gathered these statistics myself by phoning the personnel department, or the personal assistants of the editor or managing editor on each newspaper, in early 1994. I am most grateful for their assistance.

The league table reflects my interest in investigating what are still perceived as jobs for the boys – the top positions in what are regarded as the 'hard' areas of news and opinion – and to see whether women have made any inroads into them. For this reason, I have not included any of the features-supremo assistant or executive editors – such as Veronica Wadley on the *Daily Telegraph*, Brigid Callaghan on *The Times*, Sarah Sands on the *Evening Standard*, Sue Douglas on the *Sunday Times* or Hilly Janes on the *Independent* – or any of the growing number of senior women in newspaper production or management.

*

Top positions held by women on national newspapers

Independent

Editor	0
Deputy editor	0
Foreign editor	0
Political editor	0
Business editor	0
News editor	0
Sports editor	0

Independent on Sunday

Editor	0
Deputy editor	0
Foreign editor	0
Political editor	0
Business editor	0
News editor	0
Sports editor	0

Guardian

Editor	0
Deputy editor	0
Foreign editor	0
Political editor	0
Business editor	0
News editor	0
Sports editor	0

Observer

Editor	0
Deputy editor	0
Foreign editor	1
Political editor	0
Business editor	0
News editor	0
Sports editor	0

Daily Telegraph

Editor	0
Deputy editor	0
Foreign editor	0
Political editor	0

Business editor   0
News editor (called Home editor)   **1**
Sports editor   0

Sunday Telegraph
  Editor   0
  Deputy editor   0
  Foreign editor   0
  Political editor   0
  City editor   0
  News editor   0
  Sports editor   0

The Times
  Editor   0
  Deputy editor   0
  Foreign editor   0
  Political editor (aka Assistant editor)   0
  Business editor   0
  News editor   0
  Sports editor   0

Sunday Times
  Editor   0
  Deputy editor   0
  Foreign editor   0
  Political editor   0
  Business editor   0
  News editor   0
  Sports editor   0

Financial Times
  Editor   0
  Deputy editor   0
  Foreign editor   0
  Political editor   0
  Business editor   0
  News editor   0
  Sports editor   0

Top editorial jobs on the quality broadsheets
TOTAL = 63
MEN – 61 WOMEN – 2

The picture is marginally less bleak on the tabloids:

Daily Mirror
    Editor   0
    Deputy editor   0
    Foreign editor   0
    Political editor   0
    City editor   0
    News editor   0
    Sports editor   0

Sunday Mirror
    Editor   0
    Deputy editor   1
    Foreign editor   *
    Political editor   0
    Business editor   *
    News editor   0
    Sports editor   0

The People
    Editor   1
    Deputy editor   0
    Foreign editor   *
    Political editor   0
    Business editor   1
    News editor   0
    Sports editor   0

Daily Mail
    Editor   0
    Deputy editor   1
    Foreign editor   0
    Political editor   0
    City editor   0
    News editor   0
    Sports editor (Assistant editor)   0

Mail on Sunday
    Editor   0
    Deputy editor   0
    Foreign editor   0
    Political editor   0

Business editor 0
News editor 0
Sports editor 0

Evening Standard (London only)
Editor 0
Deputy editor 1
Foreign editor *
Political editor 0
Business editor 0
News editor 0
Sports editor 0

Sun
Editor 0
Deputy editor 0
Foreign editor *
Political editor 0
City editor 1
News editor 0
Sports editor 0

News of the World
Editor 1
Deputy editor 0
Foreign editor *
Political editor 0
Business editor *
News editor 0
Sports editor 0

Today
Editor 0
Deputy editor 1
Foreign editor 1
Political editor 0
City editor 0
News editor 1
Sports editor 0

Daily Express
Editor 0
Deputy editor 0
Foreign editor 0

Political editor	0
Business editor	0
News editor	0
Sports editor	0

Sunday Express

Editor	**1**
Deputy editor	0
Foreign editor	0
Political editor	0
Business editor	0
News editor	0
Sports editor	0

Daily Star

Editor	0
Deputy editor	0
Foreign editor	*
Political editor	0
Business editor	*
News editor	0
Sports editor	0

Top editorial jobs on the tabloids
TOTAL = 75
MEN – 64 WOMEN – 11

* indicates that these posts do not exist

LYNN BARBER
'AIM FOR THE TOP'

In the early 1990s Lynn Barber was the most talked about interviewer of celebrities. Her fans thought she was brilliant at capturing and dissecting the vagaries of public personalities; her critics called her an axe-woman. Perhaps her most controversial interview as star writer for the *Independent on Sunday* was with the media polymath Melvyn Bragg. She was named colour magazine writer of the year in 1986, 1987 and 1990. In 1992, she was signed up by *Vanity Fair*, and in 1993 she joined the *Sunday Times* as a columnist.

Lynn Barber is the interviewer of celebrities turned celebrity interviewer. I use the word 'the' advisedly. Before she disappeared inside the glossy covers of *Vanity Fair*, Barber was the most talked-about journalist in London.

There was a time in the early 1990s when dinner party hosts must have wondered what they did for conversation before The Lynn Barber Interview – as personage after famous personage submitted himself (and, more unusually, herself) to the merciless gaze and pungent prose of the *Independent on Sunday*'s star writer.

The vulgarity of her openings could take your breath away. Who can forget her description of Richard Harris playing 'pocket billiards', with his hand thrust into his tracksuit bottoms? Or Sarah Miles's personal beauty tip: Drink a glass of your own urine every morning, Lynn, and you, too, can have a lovely complexion. (She tried, and couldn't . . . but the reader had to read on.) She asked the questions that other interviewers still don't dare to ask (out of decorum, perhaps, or more likely gutlessness). 'Have you ever been certified insane?' – to Ken Russell; 'People say you like little girls . . .' – to Jimmy Savile. She dismissed Kirk Douglas as an 'anecdotal armadillo'. And as for Jeremy Irons – 'I don't want to give a cool appraisal . . . I just want to boil him in oil.' There was nothing even remotely objective about a Lynn Barber piece. But that was the point. Her interviews were addictive precisely because you wanted to know what she would make of her next subject.

Media students were dispatched to interview the Queen Bee of interviewers. Headmistresses of academic girls' schools invited her to give talks to their pupils. Publishers badgered her to write Fleet Street exposés. She declined, saying, 'I'm in love with journalism, I adore journalism and adore journalists. So the sort of things people would probably be eager for me to expose I probably wouldn't expose, because I think they're fine.'

But this love affair was not entirely mutual. *Private Eye* took to calling her the Barbie Doll and worse. And when the interviewer became interviewee, to publicise *Mostly Men*, the collected interviews of Lynn Barber, the headline writers had a field day: CONFESSIONS OF AN AXEWOMAN, BARBER OF FLEET STREET, HARD LINES AND HATCHET JOBS. The photographs were pretty terrible, too. In one particularly ghastly snap, she appears to be picking her teeth, fag pincered between her fingers, sharp eyes staring out from their baggy setting, puffy jowls. What delicious retribution for her victims.

When I phoned Lynn Barber to request an interview, I was momentarily taken aback by what I heard. It was the voice of a genteel, slightly peevish old lady, which is almost as unlikely as the little-girl squeaks of Julie Burchill. Both writers are considerably more assertive on the page than they are in person.

Barber lives in a large house in Highgate. When I arrive, she is on the phone to one of her editors at *Vanity Fair*. The magazine is trying to line up assignments with Arnold Schwarzenegger and/or Mel Gibson. Poor Lynn Barber. Actors are her idea of interviewing hell. And Hollywood stars, cosseted as they are by their powerful agents and American puff-piece journalism, are the pits. 'Maybe we should go for someone other than an actor next time. What do you think?' she asks breathily.

One of her teenage daughters is watching something lowbrow on telly. The other is in the kitchen chatting to her father, David, principal lecturer in media studies at Central London University, while he prepares the dinner. I go to the downstairs loo. Wellingtons and sundry other items line the floor. Lynn Barber's awards line the walls . . . Colour Magazine Writer of the Year in 1986, 1987, 1990.

The chattering classes only discovered Barber when she started writing for the *Independent on Sunday*, the favourite paper of the media in-crowd. She had, in fact, been writing and winning prizes for her distinctive interviews in the *Sunday Express* magazine for years.

Barber leads the way, up many flights of stairs, to her study at the top of the house. I am mesmerised by her appearance. One interviewer has described her as matronly. Others had referred to her 'handsome, lived-in face' or 'deep frown line'. Melvyn Bragg had written a disgusting portrait of a veteran female interviewer in the *Crystal Rooms*, widely perceived to be an act of vengeance against Lynn Barber, in which he detailed sagging rolls of flesh, and so on. I had seen the unfortunate photographs. To be candid, I was expecting Lynn Barber to look like a raddled old hackette, such is the mythology which has grown around her. But she doesn't. She has a pleasant, most unshrewish face. (She may sue. She has been known to.) She is almost 50, but looks younger to me, perhaps, because she is relaxed in her own environment.

Alistair Cooke once said that a decent interviewer is likely to have some of the mimic in him, so that he may adapt himself to his subject's tone of voice. Maybe this is what I'm doing. One consistent thread in Barber's writing is her tendency to be softer on women than on men. She invariably has something kind to say about the looks of her female subjects. Fiona Pitt-Kethley has 'beautiful hazel eyes' and 'good deportment'; Sarah Miles 'looks really good, soft and wholesome and downy as a peach'; Anita Roddick is 'potentially a great beauty with her cascades of Pre-Raphaelite hair and long, pale face – although she is 48, her skin is unlined'; Ali MacGraw is 'gorgeous at 52'.

Barber was in the vanguard of female journalists who urged Andreas Whittam Smith to include more women in the pages of the *Independent*. Yet she herself rarely chooses female subjects. I ask her why. 'I don't think I'm very good at interviewing women, and that might be because I'm more inhibited with my own sex. But it's also slightly because if they're in the position that they're famous enough for me to interview them, I tend to think, "Well done."'

She refuses to interview women who are famous by proxy, much to the chagrin of her editors. 'They are always trying to get me to do, say, Norma Major. Well, bugger that. They make this great thing about quality journalism versus tabloid journalism, but I think there's nothing crummier than to interview the wife of someone important – then to comment on her clothes and whether her hair's done like this or like that, and whether she pronounces words the right way. I hate all that. Anita Roddick may be nail-grindingly tiresome and ghastly in many ways, but she is also a woman of great achievement.'

So how did Barber become a woman of achievement? She was an only child, brought up in dreary Middlesex. Her father had come out of the army. Her mother wanted to be an actress, but parlayed her way up from teaching elocution lessons to teaching drama to teaching English – despite having no qualifications – and ended up as the deputy head of a sixth-form college. 'My mother used to say, "If you're a woman and you're going to work, then jolly well don't be half-hearted about it. Aim for the top."'

Barber won a scholarship to the academic independent Lady Eleanor Holles school, went to Oxford, discovered miniskirts and parties, met her future husband, and interviewed Bob Guccione of *Penthouse* for the student magazine *Cherwell*, who told her, 'Any time you want a job, honey, come to me.' She did, and spent her twenties learning about every aspect of magazine production and moving up the slimline hierarchy of *Penthouse*. By the time she left, she was deputy editor.

She built on her reputation as a sexpert with two books, *How to Improve Your Man in Bed* and *The Single Woman's Sex Book*. These were the source of considerable mirth among the students at Central London Poly, as it was then known. One of David's former students told me that his group assumed that their tutor always looked shagged out because he was helping his wife research her books. Her third book was a more scholarly tome on Victorian natural history.

She abandoned full-time journalism when her children were young. These do not appear to have been her happiest years. 'My theory is, the real loonies are the playgroup mothers who appear so serene and wonderful and are completely screwed up,' she told Valerie Grove in *The Times*. 'I was at their mercy for years but kept my sanity.'

Her first writing slot on the *Sunday Express* magazine was the back-page feature: 'Things I wished I'd known at 18'. She was offered an editing job or the chance of writing general features, opted for the latter, luckily, and went on to win numerous awards and widespread acclaim.

She has worked for both female and male editors. Is there any difference? 'It's quite complicated in the workplace,' she says. 'The things we complain about in men – their clubbability, and their ganging together : "We can't sack him, because he's such a nice chap" – is both their strength and their weakness. And, to be fair, I do find all the gallant public-school chaps at the *Independent* are very nice and decent. If I'd thrown some of the scenes I've thrown at the *Independent* to a woman editor, I'd be out by now.

'The women who get to the top are generally far more ferociously ambitious, far more ruthless and, also, far more self-important than men. A lot of successful women are tiresome because they make such a song and dance about their career, but I think this may be a temporary phenomenon because high-powered women are still such a rarity.'

Her advice to any writer worth her salt is to push, push, push for more money. She has never found this awkward herself. Far from it. 'I love asking for money, and I'm very, very good at it.'

She first cottoned on to the possibilities when she was a Finsbury Park hausfrau writing the odd freelance article – usually on sex – for teen magazines. Editors would offer her £200 for a day's work, she would say 'no' and miraculously the figure would shoot up to £500. 'It then became my habit to hum and ha about the fee, just to bid them up.'

By the time she left the *Express*, in 1989, she was on £38,000 a year plus car. She was sufficiently keen to join the *Independent on Sunday* to accept less money: £35,000, no car. Almost immediately she bumped it up to £45,000. When the word got round that rival papers were trying to poach Barber, her salary was boosted to £60,000, and she got a BMW. And by the time *Vanity Fair* came along, with an irresistible offer of $120,000 for six articles, Barber was on £70,000.

'For years, there has been this sort of connivance that editors should get paid more than writers. I don't see why, at all. I hope Ian [Jack, editor of the *Independent on Sunday*] is paid more than me; he certainly deserves to be paid more than me. But there are an awful lot of very mediocre people sitting around calling themselves editors, who I don't even think have a place in journalism.' She is happy to report that the trend is shifting. 'It is not so unusual to hear of an editor being paid £30,000 now, while the writer is on £40,000.'

When a man writes a strong, assertive piece, he is called a strong, assertive writer. When a woman writes a strong, assertive piece, she is called a bitch. Lynn Barber once appeared in a feature in a freebie magazine, along with a number of other tough female writers, under the headline THE BITCHES OF FLEET STREET. 'It makes me so cross,' she says. 'I don't think I'm ever bitchy. It's just a way of putting you down. No one ever says A.N. Wilson is bitchy, and if bitchy means anything at all – it's what A.N. Wilson is.'

It is women journalists who have cornered the market in The Big Interview slot. This must be the only area in journalism where it is positively advantageous to be female. 'I would certainly go along with the statement that women are better interviewers than men on the whole,' Barber says (although she admits to admiring Ray Connolly and Professor Anthony Clare). Why? 'Women are trained socially to draw people out, and to listen rather than to assert themselves. You're also in a slightly inferior position when you're interviewing somebody, and that's uncomfortable for many men.'

Some interviewers write up their encounters in such a way, placing the emphasis on the rapport between the interrogator and the subject, that the reader becomes a sort of voyeur. Lynn Barber is not one of them. Her relationship is always, first and foremost, with the reader. 'I am surprised that people go on so much about whether or not you upset your subject,' she has said. 'I am writing for the reader and what matters is being truthful.'

Orianna Fallaci, once dubbed 'the greatest political interviewer of modern times', likened a good interview to coitus. John Le Carré says, 'The real interviews are a kind of bonding, and if that doesn't take place – and between oafs, or with one oaf, it doesn't – then you're finished.' Terry Coleman who has written for most of the quality newspapers, believes that the best interviews go 'like a conversation, with a sense of to and fro'. Lynn Barber holds no truck with the idea of the interview 'as a conversation', let alone something more intimate. She simply shoots from the hip.

Richard Ingrams, the editor of the *Oldie* and formerly of *Private Eye*, told me that when he was interviewed by Barber her very first question was about his marital problems. He clammed up instantly, and she went on to describe him as a truculent interviewee. She would never dream of arguing a point; she is too conscious of wasting time. She also thinks that it is more effective to string her interviewee along than to make her own feelings known. She offers an example: 'As an interviewer, I will say, "Oh yes, so you think black people should be sent back to Africa? Gosh, um, how would you actually do it?" My instinct is to wind them on and on and on . . . and never bat an eyelid. A man would always need to say [deep, manly voice]: "Oh, but you're wrong . . ." Whereas I'll be thinking, "Oh, this is magic."'

Most interviewers have some compunction about what they will or will not include in their finished article. Does Barber ever go in for self-censorship? 'What I prefer to do is not ask about anything I don't want to know about, as it were. One of my rules is that I would never say anything that would jeopardise a marriage. But if I've got the information, then I'm torn . . .' One problem is that the subjects can treat an interview as a weird form of psychoanalysis. 'Yes, yes, it's true. People do sometimes tell me things that I'd rather not know. I always preface my interview by saying, "This is all on the record now. I'm switching my tape recorder on. Off we go."'

And yet, I point out, earlier on in this interview you asked me not to include something you'd just said. And what about this line in Valerie Grove's interview with Lynn Barber: 'She rang me later and beseeched me not to mention certain matters . . .' Barber becomes uncharacteristically nonplussed when pressed on this point, and makes vague noises about 'hurt feelings', 'distress' and 'libel writs'. Her critics might say she has double standards, but my explanation is that Lynn Barber must believe in some sort of code of honour between journalists.

It is after 8p.m. Barber's daughters are fed up with shouting up the stairs for their mother to join them for dinner. She has been an extremely patient and helpful interviewee, particularly as she is used to talking to her subjects for a brisk one hour.

Lynn Barber has since taken her column to the *Sunday Times*. She is a good columnist, but she is a brilliant interviewer; her pieces are buried in *Vanity Fair*. Which is a shame. Sunday mornings are much less fun without The Lynn Barber Interview.

SUE DOUGLAS

'WHEN YOU WIN, NOTHING HURTS'

Sue Douglas is the executive editor of the *Sunday Times*. She started her career in journalism on the *News of the World*, and graduated to the *Daily Mail*. She moved to the *Mail on Sunday* and rose rapidly to the position of features editor. In her late twenties she was promoted by Sir David English to the post of assistant editor on the daily paper. In 1991 she was hired as associate editor of the *Sunday Times*, and was soon promoted to her current position, which makes her one of Fleet Street's most senior women journalists. She is still in her thirties.

As the most senior female executive of the *Sunday Times* makes her way across the dining-room of Le Pont de la Tour, she turns the heads of the men who lunch. This is not surprising, since Sue Douglas is in full battle regalia. She is wearing a pastel, sheath-like suit – an abbreviated skirt and a moulded top. Her fair hair flops over each bony shoulder. Her shoes look positively dangerous.

There is something famished about her which goes beyond her ultra-slim appearance. Her defiant, streetwise bravado is tinged with an obscurely battered quality. It is not that she comes across as a victim exactly, more like someone who has had to harden herself against abuse. After our two-hour conversation I am left wondering whether Sue Douglas is a sell-out or a heroine. Perhaps she is a bit of both.

My first sighting of Douglas was when Andrew Neil, her boss, had left her in charge of the paper. She was sitting in her glass cubicle, dealing with a crisis. The *Sunday Times* had published an extract from the Goebbels diaries – a story which had involved the participation of David Irving, the revisionist historian who argues that Hitler knew nothing of the gas chambers. The entrance of Fortress Wapping, in a distant echo of the war between the printers and the proprietor, was sealed off by Jewish protesters and members of the Anti-Nazi League. Douglas was working on a carefully worded statement to appease the protesters. She was also flicking through her diary to fix a time to see me. I was impressed by her sang-froid. But, as I later discover, Douglas is a connoisseur of conflict.

She was born and brought up in the pebbledash suburbia of Kingston upon Thames. 'There's a great deal to be said for being brought up in the suburbs,' Douglas believes. 'It gives you a burning desire to get out . . .' And make a success of yourself. Growing up, she had no idea that there were different sets of rules for men and for women. She attended an all-girls school; the head was a woman, the science teachers were women. The first time she took an interest in politics, a woman was elected as prime minister. 'I had always thought it was possible to do anything you wanted to – as a woman,' she says.

After graduating from Southampton University in 1978, with a first in biochemistry, she worked briefly on a medical magazine and ended up following her boyfriend to South

Africa. 'At first I refused to go, but he persuaded me to come to see what it was like for myself.' She got a job on a newspaper as a feature writer and – the irony is not lost on her – edited the fashion pages: '*very* socially relevant'. To appease her conscience, she spent her weekends teaching biology to black children under the auspices of Witwatersrand University.

On her return to England, Douglas made straight for Fleet Street. But, she says, 'No one wanted to know.' She wrote an article on white South African women, sent it to the *Guardian* and was devastated by the terse one-line rejection: 'We think your piece is rather contrived.'

She settled for doing shifts on the *News of the World*. At the time, the features editor had an all-female team of reporters, whom he called 'Les Girls'. Douglas's first assignment was a dismal failure: she was dispatched to interview Malcolm Maclaren's discovery, Anabella Lwin of Bow Wow Wow. The real brief was to see how the 14-year-old singer reacted to being asked whether the rock 'n' roll Svengali had slept with her. 'I remember going through the interview asking sensible intellectual questions, knowing I would have to ask whether she'd screwed him.' She eventually summoned up the courage to ask the question and was told exactly where to go. 'It was mortifying, because I took myself rather seriously. I'd done all this committed stuff in South Africa. I cared about politics and race.'

Douglas graduated to the *Daily Mail*, writing shorts on the bottom of the features pages, until someone discovered she had a first in 'something to do with biology'. She was appointed medical correspondent of the *Mail on Sunday*, and was on her way. Eighteen months later, Stewart Steven, then editor of the *Mail on Sunday*, promoted his young and female medical correspondent way above the serried ranks of Associated Newspaper males, to the senior position of features editor. It was the start of the Sue Douglas rumour industry.

I ask her what she thinks people said about her appointment. 'Oh,' she says, matter-of-factly, '"She's screwing the editor", "She's not going to be any good", "What on earth is he doing that for?", "He's a fool", "She's stupid".'

How did she cope with the level of animosity towards her? 'It hurt in the beginning. But I learned to pretend it didn't exist. Eventually you get people on your side because you're good. I can't stand in the middle of a room, like men do, and stick my hands on my hips and scream and shout. They would laugh at me or walk out. I daren't risk it. When you're thrown in at the deep end and the sharks are all around you, you've got to analyse how you're going to succeed. I was never going to win by trying to kill them. So I fed the sharks and got them on my side.'

The rumours were hardly extinguished by the publication in 1989 of Julie Burchill's first blockbuster, *Ambition*, which chronicles the rise and rise of Susan Street, 'the young, beautiful and nakedly ambitious deputy editor', who gets intimate with dildos, dominatrixes, designer labels, male and female prostitutes in Brazil, as well as her own editor, in her single-minded climb to the top. The book's dedication is: 'For S.D. My B.F.'

I ask Douglas about the origins of *Ambition*. She looks momentarily startled, as though she assumes I must know the answer already. 'Julie and I were incredibly close. [Douglas was responsible for making Burchill one of the highest paid columnists on Fleet Street. She hired Burchill in the mid-eighties and paid her £30,000. When Douglas lured Burchill to the *Sunday Times* in 1993, the *Mail on Sunday* was paying Burchill around £100,000.] The book was based on ludicrous, drunken conversations we had over the course of two years.' What did you think of it? 'I was horrified when I first read it. She gave me the unexpurgated manuscript [the mind boggles] for Christmas, wrapped up in blue ribbon. I didn't think she was serious.'

Douglas rose rapidly in the hierarchy of Associated Newspapers: from features editor to assistant editor to associate editor of the *Mail on Sunday*. By the time she was 28, she had actually edited the paper. She was beginning to feel pretty cocky, as she herself tells me.

Hubris lay ahead in the form of Sir David English. The editor of the *Daily Mail* summoned the rising star of the Sunday paper to his office. 'You think quite a lot of yourself, don't you?' he asked Douglas rhetorically. 'Well, as long as I am editor-in-chief of this group, you will have to prove yourself to me. So I am offering you a very good job as assistant editor of this paper, and I suggest that you take it.'

She took it. 'And it was awful,' she says. 'I had this ludicrous sense of false optimism because I had had a great run, and I had been popular and successful. But at the same time there were these ghastly alarm bells ringing.'

The successful *Mail* man has cast himself in the Sir David English mould. He believes in 'creative tension' and the flatter-batter technique – build 'em up and knock 'em down. Paul Dacre, the present editor of the *Daily Mail*, learned his management style from his predecessor. In October 1992 an *Independent* profile-writer described Dacre's attitude to his reporters: 'Some were his "creatures" or favourites; others miserably suffered ritual humiliation in the hope that one day they, too, would become creatures and be given the good jobs. All, however, were singled out for the ferocious *Mail* treatment.'

Sue Douglas knew what she was letting herself in for, but was arrogant enough to think that she would get round her boss. This was one of her rare miscalculations. Her cool exposure of the cut-throat nature of newspapers, certainly at this end of the market, paints a fascinating picture of a truly loathsome world: the ritualistic game of dominance and submission, the connivance between editors, the well-crafted technique of the schoolroom bully, the grim-faced silence of his victims. But if you are hungry enough for success, you will put up with anything to get there. Or as Douglas puts it, 'I thought that I have to do this to prove that I can do it – so I haven't got a choice.'

She describes her former boss as 'a brilliant editor' and goes on to outline his version of effective staff relations: 'His trick, and it is a clever trick because it does work, is that he encourages and encourages and encourages you until you feel that you can do no wrong, and then – whack – he smacks you down. It's a bit like animal training. In the end you feel that you are reduced to absolutely nothing.'

The daily editorial conference became an ordeal. Douglas would steel herself against the inevitable humiliation in front of a room full of men in suits: 'Sue, how can you suggest that? What a stupid idea!' At first, she would stand up for herself. But this only aggravated the attack: 'I have employed you to think. Why can't you think, Miss Douglas?'

Perhaps the most remarkable aspect of her story is that Douglas put up with this treatment for three and a half years. I ask her how she survived. 'I used to go to the loo, stand in front of the mirror and say, "It's all right. You're better than this. It doesn't matter."'

Douglas's coping mechanism was, of course, rather more sophisticated than this. She learned pretty quickly that if she was going to get on, she would need to use every trick available. In the early days, she was the macho-girl – 'I can't tell you how many times I used to get pissed in the right Fleet Street pubs, roll up my sleeves and say, "I can take 14 gin and tonics like the rest of them."' Now, she says, 'I am prepared to do anything to get what I want.' Like what? 'I know how to get around men ... by being charming, by letting them think that they're cleverer than me, by being mildly flirtatious – even with somebody whom I find absolutely disgusting – if necessary, by being completely asexual, if that is appropriate, by saying my views are one thing when they are patently not. Everything is an act, a game. Everything is a means to an end.'

I ask her about her choice of wardrobe which is frankly, sexy. She has an instant reply. 'I really do think that men are, fundamentally, pretty stupid about this. Again, it's about advantages. If I can score a few points in this game, I will. If it means that I have to ruin my back by staggering around in high heels, I don't care. I'll do it.'

In the *Independent*'s Dacre profile, an anonymous female journalist on the *Mail* said she discovered a way of winning an argument with her editor. 'I used to sit on his desk in a very short skirt and sit ever closer, invading his private space. He used to lean back at such a dangerous angle I thought he was going to fall off his chair. He could cope with screaming, violence and bullying, but he just couldn't cope with little coquettish girlie behaviour. A lot of women used to do that.' This bears all the hallmarks of the Sue Douglas school of survival. What makes me think it wasn't her quote is that Douglas probably would have had no qualms about attaching her name to it.

A boyfriend, she says, is a handy accessory; just as long as he is suitable. 'I've recently been going out with someone who is a historian at Cambridge. I've used that card. When I was going out with an out-of-work actor, I didn't mention him.'

Secretaries have been Douglas's secret weapon. 'I had this absolutely wonderful secretary who was the office sex object at the *Daily Mail*. This was a great ploy of mine. I knew she would go out with all the men in the office and that she'd get all the gossip. And because she was so loyal to me, she'd come back and tell me everything. Which she did.'

In this case, the ploy backfired when Douglas discovered that the secretary had been drawing thousands of pounds of 'expenses' in her boss's name. Douglas dealt with the matter herself, with the help of the company lawyer, but without informing Sir David English. The money was paid back, and the secretary was given another chance. A few months later the same thing happened, but to another editor. The whole story came out, and Douglas was knocked back on a promotion.

It is odd that someone who is so calculating about her every move, 'in this act, this game', is also so candid about her battery of techniques. But you don't have to look too hard at Sue Douglas to see the chinks in her armour. I ask her whether she has any personal ethics or moral code. And she gives this enigmatic, slightly faltering reply: 'I do have something which is very personal to me, which is very secret. I want there to be something left that's mine, because

I've gone so far down the road in betraying what I do believe in. I think there's a little bit left of me, but I'm not even quite sure what it is.'

What she has always been sure about is that she never wanted to be sidetracked into what she calls 'The Women's Lot'. 'When I first started to do well at Associated Newspapers, someone asked me whether I was interested in editing *You* magazine. And I remember saying, "No. That's what you give to a woman. I want a paper."

'I never wanted to do features or magazines or soft "girls"' things. I wanted to do all the hard things, like sport and news and war correspondent stuff. Why one should want to take the most difficult route possible, I don't know.'

To prove she could do it, I suppose. In 1991 Douglas finally escaped from the 'tyranny' of the *Daily Mail* and joined the *Sunday Times* as associate editor. 'I really felt free. It was like taking a corset off. If you've worked at Associated Newspapers and been through that sort of shit, you think that you can deal with anything.'

But the battles were not over. While Andrew Neil has been entirely supportive, Douglas says, some of his henchmen were clearly less than thrilled by the arrival of this parvenue. In her first week at Wapping, Douglas's secretary felt the need to reassure her new boss, 'I just want you to know Sue, that we're all on your side.' It was well meant, but had rather the opposite effect to the one intended.

Not long after, Douglas asked one of her executive colleagues whether he'd like to have lunch. 'I don't do lunch,' he said. 'What do you do?' Douglas asked: 'I work out,' he said. Douglas gamely persevered, 'That's all right then. We'll go to the gym and have a drink afterwards.' 'I don't think so,' came the decisive put-down.

I ask her what difference it would make to the content of the *Sunday Times* if she were its editor. 'It's funny you should ask that,' Douglas says. 'Last Saturday, when I was editing the paper, Rupert Murdoch phoned me and said, "So are you going to make the paper very different?" I laughed and said, "How can I do that in one week?"'

'How can the first generation of women editors make a difference to the paper? The first woman who gets the job of editing a broadsheet will have to be a "man". The cv of the job is set, and she will have to do the job according to its specifications. There might be small differences around the edges, but I don't think that a woman would dramatically change the agenda. A newspaper is a product. It has to be marketed to a society which exists. It would be stupid for us to artificially change the agenda, when society isn't like that.'

So what next? Does Sue Douglas hope that she will be the next editor of the *Sunday Times*? 'Obviously,' she says. 'But it's not the be-all and end-all. The biggest problem with ambition is that if you make yourself hungry enough to do these things in the first place, there is no end to it. You're always looking for the next pinnacle.'

Five years before her appointment at the *Sunday Times*, Douglas was interviewed by one of Andrew Neil's underlings. This executive, an old Etonian, had his feet on the desk and, barely stifling a yawn, said, 'Sue . . . um . . . Douglas, what do you think you can do for the *Sunday Times*?' Quick as a flash, came the reply, 'Your job, for starters.' That was the end of the interview. Now Sue Douglas is executive editor of the *Sunday Times*; number three in the hierarchy, and rising, rising.

EVE POLLARD

'THEY DON'T THINK "GOOD BUSINESS BRAIN". THEY THINK "38-D CUP"'

Eve Pollard is the first woman to edit a mid-market Fleet Street newspaper. She started her career in journalism as assistant to the fashion editor on *Honey* in 1967. Since then she has been one of the most prominent women in journalism, working in television and newspapers, as well as on other magazines. In 1988, she was appointed editor of the *Sunday Mirror*. Since 1991, she has been editor of the *Sunday Express*.

Luckily, it took me a very long time indeed to secure an interview with Eve Pollard [the first female editor of a mid-market Fleet Street newspaper]. Week after week, I put in the phone calls. Each time, a different secretary or personal assistant came to the phone. Some were as indiscreet as they were disgruntled: 'Things have never been so bad around here'; 'She's too busy sacking people to give interviews.' A male underling later claimed, perhaps with a little poetic licence, that Pollard had been through a dozen secretaries in three months.

Mutual friends and colleagues promised to bend the editor's ear. This method had worked well, after all, on other recalcitrant subjects. But not in this case. My publisher began to suggest ever more outlandish ideas to attract the attention of busy Ms Pollard. Perhaps we could send her a fax with a drawing of a weeping woman . . .?

A year and a half later, persistence finally had its reward. I had been granted an audience with the editor who has been variously dubbed by the mickey-takers as La Stupenda, Lady Bollard and 'the senior figure of the so-called Killer Bimbos of Fleet Street'.

To the Express Newspapers building in Blackfriars Road. After waiting for an hour in the anonymous foyer, I am summoned upstairs to the open-plan office of the *Sunday Express*, where there is more waiting to do. Banks of secretaries line the walls to the left and to the right. The minutes tick by. A man with pronounced buttocks and a hectic manner – white shirtsleeves, tie slightly askew – darts in and out of the room adjacent to the editor's. This is Eve Pollard's deputy, Craig Mackenzie, now associate editor of the *Daily Express*, aka 'the Bouncing Bog Brush'. But where oh where is Eve Pollard? Just as it seems sensible to give up all hope, oh joy! she sweeps up to me. 'Ginny, I'm so sorry to keep you waiting . . .' and I am shepherded into the triangular nerve centre of the *Sunday Express*.

My pen has been redundant for so long that I am ready to dip it in vitriol. But when you eventually get to meet Ms Pollard, as the most bruiserish interviewers have found, she is so appealing that you quite forget what she has done to offend you. The Pollard brand of charm is particularly effective. She is in turn self-deprecating – and quite funny about her famous bosom – flattering, conspiratorial (we actually whisper for at least five minutes of the interview), and surprisingly un-grand. She concedes, several times, without being unduly prompted, that she is probably a demanding, difficult boss.

She sits, almost slumps, in her executive chair. What with the warm, fuggy atmosphere of the overheated office and the editor's warm, laid-back approach, it is a struggle to keep alert. Beyond her circular window, with its view of the River Thames, the streetlights throw off their eerie urban glow. It is late.

I have eighteen months' worth of stories about Ms Pollard stored up in my internal filing cabinet. Some are apocryphal, no doubt. But surely there must be a grain of truth in them. There is the one about the male fixer who was dispatched to buy Ma'am's red nail varnish. Or the one about the best-selling novelist who was invited to lunch, and was kept waiting for hours and hours. (This one has a ring of truth.) And there are many tales of temper tantrums. One persistent line is that she gets disgruntled when her subordinates omit the prefix 'Lady' when addressing their boss. (*Private Eye*'s 'Lady Bollard' was a reference to her damehood by marriage to Sir Nick Lloyd, editor of the *Daily Express*.)

'How do you like being addressed?' 'Eve,' she says. 'Not Lady Lloyd?' 'Oh, no, no,' she says, looking dismayed. 'I don't think anyone I know addresses me as "Lady". When I hear it, I don't quite believe it. But always having used my maiden name, I never quite used to believe I was Mrs Lloyd, either.

'The other day, I made everyone laugh here because we were doing a story and I said, "I could phone up and say I was Lady Muck", and somebody said, "But you are!"' She laughs.

I ask her whether she thinks there are any major differences between the way women and men operate. 'Of course,' she says. 'We've been tutored for thousands of years to be looked at in a different way to men. But I could only tell you whether there were any innate differences between the sexes when women have been regarded as equal to men for as long as they have been regarded as unequal. And how many millennia will that take? I don't think that you can throw away all those years of women feeling that they should be subservient to men, and certainly of men feeling that women should be subservient to men.'

Many years ago, Eve Pollard was pretty lowly herself. In status, at least. At a meeting I attended in November 1993, held to raise money for the Newspaper Press Fund, Joyce Hopkirk , a seasoned women's magazines editor, introduced the 'chairman/person/woman' – Eve Pollard – with the words, 'Eve started as a humble little slave on the fashion pages of *Honey* [dramatic pause] . . . Well, maybe not humble.' From the look on her face, Pollard seemed to find this less amusing than the audience.

Her first job was, indeed, as assistant to the fashion editor on *Honey* in 1967; she then moved to *Petticoat*. By the end of the 1960s she had joined the *Daily Mirror* and moved from the magazine to the paper. In 1970 she was appointed women's editor of the *Observer* colour supplement, where she stayed a year.

From 1971 to 1981, as women's editor of the *Sunday Mirror*, Pollard ran various campaigns, pro-crèches and anti-Dalkon Shield (a controversial contraceptive device which was believed to endanger women's health). She also managed to write a bestselling biography of Jackie Kennedy.

For most of the eighties she media-hopped between newspapers, television and magazines – the *Sunday People*, TV-AM and, in America (where she followed her second husband, Nick Lloyd), she launched the US edition of *Elle*. Back in England, she edited the *News of the World*'s colour supplement, and then, for 18 months, the *Mail on Sunday*'s *You* magazine, in its innovative, sharply written heyday.

In 1988, with her appointment to the *Sunday Mirror*, Pollard became one of a trio of women to edit national newspapers. During her three years at the *Sunday Mirror*, Pollard increased the paper's circulation from 2.6 million to nearly 3 million.

The *Sunday Express* was always considered to be the most male of newspapers, with a loyal, but fading readership of crusty old colonels in Haslemere. Its subscribers were once nicknamed Twirlies, because they were the sort of people who arrived two hours early to catch a train. Pollard's principal concern, when she took over in May 1991, was to reverse its falling circulation. 'Twenty-one years ago the *Sunday Express* was selling 4 million. But the circulation was going down year after year,' she says. 'When I joined it was selling just under one and a half million. It had lost touch with younger readers who fled to the *Mail on Sunday* and to the *Sunday Times* and other newspapers. So it had to become "A Good Newspaper."' A year after Pollard's appointment, the *Sunday Express* was named Newspaper of the Year. And in 1993 it was named Sunday Newspaper of the Year. Latest findings from Express Newspapers research department, May to October 1993, show a circulation figure of approximately 1.7 million.

Soon after her appointment, Pollard made the controversial, but not entirely unexpected, decision to shrink the paper from a broadsheet into a tabloid, and set about transforming its content. Kate Muir of *The Times* recorded the shifting focus of the paper during the first few weeks of Pollard's new editorship: 'pictures on the art desk include a Range Rover and an inside-the-SAS-type book cover, typical *Sunday Express* manly fodder. But the editor wants Marlon Brando. Now. At the top of the page. "Make it big," she says. "Which do you think is the sexiest picture?"'

Pollard maintains that she never set out to make the paper more appealing to women. Certainly not consciously. 'But what we do are pieces like the one by Fay Weldon, a few weeks ago, on the new celibacy. There are vast numbers of people who've lived happily together for years in an entirely celibate situation. Now who do you think will read it – men or women?'

It is her belief, in fact, that such articles are read by both sexes. Like Andreas Whittam Smith, Pollard is convinced that there is a convergence of the tastes and interests of men and women. 'Men will read about relationships. Men are trying much harder to understand their children. They are

even trying to understand themselves. Although they may
not talk about it, and very few of them would admit to it.'

I wonder whether Pollard's success has sealed her from
the discrimination which afflicts her less high-powered female
colleagues. 'Absolutely not,' she says, without hesitation.
'You suffer from it all the time. If you're successful, you must
never boast about it. Because when you do, the men will say,
"How does she get such good publicity?"

'But this has nothing to do with publicity. [She bran-
dishes a table of figures showing an increase in *Sunday
Express* sales under her reign.] These are ABC figures. But
they seem to think that you've done some extraordinary sexual favour to some editor of a trade magazine . . .'

She offers another example. 'I don't do an awful lot
of the television that I'm asked to do. But I do do some.
People say, "Oh, she likes getting made up and dolled up
and it's an ego trip." And I say, "Well, it is great fun. And
it's good publicity for the paper." But they simply wouldn't
make those comments if I were a man. No one says that
Andrew Neil [then editor of the *Sunday Times*] appears
on television because he likes to get made up and look
glamorous.'

Which brings us to the ticklish question of image. And
Eve Pollard's in particular. She believes that one of her
strengths is her business acumen. 'But when men hear that
I've got a new job, they don't think, "Good business brain".
They think, "38-D cup".'

But – ahem – surely, this may have something to do with
Pollard's past fondness for wearing perilously low-cut frocks?
'Yes, yes,' she says, assuming a sober expression. 'Hollywood stars check into clinics to deal with their health problems. I've had to check in to deal with my hopeless addiction
to cleavage.'

Pollard's neckline has risen as her newspapers have
become more upmarket. If she ever gets to edit *The Times*,
she'll probably turn up to work in a turtle-neck. Today, she is
wearing a close-fitting grey body, a tailored jacket, a tight calf-
length skirt·in navy, and what have been described as her

'kebab-skewer' heels. She is approaching 50, and wears her hair long and blonde.

In 1990, the BBC made a film ostensibly to celebrate the breakthrough of the woman editor. It was called *Killer Bimbos on Fleet Street*! Partly, perhaps, because all three women editors have blonde hair. But as Pollard says, 'Would you categorise male editors because six were bald or six wore glasses?'

Like the advertising world's Executive Tart, The Killer Bimbo has stuck because it is such a perky catchphrase. Even reasonably intelligent people are unprepared to acknowledge how trivialising this shorthand is. Somewhere, buried not too deep in all of this, is the suspicion that women should not be at the helm of the trashy end of Fleet Street newspapers. Their decision to accept such appointments makes them fair game.

In 1990 Sheila Hayman, the *Bimbos* producer, wrote an account for the *Independent* of her nightmarish filming experience. 'Eve's was quite a good interview. There was one moment when she almost got spontaneous and frank on the subject of image – this, after all, is the woman who told me she dyed her mane blonde to come over better on TV-AM.

'"You weren't rolling on that, were you?" [she said.] Actually, yes – people will be interested. "Well, I'm not signing my consent form if you do. In fact, thinking about it, I'm not signing my consent form at all until I've seen transcripts of everything you're using, and I'll need a cassette in advance of transmission as well."'

What a grisly control-freak Pollard sounds.

This reputation was reinforced by an article in the *Observer* by John Sweeney the following year. The new editor of the *Sunday Express* had apparently refused a photographic portrait by the gentle eye of Jane Bown, offering, instead, one of her own hand-picked, 'approved' photographs. The newspaper, perhaps in pique, retaliated by running the most aggressively bosomed snap of Ms Pollard they could find, which set the tone of the article.

The interview opened with this paragraph: 'Take two of the large white early-warning globes that adorn the North Yorkshire moors at Fylingdales. Hold the image in your mind. Now shoehorn them into a vacuum-packed glitzy dress, imperfectly buttoned up. The reader may now begin to comprehend something of the enormity of Eve Pollard's breasts.'

As Hayman wrote, 'The calculation that people who get difficult fail to make is that the purest journalistic intentions can be skewed by the frustration of feeling manipulated . . .'

Oddly enough, I find Pollard both co-operative and disarmingly honest on the subject of image. It is hard not to feel some sympathy with her sentiments. 'They can always have a go at you as a woman, on account of the way you look. I always joked that I knew I'd hit the wrong side of *Private Eye* when they stopped calling me La Stupenda and called me Lady Bollard. What we have to do is learn not to care.

'There is no getting away from this. It is a weakness in women, and it goes back to the same old thing. For thousands of years, you and I have been judged on how attractive we are. A certain side of our life has been regarded as a success or failure on our appearance alone. Now I must try not to think that it matters. But you've got to be very self-confident not to give a stuff about how you look.'

She sounds almost regretful about her appearance – 'I think that, in some ways, the bosom and the hair and all that stuff hasn't helped me to be taken seriously.' And she thinks now that she was probably foolish to wear low-cut dresses when pregnant. But why not? Why does society require you to become asexual just because you are expecting a child? The problem, of course, is this vexed business of throwing out conflicting signals to men. Can you be a serious career woman and a sexpot simultaneously? What is appropriate for Madonna on stage, after all, is not necessarily right for the boardroom.

'But what image are we supposed to put out?' Pollard sighs, throwing up her arms. 'How would they like us to look – me and Tina Brown and Barbara Amiel, all these incredibly successful women in the media – Bridget Rowe, Patsy Chapman? Would they prefer it if we looked like the old-time Dickens version of a schoolmarm?'

The answer is probably 'no'. Liz Forgan is not classified as a bimbo. She is merely dismissed as 'mumsy' or 'matronly'.

'It's so enviable that men just buy a suit,' Pollard continues. 'As they get more successful they buy more expensive suits to hide a multiple of sins. And it's just a navy suit or a grey suit. The problem is that if you look attractive, they think that you're trying to use your sex to help you get on. But the people who've helped me most in my career have been women.'

Do you think that you have been as helpful to women yourself? 'I hope so,' she replies. 'I try to. Listen, I am on record for saying, "I am going to pollute Fleet Street with as many women as I can." I have hired a lot of women in my time.' I ask her whether she has appointed many women to senior positions on her paper, and she rattles off a list. The assistant editor, the deputy features editor, the news editor are all women, when we meet. The magazine is run by women, but these days this is not unusual.

'From the point of view of being a feminist . . .' she starts to say. Gosh, I pounce, do you still call yourself one? 'Well,' she wavers, 'among the original four or five feminist beliefs were equal pay and equal opportunity. The trouble is that feminism has become a dirty word because it has gone too far. I don't believe that men can be removed tomorrow and replaced by sperm banks. I quite like men. Some more than others.' What she does say, naturally enough, is that she is all in favour of women working.

Some years ago, Pollard and her teenage daughter, Claudia, who was about to go off to Cambridge, were featured in the *Sunday Times*'s Relative Values. Not long after, Pollard attended a Woman of the Year lunch, and was approached by a woman she didn't know. 'She told me that the article made her feel really good. There was my daughter – and all the things we'd been told would happen to her because her mother worked – you know, that she'd be out on the streets, taking drugs, totally gone off the rails, all because I was working, hadn't happened.

'As she was growing up, I'd done all those deals that you do. That there'd be certain nights when I was always there, and so on. Somehow, in Claudia's memory bank, that had seemed to be quite enough. She has felt that I had been there for her.'

My tape has run out. I hadn't expected Eve Pollard to give me so much time, or for it to be such a jolly experience. As she is walking me to the lift, a pompous man in a bow-tie stops to tell his editor – in laborious, painstaking detail – all about his wife's latest pregnancy scan. Pollard seems so absorbed, I wonder for one moment whether it is a set-up.

After our meeting, I reread the cuttings, and find this paragraph from Michael Leapman's interview with Pollard, after her appointment as editor of the *Sunday Express*: 'Women editors have still been allowed only on to the Sunday papers, the foothills of the national press. The rationalisation for that, assiduously put about by apprehensive males, is that family commitments would not allow a woman to put in the punishing six-day routine of a daily editorship.'

He concluded that Ms Pollard could conceivably be the first through that barrier one day – maybe through a straight swap with her husband, whom she refers to as 'the man downstairs', should he decide to spend more time with his family.

When I asked Pollard whether she thought that there would be a female editor of *The Times*, the Garrick Club of Fleet Street, in her lifetime, she said, 'I bloody well hope so.' 'Do you hope that it will be Eve Pollard?' I asked. And she roared with laughter, 'I'm very happy in the job I'm in. But it would be great fun to have a go. Wouldn't it!' I shall be watching out for the turtle-neck sweater.

WHO'S GUILTY?

The Magazine Industry

'This is a day during which we might feel entitled to ask, WHY OH WHY DO WE STILL NEED TO JUSTIFY OUR POSITIONS AS WORKING WOMEN? And a day during which we might ask why women's wages are still running at little more than two-thirds of men's, and why there are still so few women at the top.'

From a speech in 1992 by Linda Kelsey, editor of *She* magazine, at a conference on stress and the working mother. *She* is one of National Magazine's most successful titles, following its relaunch in 1990 for a new readership of working mothers.

The world of magazines is dominated by women. And, more importantly, it is dominated by senior women. Most of the women's magazines have female editors and deputies. But the oldest and largest companies are still run by men.

IPC is the biggest publisher of women's magazines in this country. Its 26 titles which are aimed at female readers include *Marie Claire*, *Women's Weekly*, *Mizz*, *Options*, *Woman's Journal* and *Homes and Gardens*. The chief executive is a man, Mike Mathew. From 1985 to 1994 there were no women on the board. Now there are two . . . and ten men.

National Magazines celebrated its 75th birthday in 1985, with a special anniversary magazine extolling the merits of its publications and its personnel, past and present. On the cover was a woman in a bright yellow jacket and a phalanx of men in grey suits. Eight men; one woman.

In 1993, the personnel may have changed but the picture remains the same. Terry Mansfield is still managing director. On the board there are six men and still only one woman. Editors are not eligible for appointment because the MD wishes them to devote their energies to running their magazines, not his company.

Three of National Magazines' successful women's titles – *Cosmopolitan*, *Company* and *She* – are targeted at the modern, emancipated woman. This is a woman who aims to be in control of her life, professionally and sexually, who knows what she wants and is bold enough to go out and get it. That, at any rate, is the message.

But what is the reality for women working on these magazines? Do their experiences bear any resemblance to the mythology that they are helping to create? In short, are the editors able to practise in their own workplace the message they preach? Marcelle D'Argy Smith, the editor of *Cosmopolitan*, has publicly voiced her dismay about the under-representation of women on the board of National Magazines. And other editors are known to share her feelings.

She magazine is dedicated to the cause of working motherhood. But Linda Kelsey, who created its new look, was the first editor at Nat Mags to retain her post after having a child. Indeed, she was the first magazine editor in the company to become pregnant while editing a magazine. That was only five years ago. And in the early nineties, three journalists lost their jobs at the company after becoming pregnant. As one commentator put it, 'Are the supposed flagships of post-feminist aspiration guilty of the repressive behaviour more usually associated with chauvinist males?'

With these key issues of boardroom power and women's right to work and have children in mind, I set off to interview the managing director of National Magazines. I ask Terry Mansfield why there is only one woman on the board, and he gives me an elaborate and somewhat bizarre explanation. He could not possibly have two women, he says, because if he picked another woman, it would upset all the other female candidates who hadn't been appointed. If the MD of a company which was dominated by men applied this argument, there would be no one on his board. 'Well,' I offer, 'you could make it really easy and have no women at all . . .' 'I wouldn't think of having *no* women,' he says self-righteously. 'I *like* a woman's point of view around the kitchen table.'

He maintains that no editors, as far as he knows, have expressed any interest in being on the board. Perhaps he hasn't been listening hard enough. Rosie Boycott, the editor of *Esquire*, told me, 'Like every editor in this place, I think it would be nice to see more women on the board, particularly since most of our magazines are about women getting on in the world.'

Linda Kelsey puts it more bluntly. 'I think it's ridiculous that there aren't any women editors on the board . . . We show daily that we're capable of running our own budgets and being managers.'

If Kelsey were on the board, she would probably try to influence the company's attitudes towards job structures. Most of the senior women on her staff have had two or three children and returned to work, each time with renewed vigour and commitment to their jobs. 'Flexible hours for men and women is the way of the future,' she says. 'This company's maternity provision is more generous than other companies', but it should go much further. I don't see any point in men and women driving themselves into the ground for a lifestyle that they're too tired to enjoy, and having no time to spend with their children. We've got to work together to find a new way of working. And simply because this company produces some of the most successful women's magazines, it should lead the way. Instead, it is dragging its heels.'

When *She* was relaunched, Kelsey and two of her most senior colleagues proposed that they would work a four-day week. But the managing director proved intractable. 'It was too early,' he told me. 'We'd just invested large sums of money in the magazine.' He says that the company is experimenting with job-shares at a less senior level, but even this seems so radical to him that one suspects that he'd rather keep quiet about it, just in case it doesn't work out.

'If you're losing millions of pounds in advertising revenue,' he says, 'you can't afford to be too experimental. And I think that things are going to get worse, not better.'

I ask Mansfield about the senior NatMag women who were sacked while on maternity leave. The most publicised case was that of Noelle Walsh, the former editor of *Good Housekeeping*, who was told she no longer had her job three weeks after the birth of her son. The dismissals were reported and commented on in the press. This did not look good for a publishing company whose third major title celebrates working motherhood. An editor in the company had circulated a mock-up of the *Independent*'s media page with scary headlines around the theme: join National Magazines, get pregnant and get sacked.

Mansfield, like Andreas Whittam Smith, is a man of his generation. Ask both the bosses about the fate of women who have been forced out on maternity leave, or the women who have had to fight for their old positions when they return to work, and they say the same thing: you are confusing two issues. One is maternity leave. The other is the ability of the employee. They have nothing at all to do with one another.

In late 1993, Suzanna Taverne, the only woman on the board of Newspaper Publishing PLC, the company which owns the *Independent* and the *Independent on Sunday*, was asked to resign as finance director six weeks before she had her baby.

In early 1994 I asked Sally Gilbert, the legal officer of the NUJ, whether there had been a general escalation of maternity leave difficulties in the nineties. 'They used to be fairly regular: now they're constant. It snowballed in 1991, when the recession really hit, and is still going on,' Gilbert said. 'Women on magazines and newspapers who go on maternity leave find that their jobs have been miraculously reorganised or disappear. We're treating a lot of the cases as sex discrimination, as well as unfair dismissals. These days, if someone is pregnant, problems seem to be inevitable.'

What Mansfield says is this: 'You haven't asked me whether I think that working motherhood is a good thing . . . What I think is that to some degree you've been sold a lie. Women feel guilty if they stay at home. Women feel guilty if they go to work. If you do any research into the subject, the word "guilt" comes up a thousand times. And no one has done a book on what the children think.'

Terry Mansfield entered the magazine world at a time when rich women regarded their jobs as little more than hobbies. He has seen sweeping changes since then. Given his own ambivalence about working motherhood, it is to his credit that he backed Linda Kelsey so wholeheartedly in her mission to produce a magazine for precisely this readership.

He is also a man who speaks in PR platitudes – 'I've got this very simple philosophy that we are servants of the readers': 'My wife is the managing director of my family.' But he saves up his *pièce de résistance* for his final line: 'My view is very clear: this company is a community first and a business second. If I have learned anything in this crazy business, it is that people make magazines.'

*

Figures

Condé Nast, the publishers of *Vogue*, *Tatler* and *Brides* (and *Setting Up Home*), has a good representation of women on the board – six of the twelve members are female. But the managing director is a man – Nicholas Coleridge.

EMAP Women's Group, which includes *Elle*, *Just 17*, *More!* and *New Woman*, has a female managing director – Rita Lewis. Half of the eight-member board are women.

LINDA KELSEY

SHE-WOMAN

Linda Kelsey is the editor of *She*, a magazine which was relaunched in 1990 for a new readership of working mothers. She has worked on women's magazines since the early seventies, joining the staff of *Cosmopolitan* shortly after its launch in Britain.

Linda Kelsey is a *Cosmo* girl who has grown into a *She* woman. She tells you this herself with a completely straight face. In Nat-Mag speak this means that she is no longer a single girl looking for sex, but a mother, a worker, a lover and, most definitely, a woman.

I spend the morning before I meet the editor of *She* tramping around the various offices of National Magazines looking for a video machine that works so that *She*'s publisher, Karen Pusey, can play me the magazine's new promotional tape. SHE IS RELEVANT, the white script reads on a black background. SHE IS INTELLIGENT – splutter. SHE IS AUTHORITATIVE – crackle, crackle, whirr. SHE IS

REASSURING – at which point the picture, most unreassuringly, disappears altogether.

In *She*'s office, Kelsey and her right-hand women are in a meeting. On the wall above the editor's desk there is a spidery self-portrait by her four-year-old son, Thomas, a drawing of 'Mama' with oversized ears, and a Nat-Mag graph with the banner '*She* records its sixth consecutive rise.' The juxtaposition of artwork neatly underlines the philosophy of the magazine: successful mother; successful worker; why not?

'We haven't had any children in the fashion photos for ages,' Kelsey murmurs to her fashion director, Elaine Farmer. 'We've got this big thing in January on what makes a happy marriage, and it would be nice to have a positive image. Something hopeful . . .' They talk about Oliviero Toscani, the photographer of the controversial Benetton clothes advertisements (bloody babies, AIDS patients on their deathbed, oil-slicked seagulls, et cetera). Toscani's wife, Kirsty, is a big fan of the magazine (Kirsty and her baby, Ali, were on the cover of the second issue of the new-look *She*). Perhaps Toscani could take some more photos of his family for the next issue. 'And what have we got in the kids' spread, Elaine?' 'Pinks and reds with red hair, if that's all right. It'll be cheerful. I'm fed up with browns and greens, to be quite frank.'

More women crowd around Kelsey's desk for a postmortem on *She*'s annual conference. This year's subject was 'Stress'. It was attended by 180 people – more than the previous year's conference on 'The Family towards 2000'. The publisher relays the comments of Libby Purves, who has chaired both years' conferences – A few years ago, the issues would have been equal pay and equal opportunity. Now it was all about feelings. David Thomas told the audience that he couldn't understand why women wanted to join the rat race – I mean, what's so great about work? asked the former editor of the former magazine *Punch*. Everyone seems to argue that 'feelings' and 'emotions' are what the 1990s are all about.

Behind the sharing-caring sloganeering, of course, the

1990s are all about money, just like any other decade. The publisher says that more speakers actually mentioned the magazine this year (which must be good for product placement). The discussion moves on to whether the revenue from the £10 entry fee should go back into the company next year, rather than to charity. The question is filed away for another meeting.

Linda Kelsey has been a National Magazines employee for virtually all her working life. She read history at Warwick University (and one of her tutors' books, *The Female Eunuch*), dropped out after a year, and, while entertaining vague thoughts of journalism on local newspapers, did a secretarial course and became a typist on *Good Housekeeping*. Her bosses encouraged her to sub-edit, and in 1972 she joined the staff of *Cosmopolitan*, shortly after its launch under the editorship of Joyce Hopkirk.

'People were always taking me under their wing,' Kelsey recalls. She mentions both Maggie Goodman and Deirdre McSharry as early mentors, and describes McSharry as 'an inspiration'. 'What I learnt from Maggie was that you could get what you wanted by being nice to people,' she says. (Goodman now edits *Hello!*)

Kelsey moved from sub-editing to styling and writing for the fashion and living pages. 'I was just like a sponge,' she recalls. 'I found myself in a milieu that I absolutely loved. The whole business of putting together a magazine was fascinating. This wonderful, shiny, glossy product which incorporated words and pictures and celebrities and campaigning.' At 24, she was promoted to the position of features editor, and her six-year-old marriage to a solicitor nine years her senior collapsed. *Cosmopolitan* – the philosophy, not the magazine – was partly to blame.

Kelsey may no longer be a *Cosmo* girl, but – boy – can she remember what it felt like to be one. 'It was such a phenomenon,' she says. 'I thought, "Gosh . . . I can be financially independent *and* sexually independent." There was all this discussion about orgasms, which I hadn't yet experienced, so I was learning all the time. I was the woman in the magazine, at the same time as producing it. I really did feel that *Cosmo* changed my life, for the better.' Magazine editors don't come much more committed than this.

In the late 1970s Kelsey moved upwards and sideways on to the new title *Company*, and wondered, momentarily, whether she should rethink her career. 'I thought that if I was going to be taken seriously, I should make a move into newspapers. I applied for some jobs – on the *Sunday Express* and the *Sunday Times* – but I didn't get them.'

Kelsey's best friends tell her that she comes across as too cool or austere, and that 'people can find that a bit frightening'. And it is true that while there is an almost puppy-dog enthusiasm about the way she describes the world of women's magazines, Kelsey's manner is curiously restrained. Her eyes dart nervously down to my scribbling hand; she holds herself as stiffly as a mannequin.

What makes her appealing, however, is her reluctance to put a PR spin on The Linda Kelsey Story. She did not need to tell me, for instance, that no newspaper would hire her. And later on, when she talks about editing *Cosmopolitan*, she is extremely generous about her successor, Marcelle D'Argy Smith, 'I did an OK job – but Marcelle has made it funnier, sexier and sent it up.'

(She also doesn't tell me that the Periodical Publishers Association named Linda Kelsey Editor of the Year in 1989 for her work on *Cosmopolitan*, or that she won the British Society of Magazine Editors' Editor of the Year, Women Magazines award for the revamped *She* in 1990.)

Her comments on the shifting attitudes in newspapers and magazines are particularly illuminating in the light of my interview with Andreas Whittam Smith. 'In the late seventies, there was a feeling that magazines were fluff. They didn't count. At some point in the eighties, newspaper editors woke up to the fact that they needed to attract more women readers.' Kelsey draws a bubble in the air. 'So they think: "Women's magazines seem to attract readers, maybe we can learn from them."'

When the *Independent on Sunday* was founded, in 1990,

the editors approached a number of women from women's magazines in an attempt to find out what makes women tick. Emma Dally, the deputy editor of *She*, was one of them. 'They were absolutely clueless,' she recalls. 'They saw women as an alien group. What they wanted were lists of women who could write. The only names they could come up with were of women who had been around for years – and who they wanted to poach from other newspapers. They didn't seem interested in developing their own writers. They wanted to fix what they clearly considered to be a problem, but without going to too much trouble.'

Newspapers now routinely lift ideas or buy articles from women's magazines, from *Vanity Fair* and *Tatler* to *Cosmopolitan* and *She*. And Kelsey says that if she applied for a job on a paper today, she would no longer be sneered at because of her background. (Although, it must be said, newspapers will still trivialise magazine editors, given half a chance. When Alexandra Shulman, the editor of *Vogue*, had a haircut, no fewer than three newspapers reported the event.)

But Kelsey's knockbacks, all those years ago, only served to strengthen her commitment to women's magazines. 'I suddenly thought, "If you take a pride in women and women's issues, then you're not going to get very far in newspapers anyway – because newspapers are run by men." I decided to stop apologising for myself.'

She also decided that it was time to leave home, again – since National Magazines had become a sort of surrogate family. She moved to IPC to help launch *Options*, but hated it. Editorial meetings were held in the boardroom – 'Twenty-five people around a circular table; twenty of whom were men in suits. I quickly realised that the editor was not going to have a lot of say, which was so alien to the culture I'd come from.'

Sally O'Sullivan was appointed editor and Kelsey says she walked out – straight back to National Magazines – before she was kicked out. Terry Mansfield, whom Kelsey describes as 'very positive, very nurturing, all the things you associate with women', gave her a new health and beauty magazine to launch, *Zest*, which was eventually incorporated into *Cosmopolitan*. And in 1985, the *Cosmo* girl became the *Cosmo* editor.

When Kelsey took over *Cosmopolitan* it was losing readers. The management blamed the content; it had become too strong, the men agreed, too feminist. Kelsey took no notice. She simply updated the look of the magazine, and threw in more general-interest features. 'I always wanted the reader to go away and think, "I've learned something". Not just about relationships, but about other areas of life. Like politics, maybe.' By the time she left the magazine, in 1988, its circulation had risen from 370,000 to 400,000. Marcelle D'Argy Smith, Kelsey tells me, has further boosted it to 470,000. (It had dropped by three per cent in late 1993.)

Kelsey's son, Thomas, was born in May 1988. Three and a half months later, she was back at work. Linda Kelsey tells me that she was the first editor of a magazine in her company to return to her old job after having a baby. She emphasises that she was also the first woman in the company to become pregnant while editing a magazine. 'When I told Terry I was pregnant [she was 36], there was a long silence. Eventually he said, "If that's what you really want ... Congratulations." I set a good example. I was very healthy. I worked up to three days before Thomas was due. I was aware that I was setting a precedent.'

But on her return, to her dismay Kelsey found that she had lost interest in editing *Cosmopolitan*. 'I kept thinking, "I'm not 25 and looking for a date. I've moved on. I really should think about doing something else, before someone does it for me." And then it suddenly hit me: "Where is the magazine for women like me?" For grown-up *Cosmo* girls, if you like.'

The answer, of course, was that it didn't exist. She told *The Times* in October 1989, 'There were the domestic month-lies like *Prima* and *Essentials* and maybe *Good Housekeeping*, the "Me" magazines such as *Cosmo*, *New Woman* and *She*, and the mother and baby magazines which you buy to discover why your baby's got earache – not as a glossy treat.'

The baby may have become the Afghan hound of the nineties – in advertisements, in fashion spreads, in films – but however hard Kelsey looked, she could not find any positive images of motherhood. So she decided to produce a magazine of her own. 'I wanted it to say, "You're not over the hill at 30." I wanted it to be a campaigning magazine, but I also wanted it to be a celebration of motherhood.'

By the time she had a package to present to her boss, Kelsey's gut feelings had been reinforced by some compelling statistics. Such as: the number of births to women in the 30–34 age group has doubled since 1970; the trend towards older mothers is continuing; there is a generation of mothers who have delayed starting a family to concentrate on their careers.

Mansfield was convinced by Kelsey's arguments and research but was not prepared to invest in a completely new magazine – particularly as his bosses from the Hearst Corporation, Nat-Mag's parent company in America, were launching *Esquire* in England. Instead, he offered her an existing, ailing magazine to transform: *She*.

Kelsey was appalled. She hated the magazine and liked its editor Joyce Hopkirk, who had encouraged Kelsey at the start of her career in National Magazines: 'My instant reaction was one of panic; what it felt like was a *coup d'état*.' Nevertheless, she went away and discussed Mansfield's offer with Nadia Marks, who had designed Kelsey's dummy. The two women drew up a list of conditions, ranging from Kelsey wishing to appoint her own staff to full financial backing and promotional support from the company. The old *She*, they said would have to be totally overhauled. Mansfield agreed to meet every condition. If he hadn't, Kelsey says, she would probably have left the company.

When the first issue of the new *She* came out in March 1990, there was a flurry of articles in the national press: 'Motherhood goes glossy'; 'Labour pains for a *Cosmo* girl'; 'How I pity these poor jugglers' (predictably, in the *Daily Mail*); 'And baby makes *She*'. Buried in the largely upbeat text was this line: 'Joyce Hopkirk has been offered another role within the company', which is a euphemism for getting the sack. Kelsey says she was very upset about Hopkirk's dismissal. 'I thought this could happen to me and it might still happen to me in a year's time. [It didn't.] When Eric Bailey was replaced by Joyce Hopkirk, some of the staff wore black armbands for the first few weeks. I wondered if I'd get the same treatment.'

One of the articles quoted Peter Beauman, the media research director of the advertising agency WCRSNN, who hailed the concept behind the new *She* as 'a really radical departure' in women's magazine publishing. He supported Kelsey's analysis. 'There is definitely a gap for an upmarket glossy magazine that deals with parenthood in a sophisticated way. It is a paradox that with all the talk about the "thirty-somethings", the glossy magazines seem to have studiously ignored family life, which is now seen as a major yuppie concern.'

But, like other media commentators, Beauman questioned the thinking of pinning this 'radical' new idea onto an old title. In the first four weeks of the Kelsey regime, the editor received 1000 letters of complaint from *She* readers: 'You've become bland and boring'; 'Now you're just like any other women's magazine'; 'Just because you've become a mother, you're ramming motherhood down our throats.' It was, Kelsey says, 'pretty scary.'

The new team experimented with the format and found that every time they put a baby on the cover the sales plummeted. 'If you're a mother with a ten-year-old child, you'll think that the magazine is just for women with babies', Kelsey worked out. 'And if you're a single woman who reads *She* [interestingly, about 60 per cent of the readers do not have children], the boyfriend is going to think, "Oh, she's just going out with me because she wants a baby."'

Once the baby covers were dropped the sales went up and up, from just under 200,000 when Kelsey took over in 1990, to 236,297 by the end of her first year, 283,731 in 1991, to a peak of 288,117 in 1992. Sales dropped by ten per cent, however, in 1993, and seemed to be holding steady when I last spoke to Kelsey in 1994.

*

It is time for lunch. We walk briskly around the block to the favourite haunt of the media trendies, the Groucho Club. Kelsey phones home to talk to Thomas, and I settle into the dining-room upstairs.

There is not much point in asking Kelsey whether she likes working with women, since she has never worked with men. But she's heard enough stories from her friends who report back from the frontline of Fleet Street to reassure her that she's not missing out on much. One of the worst battlegrounds for women was – and may well still be – the *Daily Mail*. Sir David English's idea of running a newspaper was to create a hostile environment of divide-and-rule. Vicki Woods, who worked there between a stint on *Tatler* and her present editorship on NatMag's *Harpers & Queen*, told a journalist that she took to wearing ever spikier heels and wider shoulder pads as a form of protective covering.

One of Kelsey's colleagues left NatMags to join the *Daily Mail*, and was shell-shocked. 'On her first day, she was told to find four rape victims and file the copy by 4pm. "I can't do it", she said. "You need to take time to talk to women about this." The next week, she spoke to the guys who were working on some environmental stories. She said, "It must feel really good working on something worthwhile." They said, "You stupid bitch. Do you think we really care about this shit?"'

However, I counter, there are some pretty unappetising stories about the way certain women on Fleet Street treat their staff. Kelsey knows all about them. 'I just think, "Isn't it sad that this happens to women too. That you can get so taken up with your own power and grandeur, that you forget to operate as a human being."'

Back at the office, we are in a tiny room looking at a series of glowing slides of the woman who will appear on next month's cover. Linda and Nadia stand in striking parallel, dark heads cocked at different angles. The woman with the blonde, tousled curls smiles back at us – black background, red background, white background. There is a hint of red velvet off her pale shoulders; a red and black necklace. The single, most important thing, Kelsey says, is that she should look friendly.

Linda and Nadia are best friends. And like school girls, they dress identically. They are both wearing black bodies, shortish narrow black skirts, black opaque tights and pointy black suede shoes. It suddenly strikes me what a jolly thing it must be to work with your best mates on a magazine you care passionately about.

The clothes are different. The style is different. The preoccupations are different. But for one brief moment, as I watch the women sitting in a circle in the outer office thrashing out ideas, I wonder just how different this is to the collectives which ran the first feminist magazines. And then I remember. Every major decision about the future of their magazine is made by a man.

On my way out, Kelsey tells me an encouraging story. In the May issue of that year, *She*'s cover was a stunning black woman. The sales reps started running around in circles. 'Don't you know,' they said, 'that when you put a black woman on the cover, the magazines don't sell?' Linda Kelsey stuck to her decision. That month, the sales went up.

WHAT WOULD THEY DO WITH A TAMPON?

The Advertising Industry

Step into any advertising agency, and you will enter what looks like a very modern world indeed. Nearly everyone in advertising is young. The men at the top, and it is invariably men who are at the top, wear Levis and T-shirts. The women seem to favour Lycra bandages. Reception areas are full of mass-ranked TV screens and primary colour partitions.

No industry is more aware of image than advertising.

The marketplace is flooded with goods which are often indistinguishable from one another. The dream merchants are paid to manufacture an image for a product in order to differentiate it from the competition. The 'unique selling point', to use the industry's jargon, has been replaced by the 'emotional selling point'. The consumer is lured by the look and feel of what she is buying rather than by its innate superiority. Similarly the look and feel of the individual agency's environment, the logo, the dress of its employees, are all-important; the corporate image tells the client about the agency's style of business.

But behind the contemporary veneer lie some distinctly uncontemporary attitudes. In the mid-1990s it was still possible to see, on a prime advertising site in west London, a giant billboard promoting a newly built office block featuring a woman dressed in underwear; interested parties were urged to check her vital statistics. Have we really moved on that far from the 1970s, when an agency used the line: IF THIS CAR WAS A WOMAN, SHE WOULD GET HER BOTTOM PINCHED? (Which famously prompted one graffiti artist to paint under it: IF THIS WOMAN WERE A CAR, SHE'D RUN YOU OVER.)

Every industry relies on a form of shorthand to facilitate communication between employees. In the 1980s, newspaper editors started to refer to news stories as 'sexy', meaning: 'This story will sell our newspaper.' (The usage has now worked its way into the most unlikely industries. Bankers use it, computer experts use it; probably even accountants.)

In the 1960s, advertising agencies first used the choice phrase: 'Two Cunts in a Kitchen' (it was truncated, for obvious reasons, to 'Two C's in a K'; newspapers, on grounds of taste, have transformed it into the euphemism Two Tarts in a Kitchen) to describe the sort of advertisement – featuring a pair of homely women gossiping – which was made to sell anything from soap powder to gravy mix.

In the 1990s this has been updated to the Executive Tart. The ET is a successful corporate woman in command of herself and others; the pay-off is that she is almost always unappealing. She is the woman in the Peugeot commercial who humiliates the office Casanova and walks out on her husband after he asks if she has collected his suit from the dry-cleaner's. Or the bully who becomes the chairman of the board in the Kenco coffee campaign. Or the sour-faced female boss, with the clever secretary, in the Rank Xerox ads. One female account executive's explanation of the phrase was: 'It's just a crass term for men in advertising to come to terms with the modern woman.'

While I am sure it is true that advertising executives in using this sort of shorthand are not always consciously setting out to demean women, I am equally sure that a culture which relies on such catchphrases is unlikely to portray women in an interesting or even realistic way. There is something else.

Consider these statistics: 70 to 80 per cent of consumer purchasing is done by women; 50 per cent of advertisements in general are targeted at women, and 80 per cent of television commercials are aimed specifically at women; by the year 2000 women's spending power will have increased to £120 billion a year from its 1990 level of £90 billion.

And then consider these statistics: only two creative directors in the top 50 agencies – the people in overall charge of creative advertisements – are women; only 11 in total who are deputies or have the title creative director are women; and there are only 29 female creatives on the board or associate board of all IPA (Institute of Practitioners in Advertising) agencies. (The IPA represents about 230 agencies, including the top 60; it covers 80 per cent of all advertising placed.) With only three exceptions, Carol Reay, Jennifer Laing and M.T. Rainey, every major advertising agency in Britain is run by a man. This is depressing enough, but not entirely unexpected. It is decidedly more puzzling that no less than 83 per cent (and some insiders put it as high as 90 per cent) of the people who create the content and style of advertisements in this country are men. And, worse still, the number of female creatives is shrinking.

What is the impact of this male to female ratio imbalance on consumers?

Why is it that the creative nerve centre of an agency is the area where women are most under-represented in advertising?

Is there any discernible difference between an advertisement which has been devised by a woman and one devised by a man?

These are interesting and important questions, certainly, but the answers are rather elusive.

The micro-mini drama of a television or cinema advertisement has about 30 seconds in which to make its point. The teams responsible for capturing the imagination of the public have to condense the appeal of the product in a bite-sized grab. The restrictive form, one could argue, encourages the use of stereotypes. Even Barbara Nokes, who is probably the most talked about female creative director in this country because of her seniority and her bold approach to advertising, says: 'There simply isn't time in the average commercial to develop character. You have to establish who, and probably where, your actors are and start putting across your selling message from frame one.' But she emphasises: 'There are ways and ways of using stereotypes.'

One of Nokes's more mould-breaking advertisements was for Dr White's sanitary towels and tampons in the mid-1980s. Although men do work on 'sanpro' (tampons and sanitary towels) accounts, it is highly unlikely they would have taken her approach to the product. Nokes featured a hunky male model, clutching his hand to his head, dressed in silk camiknickers and bra, with the spiky legend: HAVE YOU EVER WONDERED HOW MEN WOULD CARRY ON IF THEY HAD PERIODS? (Another of hers from the same account went: IF MEN WERE SHAPED LIKE MOST TAMPONS, THE HUMAN RACE WOULD HAVE DIED OUT BY NOW.) Nokes has cited this advertising campaign, for which she won a number of prestigious awards, as one of the rare occasions where being a woman really did make a difference.

What is perhaps more significant is the comment of Philip Barnes, the former marketing controller at Smith and Nephew, who worked with her on Dr White's. 'She is not afraid to question the conventional way of doing things,' he said. 'It took someone of *her intellect* and *determination* to persuade us of the *desirability* of presenting sanpro to women in a different tone of voice' (my italics).

Barnes clearly intended this to be complimentary. But the subtext of what he is saying reinforces the extent to which those few women who are hired to make pivotal creative decisions in advertising have to be exceptional – even in the 1990s – to make their voices heard. The whole infrastructure of the business world seems to militate against women who dare to challenge and redefine the traditional way in which a product is pitched. This seems particularly extraordinary when – as in the case of sanpro – the target audience is exclusively female.

The vast majority of senior business executives are still male. Many of them are middle-aged and have wives who do not work. While they may tolerate and even appreciate the presence of a female account handler (especially if she is young and pretty) at agency meetings, it is quite another matter for them to accept that the architect of the actual campaign is a female.

Account handlers, whose role is to liaise between the client and the agency, but above all to keep the client informed and happy, are the nannies of advertising. In their nanny role, account handlers will sometimes obscure the fact that there is a female on the creative team. The second-guessing of the client's prejudices reinforces the male orthodoxy.

The problem is exacerbated by the cloning mentality. If male clients are accustomed to entrusting their accounts to other men, it may seem a radical, and even risky, departure to hand over the reins to a woman. Caution is a regrettable by-product of a shaky economy. In a recession, when agencies are already battling to persuade clients to part with their money, people are unlikely to push for change – particularly if those people are men and those changes will threaten a cosy status quo which favours them.

In 1989 the Institute of Practitioners in Advertising asked Marilyn Baxter, then director of planning at Saatchi & Saatchi, to investigate why there were so few women in top management in advertising. Her study, which was published in 1990, and has not been up-dated since, found that 'Women form only 14 per cent of the members of boards of directors and there are only 22 female managing directors and chief executives in all IPA agencies.' Baxter's conclusion was that 'There is real evidence of sex discrimination towards women in advertising, some of it inadvertent, some of it subtle, and some of it possibly unlawful.'

The following year, the Advertising Association published a booklet which had arisen out of a seminar it had held on the portrayal of women in advertisements. Sue Phipps, the writer, set out the reasons for compiling the report:

> The portrayal of women in advertisements is crucially important, not just because of the passionately held views of the lobbyists and pressure groups that keep it in the forefront of discussion, but because women's purchasing influence is rapidly extending into fields outside the conventionally female ones. [An example of this trend is car sales, which have risen 80 per cent among women since 1983, compared with 27 per cent among men.]
>
> If, even inadvertently, women are being portrayed in ways that they find negative and unacceptable, then they are going to be considerably less willing to sample whatever it is that they are being offered.
>
> It is an embarrassing irony that, whilst the last ten years have seen dramatic changes in the attitudes and expectations of women in all walks of life, and the degree of power held by women in many professions has dramatically increased, the advertising industry, which is dedicated to influencing women's purchasing decisions, is still predominantly male, especially at a senior level.
>
> That fact on its own is enough to raise the question of whether the portrayal of women in advertisements can possibly have kept up with the changes in the outside world.

Sue Phipps's preface touches on a number of key points. There are some industry insiders who say that the advertising agencies are even more conservative in their attitudes towards equal opportunities than the clients they represent. Kay Scorah, a journalist and advertising planner, is one of them. She addressed the issue in a trade magazine: 'Lots of agency people like to blame clients for the fact that there are so few female creative directors. They say that male clients might buy facts from a woman, but not ideas . . . They even say that predatory female clients expect to be tempted by tasty morsels of creative director with pony tails and Boss suits. [This is an example of the advertising world taking its own invention – The Executive Tart – and transforming it into reality.] In fact, client companies like Mars, Midland Bank, Elida Gibbs and Forte are more likely to promote women than the ad agencies that serve them.'

She goes on to quote the response of a client: Barbara Beckett, then marketing director of Forte Hotels: 'advertising agencies are effectively male bastions. A kind of fascism operates which squeezes out non-standard people. They have to have the mental equivalent of a pony tail.'

In 1992 a group of women set up the first all-woman advertising agency, in answer to the pony-tail problem. Gail Parminter, a copywriter, and Gaynor Notman, an art director, worked for BSB Dorland – one of Britain's largest advertising agencies – where clients included B&Q, Austin Rover, Heinz and Feminax. Typically, Notman and Parminter were the only women in a creative department of 38 men.

When they defected from the agency to join forces with the marketing consultants Ali Large and Anne Irwin-Brown of The Female Advantage (none of their clients defected with them), their specific intention was to make the images of women in advertising more realistic. 'Most men in the business are completely out of touch, stuck in a time warp circa 1963,' Parminter told Lisa O'Kelly in the *Independent*. 'They have no idea what it's like to be a woman today. Even the New Men among them don't know what it's like to cope with excruciating period pains in a board meeting, organise child care, juggle nannies and whizz into the supermarket on the way home from work. They don't have the language to talk to women who do that kind of thing every day.'

After their second year of trading, Notman Parminter's annual turnover is over half a million pounds. When we last speak, they have recently won the pitch for Anne Summers's new sex magazine for women, *Bite*, beating a more high-profile agency, the Banks Partnership (now called Banks Huggins O'Shea). However, the magazine subsequently folded.

The female stereotypes we see on our screens often reflect the preferences of the client, rather than those of the audience. I was told of one case where the male marketing director of a leading hosiery manufacturer did not invite one female member of staff into the consumer discussions. The initial advertisement – in which the model was dressed in black stockings and suspenders – represented the classic *Penthouse* fantasy. It is not unusual to find a male creative team, a male account handler, a male client, a male casting director and a male commercials director. As one female creative said: 'The result is that they cast women they fancy, rather than think about the consumer.'

I was able to find only one example of an advertising practitioner who had conducted a thorough investigation of women's responses to female stereotyping in advertisements. Kitty O'Hagan, then of the advertising agency GGK, conducted a survey throughout Europe. Women were given a choice of eight female faces in each category, and asked to choose which picture they thought represented the advertisers' stereotype, and which they would relate to best. O'Hagan found that consumers consistently rejected the 'ideal' stereotypes of 'career women', 'sex symbols' and 'mothers' and said they would relate better to more 'interesting' images of women in such roles.

The advertisers' stereotype of a career woman showed a steely-gazed ice-maiden with a hard mouth and brittle hairdo; the consumer favoured a fleshier woman who was smiling and looked less scrupulously groomed; the advertisers' 'mother' was the Katie-Oxo prototype – unthreatening and bordering on the frumpy; the consumer preferred a younger, more fashionable model; the advertisers' idea of a sexually attractive woman was a dyed blonde; the consumer chose a brunette.

In 1990 the Advertising Standards Authority, the advertising industry's self-regulatory body for the print medium, received 10,000 complaints. The majority of the complainants, it says, were women. The number of complaints about the *portrayal* of women, however, was not significant. The numbers have remained reasonably stable: 183 in 1987 down to 101 in 1991 and back up to 180 again in 1992. (The actual figure of complaints in 1991 was 373, but the ASA only upheld 101.) The figures, taken on their own, would tend to discredit the theory that women have finally had enough lousy advertising and are not going to take it any more.

One explanation for the low number of complaints was that women feel they don't have the power to change the advertising industry, and so complaining about it is not a high priority. 'This isn't helped by cases like the Hennes poster advertisement,' Phipps says, 'where the company, having been criticised for running a poster featuring a Swedish au pair in her underwear [in November 1990], ran a follow-up poster of a different girl (also in lingerie) with the line, 'Last time we ran an ad for Swedish lingerie, 78 women complained . . . no men!' The ASA, who did receive complaints about the ad from men, later discovered that Hennes had not logged their complainants by gender, which makes one wonder about the legitimacy of its advertising line.

The ASA – reluctant, perhaps, to draw conclusions based on figures which seem so at odds with received opinion – decided it was time to update its 1982 survey on women's attitudes. The survey, *Herself Reappraised*, took three years to complete and was published in 1990. It cost £166,000 and the findings were drawn from more than 2,245 interviews. Three-quarters of the sample believed that 'Advertising can help establish unrealistic views of the way women should look and behave', and just over half agreed that 'Advertisements always show women as sex objects.'

The most interesting material in *Herself Reappraised*, since it indicates the shape of things to come, is on the relationship between the people who complain about advertisements and the general public. As Sue Phipps emphasises: 'the research showed that the complainants and the general public had the same feelings and reactions, the former were just *further down the line* and reacted with a greater degree of sensitivity than the non-complainants.'

The ASA's conclusion was that there had been a shift in public attitude since their last survey, on the specific issue of 'equality between the sexes and the need to reflect this in advertising by not depicting women in demeaning roles'.

In 1990 the Broadcasting Standards Council commissioned a working paper on television advertising and sex role stereotyping. The communications research group at Aston University in Birmingham undertook a content analysis of about 500 prime-time advertisements on ITV. The group found that 'Youth and beauty seemed to be the distinctive features of women in television advertisements': female characters are three times more likely to be blonde than their male counterparts – which relates to stereotypical notions of beauty or glamour; two-thirds of the women looked like the kind of models who appear in a clothes magazine; men were more than twice as likely as women to be represented in some kind of paid employment, and even where women are portrayed as having particular occupational roles, 'their value depends upon their physical attractiveness'.

Women are most often shown with their men or families: 'housewives kiss their husbands goodbye, greet them when they return from work, and generally illustrate that men work in, and protect them from, an external male world', whereas men are able to integrate successfully outside the home. Men are also associated with humour to a greater extent than women. All of which reflects 'the relatively limited variety of roles played by women in advertisements'.

The stereotypes are extended to the voiceovers. Nine out of ten voiceovers are male, in which the tone is 'expert or official'. The female voiceovers, in contrast, are 'sexy or sensuous'.

The group's conclusion was that the patterns which emerged in their study 'lend strong support to the concern that women [in advertisements] exist in what is essentially a man's world'.

There is no reference in the British Code of Advertising Practice to the specific use or portrayal of women. The Authority's decisions to act on complaints are dictated by notions of offence, taste and decency, which are by their very nature contentious. I suspect that more women object to the one-dimensional aspect of the women who appear in almost all advertising than feel aggrieved by a specific advertisement. The battery of the one-note samba – tart or career girl or tarty career girl or mum or housewife – has a numbing effect. It lowers our expectations of what could be done in advertising. If only someone had the foresight to assemble the different pieces into one jigsaw, and inject some humour, we might see a truer picture of a woman.

The Oxo commercial, at least according to some of the most vociferous critics of the advertising industry, seems to have got it right. Katie has been updated in the 1990s to have a job, a family, an evening class – and, breathtakingly, a sense of humour. Barbara Nokes thinks this advertisement represents an effective use of a stereotype: 'Far from being a doormat, Katie gives the impression of being very much in control of her life. She treats her family with humour and affection and is clearly loved and respected by them.'

The first Radion washing powder advertisement in 1989, is conversely singled out as a disaster (although it won a 1990 IPA Effectiveness Award for establishing a significant 7 per cent market share within the first six months of its 'life'). Its message is not unlike the Persil commercial, from the 1960s, with its male voiceover saying: 'A mum is some-one who has a lot to put up with. And goes on putting up with it.' Marilyn Baxter says: 'The original Radion commercial was outstandingly negative for the advertising industry. It gave people a very real stick to use against the business.'

Anne Irwin Brown of the Female Advantage deplored its suggestion that 'stubborn stains' can ruin a woman's life. She, for one, voted with her purse. 'I turned away from the Radion shelves in the supermarket because I didn't want anyone to think that I or my family needed it,' she told a reporter in *Today* newspaper.

About 4 per cent of the complaints the Independent Television Commission (ITC) receives are about women in commercials. 'There has been a general reduction of complaints about women in the role of sex object, and a concomitant rise in complaints about the stereotyping of women in conventional roles,' says the ITC press officer, Stuart Paterson. (In 1991 there were 70 complaints about stereotyping, as opposed to 34 complaints about the gratuitous use of the female body to sell products. 1992, however, saw a reversal of the trend: 75 – of which 30 were about the Yorkie ad featuring a woman wearing large plastic breasts – versus 35.) Again, as with the ASA figures, the low level of complaints seems to suggest that women consumers are not too bothered by the role women play in advertisements. Or that they feel it is a waste of time and energy to write in to complain.

When Notman Parminter and the Female Advantage teamed up, they publicised their arrival with a photograph of the creative department of BSB Dorland, a leading London agency (and, incidentally, their former employer). Under the faces of 27 men, the caption read: WHAT WOULD THEY DO WITH A TAMPON? When *Campaign* magazine asked Andrew Cracknell, the agency's creative director, why there were no women in the photograph, he reportedly replied: 'She wasn't in that day.'

Many of the articles in the trade press and the media pages of newspapers pinpoint this apparent conundrum of men dreaming up sales lines for sanpro. While this is a convenient and eye-catching way of focusing the reader's attention, it misses the point. It is also dangerous. What one doesn't want to encourage, after all, is the thinking that women should work on 'girly', as ad agencies call them, accounts, leaving the men to handle beer and cars and men's products (they'll probably be bought by women, anyway). It is all too easy for women to be marginalised into what are seen as 'female' areas (which is why there are so few women political editors or news editors or foreign editors on national newspapers), when what one should aim for is equal numbers of men and women working on all accounts. But that scenario is a long way off.

All the advertising practitioners I spoke to were familiar with the expression the Executive Tart, but no one was able to identify its provenance. What is certain is that when it first emerged, the media latched on to the expression with gusto. Jonathan Glancey of the *Independent* believes he was the first journalist to write about her in the press, although he does not claim responsibility for coining the phrase. 'Executive Tart,' he wrote in April 1992, 'is a cruel label for the kind of part-make-believe, part-real, junior league, wannabe businesswoman-on-top who inhabits an expanding empire of television breaks, cinema ads and roadside hoardings . . . She is a young woman in a wide-shouldered, tight-waisted suit – dangerous red is the preferred colour – with fake Chanel earrings, handbag and heels.'

He bolsters his argument with a quote from *The Language of Clothes*, by the American novelist Alison Lurie – the ET is an uncomfortable combination of 'don't-mess-with-me career woman and sexy unliberated babe . . . the message is that she will be a tiger in the office, but a pussycat in bed'.

But Glancey himself gets sucked into the reality spin when he writes: 'As women who keep a wary eye on the would-be ET in their office know all too well, the conceit works. In any male-heavy office, the ET with her striding gait, briefcase, clipboard and fluttering eyelashes will always threaten to succeed beyond her abilities.'

In a breathtaking leap of logic, the fictional character has suddenly become a real woman. This ellipsis pinpoints the danger of stereotypes. It is only a few short steps before women start to see themselves or each other through a media-manufactured lens. It also gives men a sort of impunity in their attacks on women. The ET is a convenient put-down of the high achiever. When in doubt, pick on her wardrobe. It's so much easier to dismiss a successful female colleague as an Executive Tart, with a knowing in-media look, than to make the uncompromising statement: 'Well, she's slept her way to the top.'

If one is to attempt to understand how and why these negative images are created, it seems sensible to start with the environment in which they are concocted – and why it is so dominated by men.

Here are some comments from women who work, or have worked, as writers and art directors in the creative departments of major advertising agencies:

- 'It's very hard to be taken seriously in an environment where senior male colleagues ask you what colour knickers you're wearing. There's no way my husband would be asked those sorts of questions by a woman.' (She left.)
- 'When I came back from maternity leave, I was given a really hard time. My boss always waited until the end of the day to give me a brief, just to guarantee that I would have to work late. He eventually admitted it was to see whether I put my baby or the job first.' (She left.)
- 'Oh God, I haven't got you, have I? I wanted one with big tits.' (Greeting to a female creative from her male partner. She left.)

These three quotations exemplify the culture of the creative department. It is described, variously, as a boys' own playground, a rugger-buggers' locker room, a bastion of male prejudice. The few women who have the courage to complain about sexist remarks or stereotyping (and, as we have seen, there are only ever a few of them in a creative department) are dismissed as strident feminists or whingers.

Some talented women, nevertheless, have managed to scale the bastion. Their names come up again and again in a sort of litany of the advertising world: Barbara Nokes, Alex Taylor, Cathy Heng, Kiki Kendrick, Suzie Henry, Rita

Dempsey and 'those two who set up an all-female consul-tancy' (Notman and Parminter).

These top female creatives have all, doubtless, devel-oped their own personal strategies for survival in a man's world. It is generally assumed that they must be exception-ally tough. Precisely because there are so few of them, creative women are subjected to a peculiar scrutiny. This lens is distorting, reducing its subjects to the sorts of stereotype which we are accustomed to seeing in advertisements. Thus, female creatives can be either over-emotional or as hard as nails, and even – puzzlingly – both at the same time. Some women – perhaps not surprisingly – fall prey to believing the mythology which has been invented for them.

Anita Davis, the creative group head at Young & Rubi-cam, says: 'Most of the time, there is the expectation that simply because I am a female creative I must be hard. My male partner, in fact, is a lot less tough than me. But when something goes wrong, I'm still the one who is expected to burst into tears.' Her stomping bravado in the workplace is not always maintained when she leaves the office. 'Some-times I go home and look at myself in the mirror and say: "Did you really scream and shout like that today? Anita, I thought you'd have more intelligence. It's only an advertisement, after all."'

There are other reasons, beyond male prejudice, which are offered to explain why women find the culture of the creative department so alienating. None of them rings true to me. Women, the argument goes, find it difficult to defend their work in front of a roomful of people. They suffer from wanting to be liked. They find creative work too exposing. But there are legions of women who work as sub-editors on magazines and newspapers who have to defend their cover-lines and headlines every day. They don't seem to find it a problem. The one obstacle female creatives appear to face is working in a department which is so overrun by men that their viewpoint is likely to be marginalised or discredited.

There are some industry insiders who find reasons to be optimistic. Marilyn Baxter is impressed by the confidence of the young women who are entering advertising. 'It is noticeable that younger women, though they do perceive the differences between men and women, are significantly more self-assured and confident of their own strengths than women of earlier generations, and are more determined to succeed *through* their differences, rather than despite them.' The implication here is that as long as the numbers are sufficient, the next generation of women is more likely to remould the environment in which they work to suit themselves, rather than conform to the male orthodoxy as their predecessors have had to do.

There is a direct correlation between the lack of senior women in advertising today and the relatively small numbers of women who entered the business 10 or 15 years ago. In 1989, 45 per cent of the graduate entrants were women, which is almost double the figure for 1975. The PCAS statistics for students accepted for media and journalism courses for 1993 show a total of 1,848 women against 1,544 men. Female students have also outstripped male students in the UCCA statistics for media and journalism courses for 1993: 794 women; 469 men.

The prediction is that five to ten years from now there will be a significant increase in the number of women at the top of agencies. The prognosis looks good – but are the numbers sufficient *throughout* advertising?

Some areas of advertising are now dominated by women (55 per cent of account planners and researchers are female). The creative department, as we know, is not one of them. Here, at even the most junior levels, Susannah Richmond says, 'male/female ratios are still embarrassingly low'. And it is the only department in advertising where the female intake is actually on the decline.

Andrew Cracknell, creative director of BSB Dorland, says that only one in eight applications for a placement comes from a woman. When I repeat Cracknell's figure to Canna Kendall, one of the most prominent headhunters in the business, she laughs. Her agency is the first stop for anyone who wants to enter advertising. In 1992, 84 aspiring copywriters registered with the agency; 24 of them were women. This, apparently, is entirely representative. Which makes the female-to-male ratio of applicants closer to one in four.

But even when a female creative already has a good track record – and can prove it with her portfolio – she is likely to confront obstacles. Creative departments are made up of teams. It is unusual, and not only because of the numbers deficit, to find two women working together. The thinking here – which has a fabulous irony considering that there are creative departments which don't employ a single woman – is that you need a male point of view to balance the perspective.

Liz Whiston is the only female copywriter in a department of eight creatives at Howell Henry Chaldecott Lury. In 1992 she (and her male partner) won three British Television awards for the Mercury telephone commercials starring Harry Enfield. 'I wonder why the secretary is picking up the award,' a senior ad man said to a colleague at the celebration dinner. By the time Whiston had picked up her third award, he'd worked it out: 'Ah, she must be the production assistant.' And he wasn't joking.

Here is another explanation for the dearth of creative women. It was the opinion of Murray Partridge, when he worked in the all-male creative department of TBWA HKR (whose accounts include Gossard and Mary Quant) that 'There are not enough women creatives generally because the only girls who get interviewed are the pretty ones and they are not usually the most talented. People are always saying, "You've got to see this team, because one of them is stunning."

'The only way it will change is if we recruit more women, but at the moment women aren't going to get recruited unless the guys fancy them.'

*

The Lion's Den

So what, one may wonder, particularly in the light of comments like these, can life be like in an advertising agency in the 1990s? I ventured into the lion's den to find out.

Young & Rubicam's British headquarters is in a huge 1930s listed building in north London. Y&R is one of the top ten agencies. Clients include American Express, Pirelli, Olympus Cameras and Eurostar (the Channel Tunnel's express train).

The period during my visit is marked by an unusual degree of turbulence. The London office, under instructions from the parent company in New York, had recently replaced some of its top personnel. The new managing director, Tim Lindsay, the glamour-boy of advertising who is 36 but looks ten years younger, and chief executive, Jerry Judge, had been headhunted from Bartle Bogle Hegarty. Part of the new chiefs' troubleshooting brief was to trim the workforce. Eighty employees were made redundant, leaving a staff of 190. A number of key women – including an assistant managing director and a board account director – were among the casualties.

With the new regime came a new ethos. Any sort of change within a company tends to be accompanied by uncertainty and criticism, especially from the old guard. Nevertheless, I was startled by the level of resistance to the new hierarchy. Bartle Bogle Hegarty was described by one woman who had worked there as being particularly young, particularly male and particularly sexist. Some Y&R employees felt that these qualities were intruding on their working environment to a degree they found unacceptable. By the end of my third day there, I had begun to see their point. It is important to stress here that Young & Rubicam is considered to be a good deal less hostile to women than many other agencies. This, it transpires, is less reassuring than it sounds.

There are endless meetings in an advertising agency. Many of them amount to little more than a conversation between two members of staff. Occasionally I feel as though I have strayed on to the set of *Reginald Perrin*. Particularly on the less exciting accounts: the Yellow Fats meeting for Dairy Crest (an ersatz butter), for example, or the Welsh Water Board. The employees' ability to muster enthusiasm for these campaigns is remarkable. The favourite words of Reggie Perrin's vacuous young ad executives ('super' and 'terrific') have been updated (only marginally) to 'sexy' and a tongue-in-cheek 'groovy'.

It is when I find myself listening to an even more dated patter that I really start to worry. I ask a perfectly normal-looking man, who is a senior account handler, whether I can accompany him to a meeting in which women do not generally make their presence felt. The response – a parody of his hapless assistant – is astonishing. He turns his back, pretends to pin up a chart while hitching up a skirt and wiggling his bottom. 'My assistant,' he leers, 'certainly makes *her* presence felt.'

This little performance is disconcerting for several reasons. Not least because it is not a wind-up. The poor man even looks puzzled when one of the women in the room says, 'You said it, boy, you said it. It'll go straight into her book.' He is a middle-class, thirtysomething, totally unreconstructed male; a throwback to the sixties.

But what of the assistant herself? She is a graduate in her mid-twenties. She wears micro-miniskirts and figure-hugging tops, and flaunts her sexuality. She is very pretty. She is also very bright and very ambitious. But she probably doesn't know that she and her cohorts – who are also bright graduates – are referred to as 'office totty'. And she would probably be amazed to discover that her male colleagues wager bets on what colour knickers she is wearing.

There are two ways of looking at this. Either she is a member of the Madonna school of post-feminists, and believes she is using her sexuality on precisely her own terms. Or she is an unwitting victim of her bosses, who suggest she wear skimpy clothes to impress the client (who is usually male). Either way, she loses. The client who has been encouraged to regard her as a tasty decoration is hardly likely to entrust her with the grown-up business of handling his account.

Dress and decorum, it transpires, is a vexed issue for female account handlers throughout advertising. The IPA has held seminars on the subject. Barbara Nokes of CME. KHBB, M.T. Rainey of Rainey Kelly Campbell Roalfe and Carol Reay of Reay Keating & Hamer have given talks about it. All my interviewees have had to tackle the subject informally with female members of their staff at some time. Marilyn Baxter addressed it in her report:

> Some senior women complain that more junior women fall into the trap of dressing as if they are trying to seduce the whole office, then complaining that men do not take them seriously. Looking attractive and well-dressed is believed to be important to success, but women should not be persuaded to dress provocatively by senior agency males if they expect to be taken seriously. As several women pointed out, the problem of confusing a woman's roles is the man's problem rather than the woman's, but it seems that women are the ones who have to solve it.

It is a more complicated problem to solve than one might think. The senior Y&R account women have long, agonised discussions about how they should broach the subject with a junior member of staff. 'Perhaps she'll think I'm jealous,' one worries. Another woman, who is in her mid-thirties and has children, says: 'She may look at me and think "Christ, that's not my idea of a role model. Who's she trying to kid?"'

A giant question mark hovers over the debate. Under the present regime, its critics say, there is some justification for thinking there are rewards to be gained for behaving in a way that has little to do with professional attributes. They cite a recent example. An account team had put in long hours pitching for a lucrative piece of business and had won it. The team was rewarded with a celebratory dinner, but only the junior account women were invited, so they say.

Tim Lindsay, when I ask him about this story, says he never heard about such a dinner taking place, and if he had done, he would have reprimanded the perpetrators.

A year later I return to Young & Rubicam to speak to Tim Lindsay about advertising in general, and his agency in particular. He shows me a reel of his latest greatest hits. Two of them feature the ET.

Suchard's Twilight Mints shows a couple at a candlelit dinner. The woman is in control and really rather grim. The man – as Lindsay puts it – is a 'himbo'. 'I like my men like my Twilight Mints,' purrs ET. 'Well-dressed, smooth, rich and very, very . . . thick.'

A series of ads for Rank Xerox is a different take on the film *Working Girl*. The female boss is a hard-faced shrew; her secretary is the clever one who handles everything, but never gets the credit. 'Where's everyone going?' asks the boss. 'Home . . . remember that place?' answers secretary.

Since we last met, Lindsay has separated from his wife of the past 17 years, with whom he has a teenage son and a young daughter, and has moved in with one of his junior account handlers. He admits that the nature of the business – long hours, travel – is likely to put a certain amount of strain on most marriages. 'But in a recession, when you are operating with 25 per cent less staff and more demanding clients, there is no other way of organising the workload.'

In 1989, nearly 16,000 people worked in London's advertising industry. Now the figure is 11,100. Over a quarter of the workforce has been laid off.

We talk about the level of sexism in advertising. He seems pretty appalled when I mention some of the incidents I witnessed at his agency. But as managing director, I say, surely it is your job to create a culture in which it is clear that such behaviour is not to be tolerated. 'It's very difficult because you want an atmosphere that's fun. You know, you sometimes find yourself making jokes which aren't politically correct, too. The problem is that for some people it is a cover for views which are unacceptable.'

I ask him, with a certain amount of trepidation, about

the – ah – bonding, shall we say, between male and female colleagues, which seems to be particularly prevalent in advertising agencies.

'I think that it's a good thing,' Lindsay says, without much hesitation. 'An agency that plays together, stays together. Intense relationships, which are not necessarily sexual; groups of people getting pissed together. It's all very good for the culture. And as long as you're not hurting anyone . . . well, of course, sometimes people do get hurt if they're married . . .'

He adds, perhaps thinking that he's reading my mind, 'You can say that it's a lot of dirty old men getting off with their secretaries, or you could say that it makes the women feel more as though they are part of the agency. It's probably a bit of both. And even if you were to insist that it is older men preying on younger, defenceless girls, I certainly know powerful women who have preyed on younger men.

'Jerry and I do talk about girls a lot of the time. But women talk about men, as you must know, and the content is often a lot more clinical . . .'

And there he rests his case. In the creative department of Y&R there are 15 men and three women. Of the eleven department heads, nine are men and two are women. And there I rest my case.

*

When I first met Marilyn Baxter, she said that women with feminist leanings were unlikely to be attracted to advertising. She revised this when I interviewed her a year later. But her initial comment had rung true. Aspiring to any sort of high moral ground seems oddly incompatible with working in a service industry whose *raison d'être* is to flog products. But many of the women I interviewed felt strongly about all sorts of issues. Several of them contributed their services, out of office hours and free of charge, to a number of organisations, the Labour Party and the Anti-Vivisection Society among them.

Most – but by no means all – of the women I spoke to, particularly those in their late twenties and thirties, felt some commitment to improving the lot of women in advertising. They move by stealth, meeting up for solidarity lunches to discuss maternity benefits or how to circumnavigate male chauvinism.

The explanation they offered for this covertness is that senior men are becoming increasingly sensitive about women expressing dissatisfaction with the status quo. Like-minded women are dismissed as 'the spinster clique', or told to 'break it up'. One top creative woman was ticked off by her boss for speaking out in the press. Other women network more blatantly by joining lobby groups such as the Women's Advertising Club of London (WACL) or Adwomen.

Alison Butler, a board accounts director at Y&R, who has since moved to America, told me she fantasised about setting up her own female lobby group, since she doesn't believe the existing organisations are taken seriously by the industry. It would act as a trade union cum training consultancy, with a particular brief to look at women who are entering the business. Her belief is that unless agencies can rise to the challenge of making the working environment more sympathetic for both sexes, the women who have been trained in their twenties are likely to become disenchanted with the profession in their thirties. That is, if they get that far.

In 1990, Winston Fletcher, who was then president of the Institute of Advertising Practitioners, described an event which had prompted him to commission Baxter's report:

'In the autumn of 1988, I ran a series of eight IPA seminars for graduate trainees and other entrants into the agency business. The format of each seminar was an interview with one of the country's leading advertising people. The eight people I chose to interview – they were obvious choices – were all male. Yet the audience, all in their early twenties, was split 50/50, male and female. The young women made their disapproval of my apparent chauvinism abundantly clear. Why had I chosen no women? they asked. Because there were almost no women at the very top in advertising, I replied. Their faces dropped. Why not? Don't women ever get to the top? Many of them were so angry, and so depressed, I feared they might quit their newly started advertising careers even before the series ended.'

In 1992 Fletcher made the depressing admission that 'Little has changed since the report and the problems facing female creatives have, if anything, been exacerbated by the recession.'

Whatever one's opinion of advertising, there is little doubt that it plays a part in shaping our popular culture. There is a direct correlation between the images we see of women in advertisements, which I believe have an impact on the way we see ourselves, and the number of women employed in key positions in the advertising industry. The Executive Tart, and her beleaguered sisters in the kitchen, will only be buried when there have been generations of real-life female executives – particularly in the creative departments – to offer an alternative.

MARILYN BAXTER

OUTRAGED OF CHARLOTTE STREET

Marilyn Baxter was director of planning at Saatchi & Saatchi in the early nineties, before taking a two-year sabbatical to sail from England to Australia. When she left, she was the only woman of the 13 members of the agency's executive management committee. In 1989 the Institute of Practitioners in Advertising commissioned Baxter to investigate why there were so few women in top management in advertising. Her damning report was published in 1990.

What's a nice Labour-voting woman, with a highly tuned social conscience and a house at the shabby end of Shepherd's Bush, doing in advertising? Marilyn Baxter, the former director of planning at Saatchi & Saatchi, does not have to think about the question, since it's one she's been asked – and asked herself – at various times during her ten years in the business.

At Saatchis, where she worked for more than seven years, Baxter was known as 'the resident pinko'. Her other sobriquet was 'Outraged of Charlotte Street'. It says something about the conservative nature of the advertising world behind its sharp-edged image, that Marilyn Baxter – a mild-mannered and eminently sensible woman in her mid-forties – considers herself a militant.

When she left Saatchis in 1992, Baxter was the only female of 13 members on the Executive Management Committee. The uniqueness of her position meant she was all too often a lone voice protesting about the depiction of women in advertisements. 'It's quite hard to be the one who is constantly pointing out that these images are sexist,' she says. 'You can see your male colleagues raising their eyebrows and you know they're thinking, "Oh, bloody women". It wears you down. There are some younger women coming into the business who are much more outspoken. Our generation would tend to keep the peace, while still having an opinion.'

What are her main objections to the way women are used to sell products? 'In press advertisements, there is still too much gratuitous nudity, and women are often unnecessarily sexy or fawning. In TV ads, we still see women cast in one of the very few stereotyping roles: as an obsessive whose only concern is about the cleanliness of her kitchen; the mother-in-law nag or a pathetic creature dependent on her partner. I would think, "I don't like this, what can I do about it?" You can say, "This is frankly sexist", which I don't recommend because there will be a fight. It's much more effective to say, "This is hackneyed" because there is nothing a creative can bear less than being told his work is dull.'

Baxter is a great believer in the innate differences between men and women. In her report for the IPA, she listed nine points which illustrate why the gender differences militate against women getting to the top in advertising and, since she believes the rules of the business have been dictated by men, favour men.

'*Men* are characterised by high motivation, single-mindedness, risk-taking, preoccupation with dominance, hierarchy and the politics of power, and the constant measurement and comparison of success.

'*Women* are ambitious, but they are ambitious for different things. A woman's conceptual horizons are wider. She takes a more balanced view of life. The nature of the occupation and her own judgement of her competence at it are more important than formal achievement or financial success.'

When we meet, Baxter is changing her horizons from Soho to the limitless views of the Pacific Ocean. She and Martin, her partner of the past ten years, are taking a two-year sabbatical to sail from England to Australia in their 32-foot glass-fibre cutter.

Her decision to throw in a salary of £90,000 and one of the best jobs in advertising, particularly given the dodgy economic climate, seems to fit in almost too neatly with her verdict that women are generally not as one-track minded about their careers as men. And yet, a year after my meeting with Baxter, another of my subjects, Barbara Nokes, resigned from her job at Bartle Bogle Hegarty to concentrate on other interests. Nokes is now executive creative director of CME.KHBB: the top female creative in advertising.

This is not the first time that Baxter has abandoned her advertising career for maritime adventure. In 1981 she left her job as an account planner at McCann Erickson to go sailing across the Atlantic Ocean. When she returned two years later, she found that people were so intrigued by her escapade that it actually did her reputation good. She went back into planning, this time at Grandfield Rork. She was made a board director in 1985, and left to join Saatchis where she was promoted to director of planning the following year.

Given her passion for sailing, it is perhaps not surprising that Baxter has a tendency to describe the various functions of advertising in nautical terms. The planner is the navigator and the account handler is the captain. 'The navigator says, "We shouldn't leave today because the currents aren't good" or "Look out for those rocks" or "The best water's over here."'

The planners, she goes on to say with a straight face, are

the brains of the agency. 'The account people think we're over-intellectual. We think they're the ones who carry the clients' bags, take them out to lunch, and that they only care about keeping the client happy. The creatives are concerned about whether the advertisement will win an award and make them famous. The media buyer wants to be satisfied that the space was bought for the best price at the right time. The planner is the only person who really cares about whether the advertisement has worked.'

The majority of planners are women. They are also well represented at the top of their department. Altogether there are 74 female planners who are directors or associate directors and 17 female heads of that department in IPA agencies. Many planners, like Baxter, have a market research background. Market research tends to attract large numbers of women, which explains why so many of the candidates for planning jobs are female.

But there are other less pedestrian explanations for this unusual predominance of women. Baxter pinpointed one in her report: 'Planning is a relatively new discipline in agencies. There is therefore no historical tradition of men doing the job and women have not had to fight to be recognised in it. Interestingly, men in planning [are] judged (by women) to be more liberated and less "macho" than their account handling counterparts, though there is a tendency in some agencies (for men) to believe that real men avoid planning and become account directors!'

Baxter believes that women feel comfortable in an environment in which they play the supportive role. The planner's power is the power behind the throne. Since it is an advisory job, it would be very unusual, for instance, for a planner to have power of veto over whether or not an advertisement should go ahead.

Baxter tells me about an advertisement which the Saatchi creatives dreamed up for Habitat. It showed two naked, obviously female bottoms, with the strap line: TWO FREE SEATS FOR EVERY TABLE. '"Excuse me," I said at the meeting, "but why have you picked two women's bottoms?"' I presume that

Baxter is making the point that it took a woman to point out that the women's bodies were being used gratuitously. I make the further assumption that she believes there would be less of this sort of advertising if there were more women involved in the decision-making process. But I am wrong. 'Advertising won't automatically change if there are more women in creative departments,' she says. 'There is a mythology that all women feel the same. But the people who are sensitised to sexism in ads are pretty few and far between, and that includes women.'

An all-women creative team, she says, is just as likely to fall for a classic sitcom scenario as a male team. But surely, since she herself stresses the differences between men and women, it would have to make some difference if women had a greater say about the content of an advertisement? 'Yes,' she admits, 'in theory, if there were a lot of women writing ads you would see a different product. Barbara Nokes's Dr Whites ad is the most famous example of a woman doing it differently. But ads don't get written by one person, and they have to be approved by the creative director [male], who might say, "That's very nice dear, but where's the selling line?" And then they have to be approved by the client, who is nearly always a male.'

We discuss whether it is possible to pinpoint a feminine imprint on an advertisement. Even if there were some parity of women to men involved in the making of a commercial, this is an elusive exercise since some men have a feminine sensibility and vice versa.

Maxine Tabac is notable for being one of the very few female directors in advertising. Her ads are impressionistic, non-narrative and often full of dreamy images. She is the woman behind the *Independent*'s launch campaign ('It is. Are you?') and Lanson (black and white again, the young couple who drink their champagne on an out-of-season English beach to a backdrop of 'Chanson d'Amour'). Tabac filmed the Lanson ad for Saatchis. Baxter recalls the difficulties in explaining the script of a commercial, which essentially has no storyline, to the client.

Rita Clifton, Baxter's successor at Saatchis, cites a commercial which she believes reflects the contrasting male and female sensibility. The product was the Vivas body spray. The commercial showed a woman in a ladies' powder room, drying her hands with a hand-held dryer, lost in her own thoughts. It suddenly occurs to her that it would be marvellous to have every bit of her body buffeted. Aha. Vivas. 'Our research showed that women responded well to the idea of personal fantasy,' Clifton says. 'We were practically an all-female team. It was researched by a woman, the senior account handler was a woman, the planners were women and the creative was a woman. But when the male commercials director got his hands on it, the hand-dryer was transformed into a willy. At the end of the ad, it even droops. It seems like a subtle shift but it changed the whole tone of the advertisement, from one of female personal involvement to male observation.'

This story offers an illuminating insight into the way an advertising agency works. It shows that even when a department whose sole purpose is to provide the research which reveals the predilection of the consumer (in this case female), the information may well be ignored at a later stage. It also underlines the essential powerlessness of the planner. Or, indeed, anyone who does not have power over the image.

Where women really could make a difference, Baxter states unequivocally, is if there were more of them in senior management positions in agencies. Like Jennifer Laing, Saatchis' former chairwoman, Baxter says the culture of Saatchi & Saatchi is particularly macho and aggressive. 'I think that greater numbers of women have an effect, not just on the well-being of other women but on the environment in general.' She recalls a meeting which was held to discuss low morale in the agency. 'The men were all saying that we should hold softball matches, throw more parties, get pissed together. One woman said, "That's the most trivial thing I've heard in all my life. Don't you realise that people's morale improves when they're praised and feel that their work is of value."'

The meeting, she says, was typical: the men lined up on one side; the women on the other. 'My feeling is that if there were more women at the top, there would be better management tactics because women are better than men at motivating people. I think it's important to let people know how they're doing and keep them informed. When you make these statements, you can hear yourself sounding "caring" and in their terms "feeble".

'I don't think about my gender when I'm at work. But at Saatchis, you are constantly having it pointed out to you that you are a woman. The comment is always, "How typically girly", which is insidiously undermining because it's not just about disagreeing with your point of view.'

The first time that we meet, Baxter is wearing an unflattering, nondescript suit. She looks vaguely colourless, like a bureaucrat or a bank manager. On the day of our interview, almost a year later, her appearance is quite different. She is draped in loose trousers and a top in varying degrees of cream. She looks altogether younger and sharper. If Baxter has an Achilles' heel, it is her fear of being a beige personality. Since our first encounter, she has been on a Colour Me Beautiful course. 'It has had a dramatic impact on the way one is perceived,' she says. 'I was smart but never stylish. I used to hate shopping and I became very conservative. I always felt I looked pale and dowdy. Certainly, no one ever made flattering comments about my appearance.

'Now that I have more confidence, I'm more authoritative and people take me seriously. It's very hard to impose yourself on a meeting if you're competing with huge male door-fillers. Because the whole business is about style over content, women are much more exposed than men. We should use the way we dress as a weapon. It may be awkward to acknowledge it, but it's the one area where we can have an advantage over men.'

But just how does a woman look attractive and avoid emitting the wrong signals – particularly in an environment which seems to be electric with sexual *frisson*. Baxter laughs ruefully. 'It's tricky. Planners refer to something called "negative correlation". Take the car, for example. You cannot have a message which says a car is good-looking *and* safe or safe *and* fast. The same thing is true of women. For a woman to be clever *and* physically attractive is considered to be a negative correlation. What I tell younger women is that if they flaunt their sexuality they cannot expect to be taken seriously. There are simply not enough people who are prepared to tackle this issue and point out the pitfalls to junior employees.'

In her role as Auntie Marilyn, Baxter has regularly taken up the complaints of younger female staff. She herself has been sexually harassed by a client and knows, from her own experience, how the victim of such an attack can feel too humiliated to talk about it. On one occasion, she upbraided a senior account manager for encouraging his junior to wear a dress with a plunging neckline to a client party. '"How do you expect her to come in the next day and sell an ad or argue the agency's point of view?" I asked him. He was completely taken aback.' This has by now become such a familiar story, I am almost immune to its impact. Where do these men come from?

There must be many admen, and doubtless a few adwomen, who find Baxter's attention to such details tiresome or even irrelevant. But some of her critics accuse her of not being militant enough. When her report was published, it was condemned by certain feminists – including Adam Lury, of Howell Henry Chaldecott Lury, the self-appointed conscience of the advertising industry – because of its fundamental approach. The report was seen as a survival guide, but only for women who were prepared to conform to an agenda set by men. While I feel this judgement is too harsh, since the report never laid claim to being a subversives' manifesto, there is one moment in our interview when Baxter betrays her susceptibility to the adman's value system.

We are talking about Jennifer Laing's famous red Ferrari. Baxter says that when she was promoted at Saatchis, she too bought herself the most expensive BMW available. Why? 'I enjoyed having it because I knew the men wanted it.' Isn't that just playing the game by their own playground rules? Wouldn't it be more intelligent to rewrite the script? Baxter acts as though she has never considered this possibility before. It may be that the gesture had something to do with her desire to appear dashing rather than beige. She reconsiders the question. 'I think it was a sense that if you didn't play the game, you would be undervalued. They would say, "She bought a Fiat Panda . . . how boring."'

I wonder how effective she thinks her report has been. (It was depressing to discover that hardly any of the women I spoke to at Y&R even knew about it. This was soon remedied. An account manager made a bulk order to the IPA.) Has it had any impact on changing attitudes in advertising agencies? 'It has had some tangible results. Many more agencies have introduced formal maternity policies now, which would have been inconceivable three or four years ago,' Baxter says. 'The intangible result is that it has put the issue of women getting promoted and how they are treated at work on the agenda. The IPA now hold seminars on assertiveness for adwomen, which never happened before. A lot of women have said that the mere physical existence of the report means they have something concrete to wave at people, rather than having to fight a personal crusade. It's political with a small p.

'I've also learned a lesson. I've become less militant and more reasonable. It's not as spectacular or as fun, but it gets results.'

It may be that the surest way for a woman to get ahead in advertising is the one over which she has least control. In Marilyn Baxter's curriculum vitae, there is a section on marital status. It reads: 'Divorced 1974. Now living with a very liberated man.' It will take a huge shift in social change before women will have the same advantages in the workplace as their male peers. Baxter's advice is 'Marry the right man.' And who may he be? 'The right man wants his wife to be successful and to move up the ranks of the agency as far as she can go; he is not intimidated by his wife's success (even if it is greater than his); and he does his fair share of the domestic chores and takes his share of responsibility for them. Alas . . . few men really help their women consorts; a good man is hard to find.'

The interview is drawing to a close, and I've discovered plenty of things that Marilyn Baxter doesn't like about advertising. So what does she like about it? 'I was very active in the Labour Party in Lambeth in the 1970s. Many of my friends work for worthwhile causes, in education or for charities. But the problems they deal with are highly intractable. And, paradoxically, they're often awful places to work in. They're back-stabbing, petty and highly political. Advertising may be trivial but what people don't realise is that it is also often intellectually challenging. I like the short-term rewards. The working atmosphere is tremendous: full of amusing, creative, energetic people. I do sometimes think – "Shouldn't I be doing something else?" But I can't imagine another job which would give me such a good time.'

JENNIFER LAING

'I'VE NEVER GONE AROUND
BANGING MY DRUM FOR WOMEN'

Jennifer Laing started her advertising career in 1969. By 1987 she had risen to the rank of joint-chairman of Saatchi & Saatchi, and was known as the Most Powerful Woman in Advertising. At the end of that year she traded in her red Ferrari and position in one of the top agencies to become the first female chief executive officer in the advertising business, with the loss-making Aspect Hill Holliday. In 1990 the agency changed its name to Laing Henry.

What do you expect the Most Powerful Woman in Advertising to look like? Big hair? Power shoulders? A suit in red or black making a bold but sassy I'm-the-Boss statement? Careful make-up and a tight-lipped smile? I must have been watching too many advertisements, for Jennifer Laing, chairman and chief executive of her own agency,

Laing Henry, and formerly joint chairman of Saatchi & Saatchi, is a surprise.

She is wearing what can only be described as a frock, in billowy, pastel-sprigged cotton. Her coiffure, for a woman of 45, is oddly reminiscent of a sixth-form prefect; the shoulder-length black waves held in check by a pair of tortoiseshell combs. Her jewellery is a string of tiny delicate pearls and matching earrings. The look is as far removed from the ET prototype as is possible.

At the end of the interview she presents me with a sheaf of clippings on the inexorable rise of Jennifer Laing. The photographs which accompany the articles don't do her justice. She looks either simpering or earnest and rather plain. Like most people who aren't professional models, her face is more attractive when it is animated. Her brown eyes are larger and more intelligent; her face crinkles in an appealing way when she smiles. Which is often. Sometimes the smile is used as a weapon. It softens her response to questions she finds irritating. Questions like: what do you think of the images of women in advertisements? Are you interested in promoting women? What is your view on working mothers?

Laing's background is in account handling. While her junior micro-miniskirted colleagues may be post-Madonna feminists, Laing is a post-Margaret feminist. Which is to say, like our former Prime Minister, she is not a feminist at all. 'I've never gone around banging my drum for women,' she says. 'I don't see that as my role. It's too difficult trying to build your own career, without trying to take the whole female population with you. I'm doing my bit simply by doing this job.'

She is deeply suspicious of women's lobby groups, or any project which is prefaced by the words 'Women in . . .' That is why she initially declined to be in this book, particularly on discovering that the publisher was Virago. She was persuaded to change her mind on the recommendation of Marilyn Baxter, a friend and former colleague at Saatchis.

Her first job in advertising was with a mid-rank agency, Garland Compton. It was the early-1970s, and Laing played the advertising game by strict adherence to the men's rules. 'You went to the pub and all that. I wasn't very good at it.' It is hard to believe it, looking at her now, but in those days she even dressed like one of the guys in a range of bow-ties and waistcoats. 'You had to act like a man,' she told another interviewer. 'I refused to pour the coffee. I made a point of swearing a lot.'

One of the liberating aspects of being at the top is that, within reason, you can dress and behave how you please. Laing noticed this a long time ago. It is interesting, given her stance on women, that one of the two mentors she cites is female. Ann Burdus was the first female chairman in advertising. She had hired Laing at Garland Compton, before going on to become chairman of McCann Erickson in the 1970s. Laing observed that 'she was always very, very beautifully dressed and feminine'.

The other mentor she mentions is Tim Bell, her former boss at Saatchis. Saatchi & Saatchi bought Garland Compton in the mid-seventies. Bell was so impressed by Laing that he promoted her to full board director almost overnight. (Bell, now Sir Tim, was best known in the 1980s as Thatcher's image-maker. Perhaps his packaging tips rubbed off on his protégée: Laing's personal style has reminded more than one observer of a younger version of the former Prime Minister. But, there again, powerful, right-wing women are always going to remind someone of Margaret Thatcher.)

Laing's strengths are managerial rather than creative, although she would probably describe herself as a creative manager. Others describe her as 'an inspirational team leader', 'a motivator', 'a chivvier', 'very professional', 'a power pitcher', 'a workaholic', 'careful', 'diligent'.

She has certainly been diligent about masterminding her own career. In 1979 she left Saatchi for another agency – Leo Burnett. Two years later she was back at Saatchis, having negotiated an extremely attractive package for herself which included a bright red Ferrari worth £44,000. This Ferrari is something of a legend in the advertising industry. For many ad-people, she will always be Jennifer Red-Ferrari Laing. She says that most women would not have to play her little game today, partly because there are so many more of them in middle management now.

But the early-eighties were the shiny Thatcher years, when status was all, and nowhere more so than in an industry which is dedicated to conspicuous consumption. To anyone who works outside advertising, particularly in the pared-down 1990s, there is something risible, even faintly obscene, about ad-people's totemistic relationship with the Flashy Car. No matter. Laing is no fool. She has nil interest in cars, but knew that if she owned the best one on the block her male peers would be left in no doubt of her value to the agency.

'I wanted to go back to Saatchis and be repositioned in the male culture,' she says. 'I knew that if I had the flashiest, brightest, reddest car available, the men would recognise my status. It was a sort of shorthand. It did really get up their noses because Saatchis was and still is a very male culture. It became an amusing anecdote, especially when they discovered I never got it out of second gear.'

In the 1970s Laing progressed from account handler to team leader to deputy chairman and, finally, in 1987 to joint-chairman. She worked on the Schweppes tonic water account, Nivea (with Adrian Lyne as art director, who later went on to direct 9½ Weeks and Fatal Attraction), Rowntree Mackintosh (Don't Forget the Fruit Gums, Mum; Rolo, Jelly Tots, Quality Street, Fox's Glacier Mints) Campbells Soup, and gas central heating. In 1986, Saatchis won more than £39-million worth of new business. Laing's role in this was significant; she was leader of a successful team on corporate and takeover campaigns. Two of her triumphs were persuading Trusthouse Forte to consolidate its entire £4 million business with the agency, and winning Christie's corporate campaign. She also helped Guinness in the company's successful takeover of Bell's Whisky.

At the end of the following year, after only ten months

as chairwoman, she abandoned the red Ferrari for a more seductive status symbol. She had been offered a job which would make her the only female chief executive officer in the British advertising business. Aspect Hill Holliday was a loss-making company which ranked only 65th in the UK agency league table. She traded a staff of 850 and billings of more than £200 million for Aspect Hill Holliday's 50 staff and accounts worth only £12 million at the time. One former colleague's explanation for Laing's defection was that 'Some people in this life have a drive to get their name on the door.' In 1989 the agency changed its name and personnel to Laing Henry Hill Holliday, and a year later to Laing Henry. Max Henry, Laing's partner, is a creative who is well known for his campaigns for British Telecom (the rhino charging down the corridor), Volkswagen (cars that drop out of the sky), Carlsberg, Skol, Heinz and Kelloggs.

The agency's logo is a black ink drawing of a thoroughbred racehorse. It is an important statement. It suggests old money, breeding, elegance, good taste. It says: we are not one of your flashy, fly-by-night, sexy ad agencies. It works. Laing Henry now has £26-million worth of business. Clients include: the Meat and Livestock Commission (posters feature athletic young men in dayglo colours and the line M EAT TO LIVE); William Grant Whisky (a pair of clubbable gents in silhouette enjoying one another's company and a drink); Anne Diamond's cot death campaign; the Department of Health (repositioning nursing as a career for the nineties by killing off its Florence Nightingale image) and Taylor's Port (small, low-key ads in glossy magazines).

The office is in a converted toffee factory near Euston Station. The décor is understated. The colours are pastel. There are no hard edges, no chrome, no black matt surfaces. The sofas are made out of cane; the fabric is cheerful, not couture. This is what an agency looks like when it starts up in the 1990s. Forget about Ferraris; the board members don't even have company cars. The booze, the lavish entertaining, the general opulent lifestyle is not part of the Laing Henry culture. 'It would cause a lot of aggravation with clients,'

Laing says. 'They'd think, "You're making a lot of money at my expense."' Laing, in turn, restricts client entertaining to a monthly lunch at the agency.

The only extravagant note are the huge vases of flowers. The agency spends £200 a week at the florist's. Laing calls it her indulgence, and then toughens the comment: 'I aim to create a nice environment but it's partly exploitative. We want our staff to come in early and work late, and they're less likely to feel resentful if they're in an attractive office.' There is even a house committee which monitors the staff's more slobbish tendencies and sticks up naff notices in the loo: 'Thou Shalt Treat The Toffee Factory as if it were Thine Own Home', followed by a list of ten commandments.

Laing ushers me into the boardroom, where her assistant has thoughtfully pinned an assortment of the agency's client posters on a partition. But it is Laing, not, her secretary, who pours the coffee now she is the Most Powerful Woman in Advertising. Unlike her friend Marilyn Baxter, Laing believes it is the young 'have-it-all' generation of women in advertising who are out of touch. This view makes her unpopular. She recalls a talk she gave at an IPA meeting: 'I said that it was unrealistic of women to expect to have a happy marriage, well-adjusted children and be a chairman of an agency. I said they should redefine their criterion of success. To be happily married, have a family and be in a senior position – surely that should be enough of an achievement.

'Whew! What a response! I was left in no doubt that there were plenty of women in middle management who believe they can have it all. Perhaps they'll prove me wrong.'

Laing, who chose not to have children because of her career, admits that working mothers have to be ruthlessly efficient. But when I ask her about her agency's maternity policy, she becomes strangely incoherent: 'Er, er . . . we will have, um, well not an extra special one . . .' When I press her on her feelings about this, she replies: 'I hope that we don't have any women who are going to have children. For a smallish company, it's a very real issue. I don't think the law is necessarily that helpful. I can't run this business with part-time account handlers. I'm dreading it happening. I'm talking completely objectively as an employer. But because I'm a woman, people think it's unacceptable to even raise it as an area of concern – when I don't have a solution.'

Perhaps this is why of the agency's seven directors, Laing is the only woman. And why the male/female ratio at Laing Henry reflects the classic industry structure: 50/50 at a junior level; a third women in the middle ranks; not many at all in top management, and no female creatives. She makes no distinction between the way she treats her male and female staff. 'The only thing I would say,' she says, 'is God help anyone who came into work and complained about a period pain. I would not be sympathetic.'

There are several explanations for why women who get to the top, like Jennifer Laing, do not involve themselves in assisting other women. A young adwoman told me: 'Top women can get intoxicated by the uniqueness of their position. They have become so accustomed to finding ways of manipulating men that they can actively impede the progress of other women.' (One senior woman told me that Laing had a reputation among some people in the industry for being outrageously flirtatious with clients: fluttery lashes, sexual innuendo, suggestive body language, the lot. I find this hard to believe, but then I don't get to see her in action.)

Another possibility is that by the time they have got to the top, they may have forgotten the obstacles they encountered on the way up. When I put this question to Laing, she rolls her eyes but still manages to smile: 'I'm sick of being told by women that they're not taken seriously; I'm sick of women banging on about being women. Maybe that is because I've reached this position and I've forgotten the struggles, but I can't see it.'

It seems an appropriate moment to test this theory out. I ask her to recall some of the trickier moments in her career. Has a client ever tried to place her in a compromising position? (I hesitate to use the phrase sexual harassment, for fear of provoking more eye-rolling.) 'Yes. It's one of the pitfalls of the client–agency relationship. Men can ask other men out for dinner, but it can be hazardous for women.' How did she cope? Once she had to get the taxi driver to intervene, and on another occasion she phoned her boyfriend and asked him to drop by the restaurant. In the first instance, the client withdrew his account from the agency. In the second, the agency fired her from the account. How appalling, I say. But Laing is matter-of-fact: 'It was no great tragedy.'

How about the legendary client resistance to dealing with women? Laing does not have to rack her brains to come up with a story to illustrate this point. 'I had to do a presentation to a client who was in the booze industry. At the time, the client had never seen a woman in the boardroom. So I sat outside and had a sandwich with the secretary, while my male colleagues had lunch in the boardroom. I just laughed about it, rather than making an issue. There were quiet conversations at a senior level, and eventually the client changed his point of view. If I had protested, I don't think it would have done my credibility any good.'

The secret of Laing's success lies in the shortcomings of her earlier personal life. She says she is entirely to blame for the collapse of her first marriage. 'My husband used to work for me quite briefly, then he moved to the creative department and we grew apart. Throughout my twenties, I was building my career as an account handler, working long hours, joining every committee, really throwing myself into it. It took up a lot of emotional energy.'

At 30 she was divorced and heartbroken. But that's when her career really took off. At the key time when her peers were investing in their relationships ('Very wisely,' Laing says) and deciding to have children, Laing was spending even more hours at the office. 'The fact that I had no family life was an enormous advantage,' she says. 'It was helpful for a few years, but not to be recommended. You can lose your sense of reality.'

Which is precisely the feeling I have when watching advertisements. At the beginning of our meeting, Laing had said that she had never considered that the image of women in advertisements was an issue. 'I have never come across any campaign in which the subject of women has been mishandled,' she said. When I return to the subject later, she becomes animated, even cross. 'Look,' she says, 'advertising is not about changing attitudes to women. We're in the business of flogging products and services.'

I say I think the female stereotypes are often demeaning or ludicrous. She agrees with me that women have many roles beyond doing the housework, shopping, looking after the children or looking decorative. 'But it is perfectly reasonable to show a woman cleaning the floor, although she shouldn't look like a drudge or a bimbo.' Surely, since so many women do work, the creative whizzes, with their elliptical skills, could incorporate some suggestion of this into the ad. 'What? Put her in a suit with a briefcase, popping back from the office to clean the floor? That's nonsense. Now if you're flogging cars or computers, you can have a woman as the business manager. As long as the overall communication is about the product.' What really seems to worry the highest-flying female in advertising is that 'Increasingly, there are going to be a disproportionate number of women depicted in high-flying roles because of the pressure not to be patronising.'

Jennifer Laing's perky, breakfast DJ voice has become staccato. But something odder is happening. I am distracted from the content of her spirited defence of advertising by a peculiar nervous tic she has appeared to have developed. This most ladylike of women is scratching her arms, the back of her neck, her scalp. Why haven't other interviewers noticed this startling manifestation of neurosis?

It's catching. I start to mirror her actions, but Laing does not notice. She is in full tilt: 'not our job to reposition women ... marketplace dictates attitudes ...' How do you tell the Most Powerful Woman in Advertising that you think her elegant office must harbour a flea or some other parasite?

Somehow I do. Laing looks shocked. 'Oh my God.' Staff are summoned. The interview is over.

Laing manages to make light of it, but all the same in an image-conscious business it doesn't look good. She waves me goodbye with the words, 'This'll look great won't it? Come to Jennifer Laing's agency and get fleas.' Still smiling, but scratching.

M.T. RAINEY

'AWAY FROM ADVERTISING, I'M VERY SHY'

In 1989 M.T. Rainey became the third woman in the United Kingdom to head an agency. The agency was Chiat/Day; its boss was only 34. She started her advertising career as an account handler, but soon discovered that her skills lay in planning. In 1983 she accepted an offer from Jay Chiat, the American advertising guru, to introduce the British-invented discipline of accountplanning to his West Coast operations. The high-point of her career there was launching Macintosh's new Apple computer. Her reward for her successes in America, was the London promotion, and a commensurately hefty salary. In late 1993 she defected to set up her own agency with three colleagues – Rainey Kelly Campbell Roalfe.

Chiat/Day is almost too contemporary for its own good. The avant-garde offices of the international agency are so photogenic that they are more likely to appear in the pages of a glossy architecture magazine than in the advertising trade press.

It is the corporate wisdom of the agency's founder, Jay Chiat, that 'You can't make people do great work. All you can do is create an environment in which they believe they can.' Unconventional architecture and design is a trademark of Chiat/Day offices throughout the world. In Toronto, visitors to the agency are met by a glass-encased lead carp which hovers over a white ceramic bathtub in the reception. In London, where Chiat/Day established itself in the early 1990s, screens of shattered fibreglass conceal the entrance to the boardroom, where clients and the agency conduct meetings in an oval pit.

And just in case the prospective client may have overlooked the fact that Chiat/Day prides itself on being different, he or she will be handed a brochure which resembles something designed by Neville Brody and states:

'If you like large corner offices,
    drinks cabinets, lots of secretaries
        and thick pile carpets,
            you won't like it here.'

The client has been warned. But there is one final surprise in store. For M.T. Rainey, Chiat/Day's chief executive in London, is a woman.

Since M.T. Rainey is late for our interview, I have ample time to accustom myself to her agency's unconventional seating arrangements. The visitor arrives on the tenth floor of a refurbished West End office block and is directed to a colony of velveteen blobs. Perhaps this is a ploy to disconcert the recalcitrant client. It is hard to keep a semblance of dignity when you need every ounce of concentration just to stay upright. The problem with all this wacky design detail is that it tends to eclipse the personnel. I half expect the chief executive to appear in a witty Dadaist statement, a hat in the form of a question mark or a sheath of designer fish scales in tune with Chiat/Day's piscatorial theme. No such luck.

M.T. Rainey may wear designer clothing, but it is more likely to be Donna Karan than Gaultier or Moschino. She has a soft Scottish accent with a trace of mid-Atlantic. She has strawberry-blonde hair and ice-blue eyes. In her last Chiat/Day post in New York, she tells me, people often mistook her for Tina Brown. Since Brown, the former editor of *Vanity Fair* and editorial supremo of the *New Yorker*, is our most glamorous and high-powered media export, this obviously went down well.

When she was younger, M.T. Rainey had an image problem. She moved to America and reinvented herself, changing her name from plain old Mary Thérèse to her present keep-them-guessing prefix, and the problem was solved. 'I've always hated the name Mary Thérèse,' she has said, 'It's just so Irish Catholic.' Rainey was born in 1955 in a town on the banks of Loch Lomond, 20 miles west of Glasgow. Her parents were both schoolteachers and devout Catholics. She was educated at the local convent school. At Glasgow University, she read psychology – an unorthodox but useful training for a career in advertising.

Even as a student in the carefree seventies, Rainey was no slouch. She specialised in signal detection theory, which turns out to be the study of how to maximise people's performance on vigilance tests. Her thesis was published by Nato in 1976 and led to a PhD at Aston University in Birmingham. In 1978 she moved to London and completed her education by taking a master's degree in business.

In the trade press, Rainey's advertising colleagues tend to trot out the same adjectives to describe her: 'smart', 'gritty' and 'determined'. From an early age, she has certainly been focused about her career. Her first job was in the marketing department of IPC Magazines. While flicking through the pages of *Campaign*, she discovered the tantalising world of advertising and targeted the agency Davidson Pearce. She noticed that the agency worked on the publishing account of the *Observer*, and thought she could 'leverage' her own publishing experience to get a job. Oddly enough, the strategy worked. The rest of her story reads like the plot of a blockbuster. This is the modern equivalent of a fairytale. With one important difference: there is no guarantee of a happy ending.

Rainey started in account handling but soon discovered that her real strength was as a planner. 'It's more rewarding than being an account man,' she says, 'because it involves less selling and more problem solving.' Rainey moved to TBWA to work with the three men who would later form Bartle Bogle Hegarty – the hot British agency of the 1980s. John Hegarty, BBH's creative director, told a journalist that Rainey 'loved good advertising and knew how to develop it, instead of doing just good planning. Not all planners are like that.' And, as one industry writer observed, 'Planning is a bit of a female ghetto in Britain . . . it is rarely a springboard to upper management.'

Rainey, as we know, was different. But despite her reputation as one of the best planners in London, Rainey thinks it is unlikely that she would have risen to the top had she remained in Britain to pursue her career. Instead, she accepted Jay Chiat's offer to introduce the British-invented discipline of account planning to his West Coast operations. In 1983 she moved to California, with great expectations and a grand total of 24 pieces of luggage. In Los Angeles and San Francisco she worked closely with clients such as Nike, Macintosh and California Cooler.

Later in the 1980s she was moved to the New York base and promoted to corporate head of planning for Chiat/Day's extended empire in the United States. Part of her role was to develop new business. She worked on pitches for the $35 million New York Life account and the $20 million American Express account. She was known in the industry for her Le Carré-style strategy of developing moles at the offices of prospective clients who would keep her posted on developments.

The high-point of Rainey's career in America was Chiat/Day's advertising campaign to launch Macintosh's new Apple computer. In January 1989 *Advertising Age*, the Bible of the American advertising industry, voted it 'TV Commercial of the Decade'. The ad, which came out in 1984, featured a female athlete who uses a baseball bat to smash the face of an Orwellian Big Brother reflected on to a giant screen. It was made by Ridley Scott, the director of *Alien*, at a cost of half a million dollars.

Rainey puts her particular talent down to her feel for the business. 'I'm very confident about my work. I know instinctively what ads should do and what they should be like. And I can see ideas hidden in haystacks.' As the brains behind the agency, it was Rainey's idea to turn the launch into 'an event of social significance'. She told a journalist that 'the ad was part of a bigger ideological idea of giving computer power to the people'. The slogan read: 'On January 24th, Apple Computer will introduce Macintosh. And you'll see why 1984 won't be like "1984".'

Her thinking clearly paid off. The new Mac was sold out the day after the commercial was screened, and stock was ordered for the next six months. (I could not help noticing, however, that Rainey's contribution to the success of the campaign was not mentioned in the article she gave me from *Advertising Age*. When I ask her why she was excluded, she says: 'It was the first significant example of planning in action in American advertising. It wouldn't have occurred to the journalist to speak to the planner.')

Rainey cites the Apple commercial as an example of the way in which a planner can affect the tone of an advertisement. 'As a planner,' she says, 'there are very subtle ways in which you try to get a ring of truth into advertising.' She felt it was important that the athlete was a woman rather than a man, for instance, and that she should not be a conventional glamour-puss. The model who was eventually picked looks like a cross between Hazel O'Connor and Sigourney Weaver. Like the heroine of *Alien*, the Apple athlete is strong, muscular and makes an impact without using the admen's traditional idea of fragile femininity.

Rainey's contribution to the launch cannot have escaped the attention of her boss. In late 1989 she was offered what she called 'the opportunity of a lifetime'. Jay Chiat wanted her to set up his London headquarters. With her financial package, she bought a Jaguar XJS convertible. Rainey became only the third woman in the United Kingdom to head an agency. She was 34.

When the news of her appointment broke, eyebrows shot up in ad agencies all over town. Many insiders resented the fact that an outsider had been picked for such an influential post. One top executive was quoted in the trade press – anonymously, of course: 'There is not too much good in looking at London as a place that is waiting for the professional expertise of someone from somewhere else. London already has the most sophisticated advertising in the world – what can Chiat/Day offer that we don't already have?'

In 1990 the London office answered the question by picking up £25 million in new business, which included the two £6 million accounts of HMV and Cable and Wireless. This was more than six times the previous year's totals. Rainey's credibility was further enhanced when Chiat/Day won Midland Bank's £13 million account and topped it off with the £6 million account gain of First Direct. Other clients include Ecover (environmentally sound washing powder – recycled black and white ads from the 1960s, with absurdly dated actors and amusing voiceovers); Toshiba; Reebok International and Neutrogena. This last account is an interesting example of the impact top women can make in furthering the careers of their peers. Neutrogena's managing director is a woman. Rainey tells me that the MD specifically chose Chiat/Day because she wanted a senior woman's perspective on her business account.

By the time I started researching this book, almost everyone I contacted in the advertising industry said I should interview M.T. Rainey. She was 'radical', 'different', 'innovative', they said, and 'one of the few Young Turks to make it to the top'. (Rainey herself points out that she was named Advertising Woman of the Year in 1990. It is only later that I discover that the tribute was paid by an American trade magazine, *Adweek*.) But what strikes me most about the Young Turk, when we eventually meet, is her vulnerability about her status.

It is the outward characteristics of Chiat/Day – the office with its blobs and vertigo-inducing colour scheme; its business approach of involving the client in every step of the creative process; its corporate decision to ban all departments and work in multi-functional teams – which are radical, different and innovative. Its chief executive, in contrast, seems almost old-fashioned. It is clear, for instance, that she has not yet come to terms with her high-powered position. But then it is still early days.

'The hardest thing of all is managing people,' she says. 'To deal with conflict and ambition, different ethics, different working patterns. This is a very, very, very difficult job, and I think that it's been made a bit more difficult because I'm a woman. Women are so unused to being given legitimate leadership that it's rather shocking when it happens. It's hard to know how I should behave in the office or how I should present myself. It is not as though I have worked for any women I can imitate. I sometimes wish I wasn't at the very top because it is lonely and isolating and there is so much responsibility.'

Rainey's propensity for public soul-searching may be a legacy of all those years in California, where the natives emote in the same way that the British crack jokes to mask their insecurity. For an interviewer, of course, Rainey's willingness to admit her vulnerability is engaging. It makes her instantly more likeable. Many of her high-powered peers share her anxieties, no doubt, but have learned to bury them over the years. It is rare to glimpse the human being behind the carapace of power. But the danger in her being so open is that I am left wondering about her leadership ability. This seems horribly unfair, but there you go.

When Rainey first arrived back in England, she would tend to deflect questions about chauvinism in advertising. 'I suppose women's liberation and its effects are more apparent in the States, but I don't really think about these things,' she told one interviewer. Six months later, it was a different story. 'I can be the most important, the most committed, the most knowledgeable person in the room [in advertising meetings in Britain],' she told *Adweek*'s London stringer, 'but people will still address their comments to my male colleagues.'

One of Rainey's frustrations is that she has been unable to make an imprint on the sexist culture, even in her own agency. How does she react when her male staff make obnoxious comments about women? 'I've tried saying nothing. I've tried saying, "That's outrageous". And I've tried taking them out to dinner to discuss the matter in a civilised way. But nothing seems to work.'

One can't help but notice, however, that she has not exactly surrounded herself with other senior women. The photographs in Chiat/Day's brochure seem to play on M.T. Rainey's unique female presence: her diminutive form in a zappy designer jacket is flatteringly flanked by five men in suits. The finance director, the business development director, the client services director and the joint creative directors are all men. There are seven male creatives and one female. *Plus ça change* . . . This seems odd since she often makes comments like, 'Women are very rigorous about doing their jobs right. They often outshine their male colleagues.'

When I put this to Rainey, she says that she has employed women in senior positions but they have all left to pursue other options. She doesn't have a mission to help other women along, she adds. Later, she seems to change her mind. She thinks that the culture of the agency would be more dynamic if there were more women around. Next time a job comes up, she says, she would like to appoint a female. 'I want someone near me to whom I feel some personal responsibility,' she says. 'I want a "sister", someone I can relate to. I'd like to see if I was capable of encouraging a younger woman along.' (When we speak again, eight months later, I ask her whether she's appointed her protégée. Well, not exactly. But she's trying. Shortly after the interview, Rainey says, she appointed a woman as the account manager of one of the agency's biggest and most prestigious clients.

Rainey's biggest shock in becoming chief executive was

the extent to which her employees felt that they had to follow her lead. She prefers to work late because she is at her least productive in the mornings. 'I got into a lot of trouble with the men here. Most of them have families and want to leave at seven. Because I am single and childless and they assume I have no outside interests, they thought I was being unfair. But I didn't expect them to follow my work pattern. What is painfully clear – and what women may not realise – is that in the top job you really are expected to lead by example.'

We talk about the negative images that are thrust on to the single career woman in films, in TV series and in advertising. Would the images of women change if there were more key women in her industry? 'The way people respond to an advertisement is completely different to the way they relate to a film,' she replies. 'An advertisement is a sales tool. It's seen as intrinsically manipulative. It's not as simple as replacing one image with another, because the bottom line is that you are trying to sell something.'

And how about real life? How has she managed to balance her personal life with her professional demands? 'I'm particularly sensitive to the image of the single professional woman,' Rainey replies. 'Because it is such a cliché, it's very hard not to feel that people are projecting their values on to you – which may or may not be true. People look at me and say, "The reason why M.T. hasn't married is because she's such a careerist." It's true that I was only 34 when I became chief executive, so I haven't really had the balance of a home life. Also, a lot of my success has been about my willingness to move around, and men won't necessarily follow a woman.

'I honestly think that a lot of men aren't interested in going out with a woman like me. It may be an ego problem or maybe they'd think I'd talk about work all the time. I do have a boyfriend, but he isn't a high-flyer and he works in a completely different industry – which is probably why I find him sexy.

'There is a subtle disapproval directed towards people

who aren't married in this industry. There are very few single men in positions of power. Certainly, the men in my business life have wives who organise all sorts of things that I have to do myself. There is also a sense that it is an impoverished lifestyle, not having a family.

'There have been times when I've worked too hard and been too dependent on work and have not had enough of an existence outside. Away from advertising, you see, I'm very shy. But when I look at my life ... I've lived all over the world, my brain has been engaged, and I have had relationships with some fabulous men. Marriage has always been on the horizon ... It would be horrible to think that there wasn't any hope of it happening. It would be even worse to think that it was God's way of punishing me for having made the choice to be a career woman.'

And on that downbeat note, the interview ends. M.T. Rainey returns to her up-to-the-minute, open-plan console. She has work to do. The End. . . .?

CHRISTINE WALKER
SHE WHO MUST BE OBEYED

Christine Walker is the top media buyer of the top media agency, Zenith, at the toughest end of advertising. Turn on the television or read the newspaper and the chances are that the advertisements you see have been placed by Christine Walker.

When Christine Walker commands, you feel an eerie compulsion to obey. This must explain why, within minutes of walking into her glass-cubicle office, we are crawling around on our hands and knees. Walker has been playing too many party games. Picking up cornflake packets with her teeth. Clenching her buttocks round a coin and dropping it in a jam jar. That sort of thing. Great fun, apparently, but murder on the back. I make the mistake of mentioning some post-labour exercises I found helpful for back pain, and – hey presto – here we are with our bottoms in the air.

I get off lightly. Christine Walker is the top media woman in the top media agency at the toughest end of advertising.

So the stories about her are legion. Like the one about the hapless salesman. Walker negotiated with him till 10p.m. took him home, put him in her spare room, drove him back to her office at 7a.m. the next day, and continued to bargain with him until she got the price she wanted. Or the one about the prospective employer who tried to woo her over tea at the Ritz – 'The red Porsche outside is yours,' he told her, 'if you take the job.' She didn't. Or that she was so involved in setting up her company, Zenith, that she didn't realise she was five months pregnant. And that she was back at work a month after her daughter Jacqueline was born.

Her biscuit-coloured hair is tied back in a loose pony-tail. She is wearing a baggy floral shirt, loose trousers and leather flip-flops. Christine Walker does not look frightening. But then she is probably canny enough to know that it does not pay to intimidate the interviewer.

This is not to say that Walker minces her words. In fact, there's nothing mincing or frilly about her. (It is somewhat disconcerting to discover that her pride and joy is her doll's house. Sky-diving, you would have thought, might be more her line.) She's vulgar. She's ballsy. She's chummy, when it suits. And she can be lethal. A colleague from her first advertising job recalls, 'She was always one of the blokes. She didn't have to be asked down to the pub. She led the way. Later, when she got a bit of power, it was like a tap being turned on – she enjoyed authority.' Another says, 'She's got more bollocks than most departments full of men.' She swears like a trooper, chainsmokes, drinks too much for her own good (she says), spends most evenings with her clients, and if she's at home before midnight, there's something wrong.

Her gung-ho attitude means that, on occasion, she can sound like one of Mike Leigh's female caricatures. If I close my eyes, it is Alison Steadman talking. 'The funny thing about me,' sharp intake of breath as she sucks on a cigarette 'is that I get on very well with male shits. Take Sam Chisolm [the managing director of Sky Television]. He operates through fear. Goes for the jugular. These blokes are just like me. They make quick decisions and don't pussyfoot around.'

In Walker's office there is a low sofa into which the visitor sinks. The chief executive towers above you from behind her large desk. This is all part of the strategy. If you are a male client, and Walker wants to get a spectacularly good deal (which is all the time), you will be seated at a particular angle. When you look up, you will see a giant naked female breast on the wall next door to you. This happens to be an advertisement for breast cancer screening. But it should have the desired effect. You will not know where to look. This places you at a momentary disadvantage, and allows Walker to go in for the kill.

Turn on the television or read the newspaper and, as one journalist put it, the chances are that the advertisements you see have been placed by Christine Walker. Zenith places about 15 per cent of all media time and space in the United Kingdom. Clients include BSkyB; Kraft General Foods (an appointment worth £35 million, and one of Walker's personal coups); British Telecom; Amstrad; Dixon's; Woolworths; Mirror Group Newspapers; Safeways and Mars.

At home, Walker has three TV sets: a Ferguson, an Amstrad and a Sony. She can tell you exactly how much money commercial breaks generate. In 1992, for instance, a 30-second prime-time spot in *Coronation Street* cost a staggering £90,000; the equivalent 'coffee-time' slot on *This Morning* cost £11,000. She explains that TV time is largely sold on a futures market; that airtime buying operates on an auction system; that 47 per cent of British households have two or more televisions and that 52 per cent have a VCR. (In the print medium, as she will tell you, the *News of the World* reaches 850,000 of the prestigious AB readership, which is 514,000 more than the brahmin-business readership of the *Financial Times.*) She compares negotiating with national newspapers to a poker game. 'Will they sell the space to somebody else at a higher price if we hold off? Will they produce a small issue and therefore just sell less space? Will they risk losing our clients' revenue by holding out for a higher price when their competitors are talking to us at the same time?'

Walker knows that the average adult watches about three and a half hours of television each day, and that women watch considerably more TV than men. She also knows that more children watch *Neighbours* and *Coronation Street* than *Disney Club*. She can predict who will watch certain types of programme, when and for how long; which programmes are likely to attract light viewers; when programmes are viewed live, and so on.

But audience patterns are not always so easy to predict. As Walker herself once wrote in a trade magazine, time-buying can be a precarious business. When Channel 4 ran a Hitchcock season, for example, no time-buyer could have anticipated that *Psycho* would be watched by 30 per cent fewer viewers than the much less well-known *Rear Window* and *The Man Who Knew Too Much*. Or that *Land of the Giants* – a 1960s sci-fi soap opera – would attract similar numbers of ABC1 male viewers in Yorkshire as *News at Ten*. Or that when TV-AM showed an endless diet of *Happy Days* and *Batman*, as a result of an industrial dispute male viewing would increase. Walker made the breezy point that, 'A feminist would conclude that men are simply grown-up boys. A time-buyer knows it's true'. This must be about the only occasion when Christine Walker's opinion could be said to coincide with a feminist view.

A young ad-exec. told me that some of the top women in advertising 'get intoxicated by the uniqueness of their position'. She may well have had Christine Walker in mind. I ask Walker whether she feels any obligation to assist other women. 'No!' she says emphatically. 'I find the notion of positive discrimination very distressing. Where on earth does it stop? If two people are coming for the job, why should one be prejudiced against?

'Although they don't say it to my face, I know that women see me as unsympathetic. But I'm not one of those people who play to a political agenda.'

A journalist once asked Walker which living person she most admired. 'Call me unfashionable – Margaret Thatcher' was her reply. Like Jennifer Laing, chief executive of Laing

Henry, Walker believes that she is advancing women's status in advertising simply through her own example. In 1989 she won the Advertising Woman of the Year award. This was presented by Adwomen, the largest advertising women's club in the UK. Perhaps, since there are only a handful of top adwomen, they pass the award on to each other, and then start all over again. Walker would like to be remembered, she says, as an inspiration to women with ambition. Ask her what she considers has been her greatest achievement, and she replies: 'Running a large successful company in an industry dominated by men.'

The media department has traditionally been considered the most chauvinist in the agency. As Marilyn Baxter wrote in her report, 'Media buying calls for aggressive negotiating skills and tends to attract a similar kind of "wheeler-dealer" type that is found in many City institutions. This stereotype is overwhelmingly male.'

The picture, however, is changing. After planning, agency media departments now have the next highest proportion of women. It was 42 per cent in 1989. But it is only recently that women have begun to occupy more senior roles. There are 61 female media people on agency boards and associate boards, and only three female heads of media departments in large agencies. (Eight of Zenith's 22 directors are women – which is not bad going by most ad agency standards.) Increasingly, Baxter observes, the job is seen as more of a 'thinking job' and is beginning to attract the same numbers of women as the planning departments. 'One agency reported that there were so many young women entering media now,' Baxter was told, 'that they were having positively to discriminate in favour of men to maintain a balance.'

Christine Walker joined Benton & Bowles, a large American advertising agency, in 1976, after graduating from Exeter University in English, history and sociology. In those days, the business was completely dominated by men. Did she find that alienating? 'No, I liked it,' she says. 'It was – and still is – a big plus to be a woman because you'll always be remembered if you're only one of a few.'

As a graduate trainee, Walker was rather vague about her job definition. She thought she might write the odd slogan but found herself buying airtime. 'I remember thinking what a strange occupation it was buying *Crossroads* in the morning at £X only to find that by the evening I no longer "owned" it because someone else had outbid me.' (ITV companies had such a monopoly then, she says, that they didn't tell you when your airtime had been pre-empted or moved into a low-rating slot.)

She believes that most women don't get on because they're not prepared to take risks. She has never been one of them. From an early stage in her career, she decided to keep her mouth shut and play the game by her own rules. If she had been caught, she says, she would have been fired. 'My well developed sense of preservation caused me to indulge in the highly dangerous and very secretive pastime of overcommitting clients' budgets in order to calmly take pre-emptions without ever apparently redeploying money. And I quickly learned never to have lunch on a Friday in order to capitalise on the distressed weekend market.'

She also learned to seize the opportunity, whenever it presented itself. In a cut-throat business, she has always had the capacity to out-thrust her senior male colleagues. When her boss went on holiday, she persuaded the agency supremo to let her handle their biggest client, *Maxwell House*, which was a top-ten selling brand. 'When my boss came back,' she says, 'he found that I was still in charge of his account.'

In the mid-1980s B & B merged with another company in America. Four of the original staff, including Walker, broke away and formed Ray Morgan & Partners, which soon established itself as the number two media independent in the UK. Three years later the company was sold to Saatchi & Saatchi for £3 million, and emerged as Zenith Media UK – a wholly owned subsidiary of Saatchis. In 1991 Walker was promoted to chief executive.

'I couldn't say that I've done all this on my own,' Walker says. 'In the 15-odd years I've been in the business, I've worked with an incredibly talented, wonderful man.' She is talking about Zenith's chairman, Derrick Southon, who was her first boss. Walker talks about his amazing work ethic and recalls the time he phoned her at midnight to talk business. 'My husband told him to fuck off – "You can discuss it with her in the morning, Derrick," he said.'

Walker's advice to any woman who wants to get ahead in advertising is, 'Find yourself a male mentor.' Why is this still necessary in the 1990s? 'Because however talented you are as a woman, you can only open so many doors by yourself.' Isn't it about time that women like Christine Walker became mentors themselves? Apparently not. Most women simply don't have the requisite drive to get them to the top. 'I've come across very, very few females who really want to make it,' Walker says, 'who will cancel their weekends, who will stay until midnight, who will say, "I'll put myself in charge". Very few women are prepared to take the ball and run.'

The Walkers' daughter was born on a Saturday night. 'On Monday morning,' Christine Walker recalls, 'Derrick sent me a batch of papers and asked me to sign and return them immediately.' Oh, and by the way, he wrote in a postscript, 'Congratulations'. In the four years since the birth of Zenith, only one middle-management executive has become pregnant. 'She came to talk to me about what she wanted to do. By our standards, we took a generous approach. We said, "Take as much time as you need." Of course I knew that she was such a careerist that she wouldn't take six months. In fact, she came back to work two months after her baby was born.'

Walker's line on maternity provision is much the same as Jennifer Laing's. 'When you're running a company on a bare minimum of people, it's hard to justify being generous. It's very difficult to keep jobs open in a service-based industry in which people are your only assets.' Her general feelings about maternity are prescribed by her own experience. Since she had such an easy pregnancy, Walker is honest enough to admit that she would find it difficult to be sympathetic if one of her female colleagues were less fortunate. 'I think I'd probably be quite harsh. I'd certainly have to be convinced that the woman was genuinely having a bad time.'

What impressed Walker about the way Southon ran B&B was that he ruled his employees with a rod of iron. Walker, one senses, has moulded herself in his image. There is no margin in the streamlined nineties for human error. And Christine Walker has no compunction about penalising employees who slip up. She illustrates the point with a story. One of the female directors drove her company Mercedes without topping up the oil. The repairs cost Zenith in excess of £2,000. 'We took a tough line,' Walker says. 'We told her the money would have to come off her profit share. She has a daughter and has recently become a single parent, so she was mightily pissed off. But why should we have to pay for her incompetence?'

Walker's single-mindedness about her career inevitably impinges on her private life. She has to make a concerted effort, she says, to avoid becoming too one-dimensional. She gave me a copy of a speech she had prepared for an industry awards ceremony; it included a rundown of her personal achievements in 1991. Out of a list of eight, only three related to work. The others were – rather endearingly – along the lines of: 'Helped my 5-year-old daughter, Jacqueline, to do "joined-up writing"'; 'Held four dinner parties at home, a 50 per cent improvement on 1990' and 'Held my marriage together.'

Walker has always been the family breadwinner. Her husband, Robert, used to run a factory which made large dog kennels. She says he has never been as ambitious as her, partly, she supposes, because he came from a wealthier background.

Towards the end of the interview, Christine Walker becomes more reflective. She tells me that her husband has developed a brain tumour. There is no suggestion whatsoever that she is playing for sympathy. In fact, I have the peculiar sensation that she is testing the impact of what she is saying on herself, rather than the interviewer. 'Even when he was in intensive care, I didn't leave work because I thought, "Why should I?" Maybe I'm selfish, but we've always led separate lives. His illness has hardened me, if anything. But when the time comes, I hope my senior colleagues will give me leave of absence.'

BARBARA NOKES
CREATIVE GENIUS

Barbara Nokes is the executive creative director of CME.KHBB; she is the most senior female creative in the advertising industry. Her most controversial advertisement was for Dr Whites, which featured a man dressed in silky underwear with the strap line: HAVE YOU EVER WONDERED HOW MEN WOULD CARRY ON IF THEY HAD PERIODS?

In the reception area at Bartle Bogle Hegarty there is a bank of multiple TV screens. Each screen reflects the same image of a rock 'n' roll dinosaur. It is a heavy-metal hero who jumps around the stage in groin-hugging leggings, flicking sweat on to the female members of his adoring audience. Mercifully, the volume has been turned down. The clients, in their unstructured suits, watch half-heartedly.

The Soho-based agency, with its primary colour columns, TV screens, MTV music videos and high-tech furnishings is the height of eighties fashion. This is appropriate, since the eighties was the decade when BBH established itself as the hottest shop in advertising. Its award-winning Levis commercial was perfectly in tune with the postmodern sensibility. It led to the grand-scale comeback of 501 jeans, and was at the forefront of the Tamla Motown revival. The ad's backing track, the Marvin Gaye classic 'Heard it through the Grapevine', re-entered the Top Twenty. John Hegarty, the creative director, became the industry's answer to the late A.J.P. Taylor and Christopher Ricks. Television producers were thrilled to discover another photogenic pundit, who could pontificate on knotty issues such as 'Whither Advertising?'

I am shepherded downstairs to a smaller, more intimate waiting room, which still offers 1980s-style hospitality: a bottle of New World Chardonnay and plates of designer-twiddled sandwiches. My subject is Barbara Nokes. She is vaguely left-wing, vaguely feminist and vaguely vegetarian. Or so the papers say. One claim they cannot make is that she is vaguely committed to her job.

Nokes is almost as famous as her boss John Hegarty, principally because she is that rare phenomenon: a Top Woman in Advertising. Several months after we meet, in the lukewarm summer of 1992, the headlines changed. She was made executive creative director of CME.KHBB. Barbara Nokes is now *the* top female creative in the industry. Her appointment proved that it is possible for women to rise to the very top even in the male bastion of the creative department.

Vague is not the first word that comes to mind when one meets Barbara Nokes for the first time. Quite the opposite. There is nothing vacillating or equivocating about her. She has a reputation in the industry for being fierce, tough, formidable . . . oh, all the usual adjectives which are foisted on to successful women.

And here are some more. Warren Brown, one of her art directors at BBH, recalled his apprehension in meeting the 'tough lady who could make Margaret Thatcher seem like a Cabbage Patch doll'.

'She has a reputation for eating planners and account

men alive, but she only eats the ones who aren't very good' (John Bartle).

'I wouldn't like to be in the account man's shoes who didn't give Barbara a proper brief' (Suzie Henry, copywriter).

There is a story about an account director who presented Nokes with a brief and the words: 'I don't know much about this but I have written it anyway.' Her reaction was to stare at him and ask him to repeat what he had just said.

Barbara Nokes is a clever woman. I suspect that she actively encourages the circulation of these stories. In the boys' own club of the advertising world, it is useful to be known as a woman who is not easily intimidated. Only a masochist would ask Nokes what colour knickers she wears.

The favourite term is: 'she does not suffer fools gladly'. As the journalist Martin Wroe observed in an interview with Nokes he wrote for *Campaign*, 'This exact phrase was volunteered by more than two-thirds of the people interviewed for this article. And Nokes herself, no obedient slave of statistics, followed this one, and used the phrase of herself.'

Nokes eventually arrives with a grin and an apology. Her art director has been working long hours and she wanted to buy him a drink. Champagne, as it happens, in a wine bar – since Nokes loathes pubs. She has spiky hair and an attractive, piquant face. She is dressed in cleverly understated clothes. The only extravagant detail is a brace of born-again-sixties silver medallions and a crucifix. It is a genuine surprise to discover that she is 50.

Barbara Nokes's manner is genial and accommodating. She is given to expressing herself in pithy, epigrammatic sayings, which may be a legacy of all those years inventing spot-on slogans for commercials. She agrees that it is unusual in any industry, let alone advertising, for women to rise to the top and bring up a family, as she has done. 'When a man works 15 hours a day, he gets the support of his family,' she quips. 'When a woman works 15 hours a day, she gets divorced' – a phrase which has an awful ring about it in the light of future events.

It is her voice, oddly enough, which can make her seem distant. At times, it sounds clipped and even stilted. More often there is a certain languorous hauteur about its tone, which gives the impression that she can hardly be bothered to answer a question. She also has a disconcerting habit of pausing – just long enough – to make the interviewer feel uncomfortable. One has to fight the urge to fill the gap by prattling on.

Nokes fell into advertising when she was in her late twenties. Unlike the Laings and Raineys of the ad-world, Nokes seems to have been almost haphazard in her ambition. Or perhaps it would be more accurate to say that she has made the conscious decision to mould her career rather than let it mould her. When her two children were young, for instance, she was offered a number of creative directorships and turned them down. 'I just didn't think I could handle that,' she says. 'There are only 24 hours in a day.'

Her ability to rise to the very top, but only on her own terms, makes Nokes a particularly fitting role model for the new generation of women entering advertising. Certainly, what strikes me most about the young women I interview across the media is the equal intensity of their ambition and their concern that professional success will not preclude them from having children – and enjoying them. As Jennifer Laing observed at her IPA seminar, the women steering their upward path through middle management are convinced that they can Have It All. Barbara Nokes is their talisman.

There were no early warning signs that she would grow up to be an exceptional professional. Her teens and twenties represented a series of escapes from tedium. She won prizes for writing at school, but discovered make-up and high heels at 14 and walked out. She got a job with the English Guernsey Cattle Society by lying about her age, and walked out of that too, when she discovered that office junior work was 'as boring as school'. It was the first of eight jobs in two years.

At 15, she was working as a secretary for a knitwear manufacturer and her design for a hotwater-bottle cover appeared in the *Daily Express*. Her Hollywood script break came later, when she was working as a secretary in the creative department of G.S. Royds. As she tells the story, the whole creative department of the agency was off sick and the client wanted an ad there and then. 'I said, "What do you want?" and it was a trade ad for Mum Rolette, so I did it myself and it ran. [Mum Rolette Sales Go Up with the Temperature] When the creatives came back they were all very encouraging and asked if I wanted to do a bit more of this . . . so I did a bit of both for a while.'

But, unlike a Hollywood script, Nokes did not have a meteoric rise. She worked for a series of different agencies where her writing talent became submerged in the bureaucracy. Her career only took off when Roger Nokes, the man who was to become her second husband, introduced her to the agency Doyle Dane Bernbach (which is now called BMP DDB Needham).

It was at Doyle Dane Bernbach that Nokes developed her distinctive approach to writing ads. She is known for her combination of risk-taking and exhaustive personal research. While other creatives rely on market research, Nokes prefers to carry out her own idiosyncratic investigations. Nokes once talked to a production-line worker in a china factory whose job it was to smash sub-standard plates. He told her that there was no difference in the quality of china, which was not always reflected in the price. This conversation led to her slogan: 'Before you choose the pattern, choose the china.' 'Barbara just keeps digging deeper and deeper until she finds what she's looking for,' Warren Brown says. 'She doesn't spend her day dreaming up wacky ideas, but delving into the product.'

Nokes first made an impact at DDB with her work for Volkswagen ('You're in this cell for your own protection') by reversing the received opinion that only large cars can be sold on the safety angle. It was her idea to turn the car upside down; her account manager said he thought the client would call it vandalistic. He was wrong. Volkswagen went even further, and suggested the car should be bashed at both ends to reinforce the point.

As Nokes's reputation grew, so did the job offers. She defected to Collett Dickenson Pearce where she was appointed creative group head, and was lured back to DDB where in her last three years she was deputy creative director with a seat on the board. Along the way, she was instrumental in advancing the careers of other talented female creatives. She hired the late Lynda McDonnell and Suzie Henry. (She has rehired Henry at KHBB.) This is not to say that she is in favour of positive discrimination. Nokes may call herself 'a feminist, of sorts', but she is not easy to pigeonhole. 'I can't claim that I would positively appoint a woman over a man,' she says. 'But I wouldn't do it the other way round, which is what usually happens.'

It was around this time that Nokes, like her high-flying peer Suzie Henry, decided to have a family. 'The beginning of the end for many successful career women,' as one writer put it, 'of the career, that is.' Well, not in this case. Nokes turned down the creative directorships, but became a shareholder and founder member of Bartle Bogle Hegarty in 1982.

And so to the famous Levis commercial. For those who may have forgotten this seminal slice of advertising, it featured a bare-chested James Dean lookalike who whips off his 501s in a 1960s laundromat. Barbara Nokes, who co-wrote it with John Hegarty, based the storyline on an incident she had stored in her memory bank. In 1976 she was doing a wash at her local launderette on a Sunday morning when a labourer came in, stripped off his jeans, stuck them in the machine, and casually sat down in his underpants. 'I stared at him and thought, "One day I'll use that."'

She was also responsible for the casting. This conjures up the splendid vision of Nokes in her director's chair auditioning hundreds of young men in their underpants. It is a strangely satisfying image, precisely because it is such a reversal of the norm. But this is where the differences end. For Nokes's significant contribution to the ad, it strikes me, is invariably eclipsed by that of her male colleagues. (It is the account man Tim Lindsay, after all, who is known as Mr Levis.)

It is a point that has been put to Nokes before. Her contribution to the rise of BBH in the eighties, it has been argued, has been overshadowed by the presence of BBH's creative director, John Hegarty. When Martin Wroe asked Nokes to comment on this, her response was magnanimous: 'I couldn't think of a better shadow to be in,' she said. 'John has become a marvellous public face not just for the agency but also for the industry. If you're going to be in a shadow, this is the one.' Nokes, you notice, does not refute the allegations.

There has been only one advertisement in Nokes's career which she has persistently cited as an example of the female sensibility at work. It is the ad everyone mentions in the same breath as her name, and has almost the same legendary status in the business as Jennifer Laing's red Ferrari. It took Barbara Nokes no less than 18 months of haggling to persuade the client, Dr Whites, to go with her campaign. The poster featured a man in silky camiknickers and bra, clutching his head, with the now famous line: HAVE YOU EVER WONDERED HOW MEN WOULD CARRY ON IF THEY HAD PERIODS? It won several awards. But Nokes was even more gratified when the young women readers of *Mizz* magazine, a sort of junior *Cosmopolitan*, voted it ad of the month. Making an impact on the consumer, in her book, has always carried more weight than impressing her peers.

The Dr Whites campaign is the most flamboyant example of the woman behind the ad. But there are other examples in Nokes's portfolio where, it seems to me, it makes a difference that there was a woman behind the ad. Sometimes they are a neat inversion of clichés from the male world. Like her controversial slogan for the 1987 launch of the short-lived leftish tabloid, *News on Sunday*: 'No tits, but a lot of balls.'

Sometimes they go straight for the emotional jugular. The BT campaign is a perfect example of Nokes's greedy magpie imagination and shows that, on occasion, her personal research need go no further than her office. Charlie Robertson, BBH's former head of research, told Nokes that his daughter had sketched her family for a teacher but had left daddy out. Nokes, it is said, pounced on the story 'like a pirhana'. It hardly needed a rewrite. The ad shows a child's drawing of his family *(sans* daddy) and the strap-line: 'If your five-year-old son were asked to draw a picture of his family, would you be in it?' The text underneath read: 'I was really choked. He gave it to me at breakfast one Saturday. Really proud of it, he was. There was his mother, his big sister and him. I just wasn't in the picture.' Gulp. It must have had absentee fathers picking up the phone all over the country.

Roger Nokes felt compelled to do more than pick up the phone. When we speak, he is in his fourth month of being a house-husband. As soon as Mrs Nokes was appointed creative director of KHBB, with a commensurately hefty salary, Mr Nokes resigned from his job as director at McCann-Erickson (the agency which invented the Gold Blend soap opera). The couple are looking upon the role change as an experiment. He is finding it trickier than he anticipated. 'It's the business of not having your own money,' he explains. 'To have to ask for it, which is effectively what you're doing, makes you feel very vulnerable.' Never mind. There's probably an ad campaign in there somewhere. *Circa* 2001.

In 1985 Barbara Nokes dreamt up a commercial for the Audi-Quatro 4-Wheel Drive. The rugged car is driven very fast, with great expertise, over a treacherous terrain. The driver is – how shocking – a sharply dressed woman. Nokes says, proudly, this was the first car ad which didn't show the female driver picking up the household shopping or the kids from school. Her comment underlines the divide between the ad-maker and this consumer. It seems slightly woeful to me that a woman of Nokes's calibre considered this ad a breakthrough. From my vantage-point, she should be berating the ad industry for taking so long to respond to reality.

Nokes has heard the criticism before. When she was interviewed by Jenni Murray for *Woman's Hour*, Murray objected to the ending of the Audi commercial. The woman passes her mobile phone over to the pilot of a glider which is circling her car. 'Roger, it's your mother on the phone,' she says. In the final frame, the intrepid female driver is reduced to the stereotype of secretary or wife. But Nokes says that the idea of advertising being used to advance the cause of women 'seems morally wrong to me. To do advertising really well you must be right up with the changes in society, not at the forefront. You only have 30 seconds to make your point. You have to use stereotypes. You have to have a shorthand.'

Most people seem to grow more conservative as they grow older. In some respects, Nokes appears to be reversing the trend. For years, she turned down the invitations to join the elitist adwomen's club WACL (Women's Advertising Club of London). Six months before we meet, she changed her mind. She has found all the support from other women quite nice, actually. 'I've enjoyed getting the phone calls and lunch invitations. It's a new feeling to sense that people are on your side, because you're another woman.'

Nokes does not see herself as a female pioneer. But she is, simply by being one of the first high-powered women in advertising to combine a family life with work. She was responsible for introducing maternity provision at BBH, and is a solid if discreet champion of her junior working mother colleagues. At the end of our interview she introduces me to her lunch pack. Its members are three young women in their early thirties, who are pushing to work part-time so that they can see more of their children. Nokes is offering advice and support, and assisting them in their negotiations.

We are discussing tactics. 'It's no good moaning and complaining,' Nokes says. 'Women have to be cleverer than that. The big difference between women and men is that women seem to have four things going on in their head at one time. Men are more one-track-minded, which is maybe why they're more successful. There's a lot of time wasted in meetings. So I use them to write my lists to organise dinner parties, holidays, shopping, school runs and so on. It's always assumed that I'm diligently taking notes.

'As a working mother, you are always vulnerable to the received notion that "Oh, she'll be off as soon as her son has broken his leg." And, of course, you will. But if you lie and say that you have an appointment with the builder or you have to take the car to the garage, that's more acceptable. So

I do. It could be said that by lying I'm simply pandering to male prejudice as opposed to furthering the cause of working mothers. But I'm a very practical person. And I make no apologies for it.'

When Nokes finally decided to escape from John Hegarty's shadow in 1992, she did not have a job lined up. She fancied a sabbatical, she said. When we last spoke, before her appointment at CME.KHBB, she had completed an interior design course, a screenwriting course and a computer literacy course. She had also rediscovered her children, Luke and Daisy. (Daisy's middle name is Lysistrata, after Aristophanes' heroine, an Ancient Greek peace activist, who organised the women in her village to withhold sexual favours until their men stopped fighting.)

Barbara Nokes's story is a rare example of how a female creative can succeed in advertising without going to the pub. But then, Barbara Nokes is a rare woman altogether.

CONCLUSION

At the beginning of 1994 I was working on the final draft of *The Executive Tart* – the culmination of two years' research and interviewing.

The statistics showed unequivocally that women were not getting their fair share of the top jobs in the media, but – maybe – perhaps – it was just possible that, by concentrating on such specific issues, my own media lens had become distorted. My fears, in the event, proved groundless.

On 29 January *The Times* magazine's cover story was an interview with Norman Lamont. It was newsworthy because the former Chancellor of the Exchequer's description of the Prime Minister as 'weak and hopeless', over lunch at a West End restaurant with the *Times* journalist, coincided precisely with John Major's very public attempt to reassert his leadership. To use newspaper parlance, this was a story with 'legs'; one that ran and ran. The interview was rehashed and raked over not just for its political dimensions, but as a dramatic event in itself. Every single reference to the *Times* article mentioned the gender of the journalist. Ginny

Dougary, I was astonished to read, had 'pretty curves', and was a 'flame-haired', 'alluring' temptress who had enticed poor, helpless Norman into a 'tender-trap' using those shameless, age-old feminine wiles. Dougary had even, or so I read, 'won Norman's heart'. Ah, of course, that must be why she got a good interview.

What symmetry! For a journalist writing a book that explores the insidious way in which women are mythologised and diminished by the media, to find herself transformed into a ridiculous stereotype – a killer bimbo and a tart *or* a harpie and a harridan – by her own Fleet Street colleagues. It offered a fascinating, if unappetising, insight into how these myths are created, and the enthusiasm of newspaper editors to present what they know is distortion as reality.

As the weeks went by 'The Lamont Affair', or 'Lunchgate', as it became known, moved upmarket from the tabloid comics to the more influential newspapers. And this was the most worrying aspect of the coverage. For it was here – at what is supposed to be the responsible end of Fleet Street – that the nastiest, most personal attacks appeared, culminating in a column by David Mellor in the *Guardian*. This is what he wrote:

> Norman Lamont is not the only one to have been *propositioned* by Ginny Dougary. [My italics. He is referring to a request from my editor for an interview.] ... To cut a long story short, I said no ... I'm off profiles ... Why not wait for the Last Judgement to get your come-uppance. Why let some judgmental harpy conduct a dress rehearsal for you years ahead of time.
>
> Take the erstwhile doyenne of the profiles industry, Lynn Barber. She's a sabre-toothed old harridan who by the look of her has lived a bit, and none too wisely either ... In a rational world you wouldn't want her in the same town as you, let alone the same room.
>
> Now along comes Dougary, the sorceress's apprentice, an antipodean secretary and mother of two who

has gone down in the world as well as across it to develop her new career profiling British politicians . . .

Quite what it is in Ms Dougary's CV that qualifies her for all this advanced superciliousness is beyond me. But I'm steering clear of her, and I suspect after this, even old Norman will too.

The column was flagged on the front page of the newspaper, under the heading 'Who Needs Old Harridans?' It was, in the opinion of the paper's editors, something to whet the reader's appetite. I must thank David Mellor, and the *Guardian* who employ the disgraced Tory minister as their arts columnist, for reassuring me that this book is necessary. And for providing me with such a perfect ending.

EPILOGUE

Linda Agran

In mid-1994 *The Diaries of Samuel Pepys*, Linda Agran's pet project, with Kenneth Branagh as star and director, was in development with the BBC.

Lynn Barber

In March 1994, Lynn Barber was a columnist with the *Sunday Times* and an interviewer with *Vanity Fair*. She was also writing a book on the Royal Family for Viking publishers, to be published in early 1995.

Marilyn Baxter

In March 1994, Baxter and her partner, Martin Smith, had just left the Galapagos Islands and were sailing towards the Marquesas. They are due back in England in December 1994.

Antonia Bird

In 1994, Antonia Bird was hired by Touchstone Pictures in Hollywood to direct a feature film called *Mad Love*, a psychological love story, scripted by a British writer, Paula Milne, and starring Drew Barrymore. It is due for release at Christmas 1994.

Louise Chunn

In March 1994, Louise Chunn was in her fifth year of editing *Guardian* Women and had launched a bi-annual colour magazine for the newspaper called *Madame Figaro*/the *Guardian* in October 1993.

Sue Douglas

In January 1994, Sue Douglas and her partner, Dr Niall Ferguson, the historian and *Daily Telegraph* columnist, had a baby son, Felix. In April 1994, she was back at the *Sunday Times* as executive editor.

Liz Forgan

In March 1994, Liz Forgan was still at the BBC as Managing Director of Network Radio.

Phillippa Giles

Her latest project is *The Buccaneers*, adapted from Edith Wharton's novel. The five-part series for BBC1 will be screened in early 1995.

Linda Kelsey

In March 1994, Linda Kelsey was still editing *She* magazine.

Beeban Kidron

She is working for Steven Spielberg's company, Amblin, in Hollywood, on a 'major motion picture' called *To Wong Fu* starring Wesley Snipes and Robert Downie Jnr. It will be released in 1995.

Jennifer Laing

In October 1993, Laing Henry acquired the advertising agency Alliance London from Lopex PLC, as well as winning other new business. New clients include: Twinings, British Coal, Vauxhall and New Zealand Tourism. The agency now has £35 million worth of new billings. Jennifer Laing's long term companion, Tony Dalton, who is also in advertising is now a non-executive director of her agency.

Verity Lambert

Cinema Verity started filming Lynda La Plante's third series of *Widows* – *She's Out* – in mid-1994. To be transmitted on ITV in 1995.

Tim Lindsay

Joined Lowe Howard-Spink in February 1994 as managing director; his colleague at Young & Rubicam, Jerry Judge, also joined Lowes as chief executive. In January 1994, Lindsay's divorce was finalised.

Terry Mansfield

In March 1993, Terry Mansfield was appointed to the board of directors of the Hearst Corporation in America. He was the first non-American to join the board since the company started 106 years ago.

Barbara Nokes

Has been the executive director of CME.KHBB since January 1993. Her most successful campaign at the agency has been her work for Pernod, featuring Graham Rawle's artwork and the dropped 'D'. In March 1994, she was in the process of organising an amicable divorce from her husband, Roger.

Eve Pollard

In September 1993, Eve Pollard launched the *Sunday Express* Section 3. In 1994, it won a top award for best colour supplement in Europe.

M.T. Rainey

In the few months following the setting up of the new agency in late 1993, Rainey Kelly Campbell Roalfe attracted major blue-chip clients such as BT, Virgin Atlantic and Emap. In March 1994, the agency was working on a new television campaign for Virgin Atlantic featuring Terence Stamp.

Brenda Reid

In January 1994, Anglia Television no longer had a Head of Drama. Brenda Reid was appointed one of the station's six independent drama producers with a development deal to make films and series throughout Britain and Europe. She remains an extremely active chairwoman of the increasingly political Women in Film and Television organisation.

Yvonne Roberts

Her first novel, *Every Woman Deserves An Adventure: The Tales of a Female Would-be Casanova*, was published in 1994 by Macmillan London.

Andreas Whittam Smith

In March 1994, Andreas Whittam Smith was still editor of the *Independent*, the newspaper he co-founded in 1986. His consortium bid for control of the paper, involving a partnership with the Mirror Group Newspapers, was secured in the same month.

Janet Street-Porter

In January 1994, Janet Street-Porter was appointed Head of Independent Productions for the Entertainment Group. She is responsible for the commissioning of independent entertainment programmes across all genres for BBC1 and BBC2. In the same month, her production *The Vampyr*, won the classical music programme of the year award at the inaugural Classical Music Awards. In March 1994, she was made a fellow of the Royal Television Society.

Christine Walker

At the end of 1993, Walker was appointed a governor of the National Film and Television School. In the same year she expanded her management responsibilities at Zenith by becoming a director of two of Saatchi's subsidiary companies, Meridian Outdoor Advertising Ltd and Acme Media.

Index

Acker, Kathy, 13
ACTT, 40
Advertising Age, 215
Advertising Association, 172
advertising industry, 167–240
Advertising Standards Authority
(ASA), 175–6, 178
Adwomen, 189, 225
Agran, Linda, 4, 26, 73–82, 245
Amiel, Barbara, 138
Amis, Kingsley, 53
Anglia Television, xii, 20, 81
Antonioni, Michelangelo, 92
appearance, personal, 136–9,
185–6, 197–8
Appleyard, Christina, 111
Arena, 110
Armstrong, Fiona, 9
Arnold, Eve, 40
Aspect Hill Holliday, 201,
205

Aspel, Michael, 50
assertiveness, 199
Associated Newspapers, 144,
148
Aston University, 176

Bailey, Eric, 164
Balhetchet, Sophie, 11
Banks Huggins O'Shea, 174
Barber, Lynn, xv, 100, 102–3,
111, 112, 114–15, 121–9,
242, 245
Barnes, Philip, 170–1
Barron, Janet, 10–11
Barrymore, Drew, 246
Bartle, John, 233
Bartle Bogle Hegarty, 184, 214,
231–3, 236–40
Bates, Kathy, 41
Bauwens, Mona, 103
Baxter, Marilyn, xv, 171–2, 177,

181–2, 186, 188, 189, 191–200, 202, 225, 245
Bazal Productions, 6
BBC, xi, xii, xiii, xv, 4–8, 9, 19–20, 29–31, 50–5, 68–9, 74, 84–91, 93–4
BBC Wales, 53
Beauman, Peter, 164
Beckett, Barbara, 173
Bell, Tim, 203
Beloff, Dr Halla, 105
Bennett, Alan, 59
Benton & Bowles (B & B), 225–6, 228
Berlin Film Festival, 45–6
Bernstein, Sidney, 28
Bigelow, Kathryn, 42
Bird, Antonia, 11, 12–13, 57–63, 246
Birt, John, xi, 7, 74, 80, 86, 90
Black, Helen Anty, 8
Blackeyes, 13–14
Blake, Juliet, 3
Blanford, Linda, 66
Bleasdale, Alan, 25
Blonstein, Laurence, 28
BMP DDB Needham, 235
Bogdanov, Michael, 59
Border Television, 20
Bowden, Sylvia, 29
Bown, Jane, 137
Boycott, Rosie, 153
Bragg, Melvyn, 11, 13, 51, 121, 123
Branagh, Kenneth, 81, 245
Brides, 156
British Code of Advertising Practice, 177
British Society of Magazine Editors, 160
Broadcasting Bill, 70

Broadcasting Standards Council, 70, 176
Broadcasting Union, 5
Broadside, 69
Broke, Richard, 55
Brown, Andrew, 33
Brown, Maggie, 72
Brown, Tina, 138, 213
Brown, Warren, 232–3, 235
Browne, Coral, 34
Bryden, Bill, 55
BSB Dorland, 173, 178, 182
BT, 237–8
Bucksey, Colin, 34, 35
bullying, 145–7
Burchill, Julie, 123, 144
Burdus, Ann, 203
Bush Theatre, 59
Butler, Alison, 189
Byrne, John, 82

Calderwood, Andrea, 55
Caleb, Ruth, 53–4
Callaghan, Brigid, 115
Cameron, James, 110
Campaign, 178, 213
Campbell, Beatrix, 111
Campbell–Hill, Corin, 54
Carlton Television, 20
Carry Greenham Home, 39, 40, 45
Cartwright, Jim, 40
censorship, 70
Central Television, 20
Channel 4, 20, 68–9, 70–2, 224
Channel Television, 20
Chapman, Patsy, 96, 138
Cheetham, Nikki, 6
Chiat, Jay, 211, 212, 214, 216
Chiat/Day, 211–13, 214–20
children, 49–50, 234; childcare,

72; combining with work, 44–6, 53–4, 239–40; maternity leave, 154–5, 199, 206–7, 227–8; motherhood, 163–4; pregnancy, 153, 154–5, 162, 227–8; success and childlessness, 4, 62–3
Chisholm, Sam, 222–3
Christie, Agatha, 80
Christie's, 204
Christmas, Linda, 110
Chunn, Louise, 104–5, 106–7, 108, 109, 110–11, 246
Cinema Verity, xii, 23–6, 28, 34
City University (London), 6
Clare, Professor Anthony, 127
Clarissa, 10
Cleese, John, 34
Clement, Dick, 60
Clifton, Rita, 196
Cole, George, 34
Coleman, Terry, 127–8
Coleridge, Nicholas, 156
Coles, Joanna, 112
Collett Dickenson Pearce, 236
Coltrane, Robbie, 82
Columbia Pictures, 76
Company, 152, 160
complaints, advertising, 175–6, 178
Condé Nast, 156
Connolly, Ray, 127
Conran, Shirley, 93
consumers, 169
Cook, Sue, 7
Cooke, Alistair, 124
Cosmopolitan, 152, 157, 159–60, 161, 162
Cowgill, Bryan, 33
Cox, Brian, 53

Cracknell, Andrew, 178, 182
Crimewatch, 6
Crisp, Quentin, 32
Cvitanovich, Frank, 87

Dacre, Paul, 145
Daily Express, 119–20
Daily Mail, 93, 108, 111, 118, 141, 143, 144–8, 163–4, 165
Daily Mirror, 10, 118, 134
Daily Star, 120
Daily Telegraph, 97, 98, 111, 115, 116–17
Daley, Janet, 112
Dally, Emma, 161
Dalton, Tony, 247
D'Argy Smith, Marcelle, 152, 160, 162
Datar, Rajan, 85
Davidson Pearce, 213–14
Davies, Andrew, 16, 53
Davis, Anita, 181
Day-Lewis, Sean, 80
De Caunes, Antoine, 85
De Vine, Magenta, 85
DEF II, 85
Dejevsky, Mary, 111
Dempsey, Rita, 180–1
Dineen, Molly, 44–5
Director of Public Prosecutions, xii
discrimination, positive, 68, 74, 224, 236
Dispatches, 70
Dr Whites, 170–1, 195, 231, 237
Dr Who, 30–1
Douglas, Kirk, 122
Douglas, Sue, 95, 115, 141–9, 246
Doyle Dane Bernbach, 235–6

Dunaway, Faye, 31
Dyke, Greg, xi, 8, 74

EastEnders, 59
Edinburgh International Film
    Festival, 62
Elle, 104, 156
Elliott, Nick, 81
Elliott, Tony, 87, 93
EMAP Women's Group, 156
Enfield, Harry, 183
English, Sir David, 141, 144–7,
    165
eroticism 14–17
Esquire, 110, 163
Essentials, 162
Euston Films, 33, 75, 76–7, 78,
    80, 81
Evans, Kim, 93–4
Evening Standard, 66–7, 87, 93,
    105, 115, 119
Everywoman, 106
Executive Tart stereotype,
    xii–xiii, 168–9, 173,
    179–80, 187, 190
Express Newspapers, 135

Faith, Adam, 31
Fallacci, Orianna, 127
Family Planning Association,
    113
Farmer, Elaine, 158
Fatal Inversion, 16, 62
Fellini, Federico, 14
The Female Advantage, 178
feminism, 104–9, 139
Ferguson, Dr Niall, 246
Financial Times, 111, 117, 223
Finch, Nigel, 87
Fletcher, Winston, 189–9
flexible working hours, 153–4

Ford, Anna, 5, 7, 17
Forgan, Liz, 26, 65–72, 139, 246
Forsyth, Bill, 34
Forte Hotels, 173
Fox, Edward, 32
Franks, Lynne, 87, 92
Frayn, Michael, 34
French and Saunders, 3
Full Stretch, 60, 61

Garland Compton, 203
Garnett, Tony, 29
Gaultier, Jean-Paul, 85
GBH, 24–5
gender convergence, 110
Gibson, Mel, 123
Gilbert, Sally, 155
Giles, Phillippa, 16–17, 42, 43,
    46, 49–53, 55, 62, 246
Gillen, Aidan, 62
Gilliam, Terry, 92–3
Glancey, Jonathan, 179
glass ceiling, 81
GMTV, 8–9, 20
Good Housekeeping, 154, 159,
    162
Goodman, Maggie, 92, 159
Gough, Piers, 91
Grade, Michael, 17, 18, 70, 74
Grampian Television, 20
Granada Television, 20, 28
Grandfield Rork, 193
Greer, Germaine, 13–14
Griffiths, Trevor, 33
Grove, Valerie, 125, 128
Guardian, 66, 67, 68, 70, 98,
    100–1, 104–9, 110–11, 112,
    113, 116, 143, 242–3
Guccione, Bob, 125
Guha, Sankha, 85
Guinness, 204

Habitat, 195
Hampstead and Highgate Express, 66
Hardie, Kate, 58, 62
Harpers & Queen, 165
Harris, Richard, 122
Haslam, Carol, 5
Hastings, Max, 97
Hayman, Sheila, 137, 138
Hearst Corporation, 163
Hegarty, John, 214, 232, 236, 237, 240
Heller, Zoë, 86, 88
Hellings, Sarah, 44
Hello!, 159
Heng, Cathy, 180
Hennes, 175
Henry, Georgina, 107
Henry, Max, 205
Henry, Suzie, 180, 233, 236
Henry, Wendy, 96
Herself Reappraised, 175–6
Hewland, Jane, 87
Homes and Gardens, 152
Honey, 131, 134
Hopkirk, Joyce, 134, 159, 163, 164
Howell, Jane, 28, 29
Howell, Liz, 9
Howell Henry Chaldecott Lury, 183
HQ, 14
HTV Wales, 20
Hurt, John, 32

IBA, 69, 78
image, 136–9, 197–8
Independent, 44, 72, 98–100, 102–3, 111–12, 113, 116, 124, 126, 154, 195
Independent on Sunday, xv, 88, 100, 116, 121–2, 123, 126, 160–1
Independent Television Commission (ITC), 178
Ingrams, Richard, 128
Inside London, 66
Institute of Practitioners in Advertising (IPA), 169, 171–2, 177, 186, 189–90, 191, 199
interviews, newspaper, 127–9
IPC Magazines, 152, 161, 213
Irons, Jeremy, 122
Irving, David, 142
Irwin-Brown, Anne, 173, 178
Isaacs, Jeremy, 32, 33, 65, 69, 70
ITN, 20
ITV, 176, 226

Jack, Ian, 126
Jackson, Michael, 93
Jackson, Penny, 99
Janes, Hilly, 115
Jenkins, Simon, 114
job-sharing, 154
Judge, Jerry, 184, 247
Just 17, 156

Kahan, Marcy, 41
Kelsey, Linda, 151, 152–4, 155, 157–66, 247
Kendall, Canna, 182–3
Kendrick, Kiki, 180
Kennedy, Jackie, 134
Kidron, Beeban, xvi, 16, 39–47, 247
Killer Bimbos on Fleet Street!, xiii, 137
Kotcheff, Ted, 28, 29

La Frenais, Ian, 60

La Plante, Lynda, 53, 73, 77–8, 246
Labour Party, 63, 200
Laing, Jennifer, xv, 169, 196, 199, 201–10, 225, 234, 247
Laing Henry, 201, 205–10
Lambert, Angela, 111
Lambert, Verity, xii, xv–xvi, 4, 11, 23–37, 50, 52, 73, 76–7, 78, 246
Lamont, Norman, 241–2
Lamson, Laura, 11
Lansing, Sherry, 34
Large, Ali, 173
Le Carré, John, 127
leader writers, 100
Leapman, Michael, 140
Leavitt, David, 53
Leo Burnett, 203
lesbianism, 15
Levis, 236–7
Lewis, Rita, 156
Liddiment, David, 94
Lindsay, Tim, 184, 187–8, 237, 247
Lipman, Maureen, 17
Lloyd, Innes, 59
Lloyd, Sir Nick, 133, 134
London Business School, 8
London Weekend Television (LWT), xii, 8, 17, 21, 31, 32, 75, 80–1, 82
London's Burning, 80, 82
The Look, 86
Lowry, Suzanne, 110
Lumley, Joanna, 29
Lunghi, Cherie, xii
Lurie, Alison, 179
Lury, Adam, 198
Lwin, Anabella, 143

Lyndon, Neil, 107
Lyne, Adrian, 204

McCann Erickson, 193, 203, 238
Macdonald, Gus, 81
McDonnell, Lynda, 236
McGowan, Frankie, 92
MacGraw, Ali, 124
MccGwire, Scarlett, 113
Macintosh computers, 215
Mackenzie, Craig, 132
MacKenzie, Suzie, 31
MacLaine, Shirley, 39, 41
Maclaren, Malcolm, 143
McSharry, Deirdre, 159
MacTaggart, James, 29
magazines, 151–66
Magee, Bryan, 107
Mail on Sunday, 118–19, 134, 135, 141, 143–5
Major, John, 101, 241
Major, Norma, 124
Mansfield, Terry, 152, 153, 154, 155, 161–2, 163, 247
Marie Claire, 152
Marks, Nadia, 163, 166
Marschner, Heinrich, 86
Marshall, Penny, 42
Martyn, Shona, 14
Massiter, Cathy, 69
Mastroianni, Marcello, 39, 41
maternity leave, 154–5, 199, 206–7, 227–8
Matheson, Margaret, 51, 55
Mathew, Mike, 152
Maxwell, Margaret, 111
Maxwell, Robert, 96
Mellor, David, 242–3
The Men's Room, 11, 62
mentors, 227
Meridian Broadcasting, 21, 60

MI5, xii
MI5's Official Secrets, 69
Miles, Sarah, 122, 124
Miller, Sharon, 45
Mills, Liz, 6
Milne, Claudia, 69
Milne, Paula, 246
Minder, 33, 77
Mirror Group, 97
Mizz, 152, 237
Moir, James, 94
Moore, Suzanne, 111–12
More!, 156
Mortimer, John, 32
motherhood *see* children
Muir, Kate, 135
Mullholland, Clare, 78
Murdoch, Rupert, 96, 148
Murray, Jenni, 238–9

National Magazines, 151, 152–5,
    157–66
National Union of Journalists
    (NUJ), 115, 155
Neeson, Liam, 53
Neil, Andrew, 136, 142, 148
Neill, Sam, 24
Network 7, 85
New Woman, 156, 162
Newman, Sydney, 29–30, 31,
    33, 35
News Limited, 96
News on Sunday, 237
News of the World, 96, 119,
    134, 141, 143, 223
newspaper advertising, 223–4
Newspaper Press Fund, 134
Newspaper Publishing PLC, 155
newspapers, 95–149
Nicolson, Harold, 15
Nighy, Bill, 62, 63

Niven, David Jnr, 75, 76
Nokes, Barbara, xv, 170–1, 177,
    180, 186, 193, 195, 231–40,
    247–8
Nokes, Roger, 235, 238, 248
Norman, Philip, 107
Notman, Gaynor, 173, 181
Notman Parminter, 173–4, 178

Oakley, Ann, 11
Observer, xiii, 98, 101–2,
    113–14, 116, 134, 137, 214
O'Hagan, Kitty, 174
O'Kelly, Lisa, 173
Opportunity 2000, xii, 101
Options, 152, 161
Oranges Are Not the Only Fruit,
    15, 16–17, 41, 50
O'Sullivan, Sally, 161
Oulton, Caroline, 52, 55, 59
Owen, Clive, 40
Oxo commercials, 174–5, 177

Ps and Qs, 86
Palin, Michael, 25
Paramount, 75, 76
Paravision UK, 75, 77, 81, 82
Parminter, Gail, 173–4, 181
Parris, Matthew, 108–9
Partridge, Murray, 183
Paterson, Stuart, 178
Penthouse, xv, 100, 125, 174
The People, 96, 118
Periodical Publishers
    Association, 160
Petticoat, 92–3, 134
Phipps, Sue, 172–3, 175, 176
Pinter, Harold, 30
Pitt-Kethley, Fiona, 114–15, 124
Platell, Amanda, 97
Polan, Brenda, 104

Pollard, Eve, xiii, 92, 96, 97, 131–40, 248
Pope, Angela, 53
Portrait of a Marriage, 15
positive discrimination, 68, 74, 224, 236
Potter, Dennis, 13–14, 29, 34, 104
Powell, Jonathan, 87, 91
power, 4, 32, 172, 196, 204
pregnancy, 153, 154–5, 162, 227–8
Prima, 162
Private Eye, 100–1, 122, 133, 138
Producer's Choice, 90
Punch, 158
Purves, Libby, 158
Pusey, Karen, 157

Queen, 93
Question Time, 99

Radio 5, 72
Radion, 177–8
Rainey, M.T., xv, 169, 186, 211–20, 248
Rainey Kelly Campbell Roalfe, 211
Rank Xerox, 187
Raven, Simon, 32
Rawle, Graham, 248
Ray Morgan & Partners, 226
Reay, Carol, 169, 186
Redgrave, Lynn, 45
Redway, G.A.C., 76
Rees-Mogg, Lord, 10, 11, 17, 70
Reeves, Saskia, 41
Reid, Brenda, 1, 17–19, 248
Rendell, Ruth, 50

Rhys Jones, Griff, 34
Richardson, Amanda, 40
Richardson, Miranda, 53
Richardson, Samuel, 10
Richman, Stella, 31, 33
Richmond, Susannah, 182
Right to Reply, 69
Roberts, Michael, 92–3
Roberts, Yvonne, 101–2, 111, 113–14, 248
Robertson, Charlie, 238
Roddick, Anita, 124
Roedean, 27
role models, 4, 66, 76, 234
Rook, Jean, 96
Rosenthal, Jack, 32, 80, 82
Ross, Tessa, 55
Rowe, Bridget, 96, 138
Royds, G.S., 235
Rushdie, Salman, 79
Russell, Jenni, 5
Russell, Ken, 122

S4C, 20
Saatchi & Saatchi, 171–2, 191–2, 193–7, 201, 203–5, 226–7
Sackville-West, Vita, 15
Safe, 62
Sands, Sarah, 115
sanitary products, advertising, 170–1, 178, 237
Saunders, Kate, 104, 105
Savile, Jimmy, 122
Schepsi, Fred, 24
Schuman, Howard, 32, 33
Schwarzenegger, Arnold, 123
Scorah, Kay, 173
Scott, Ridley, 215
Scott, Sandy, 79

Scottish Television, 21
Sessions, John, 82
Setting Up Home, 156
sex: eroticism, 14–17; in newspapers, 113; nude scenes, 16, 62; sexual harassment, 198, 207–8; on television, 10–11
She, 151, 152, 154, 157–9, 160, 161, 162, 163–6
Shulman, Alexandra, 161
Siann, Dr Gerda, 105
Simmonds, Posy, 66
Sissons, Peter, 99
Slater, Richard, 33–4
Slaughter, Audrey, 92
Smith, Andreas Whittam, 98–100, 102–3, 110, 124, 135, 154, 160, 248–9
Smith, Joan, 105
Smith, Julia, 59
Smith, Martin, 245
Smith, Mel, 34
Souter, Fenella, 14
Southon, Derrick, 227, 228
Staunton, Imelda, 41
Stephen, Jaci, 2
stereotypes, 12–13, 60–2, 242; Executive Tart, xii–xiii, 168–9, 173, 179–80, 187, 190; television advertising, 170, 174–8, 179–80, 192, 209, 239
Steven, Stewart, 143
Stock, Francine, 5
Stoddart, Christopher, 8–9
Streep, Meryl, 24
Street-Porter, Janet, xii, 3, 4–5, 7, 83–94, 249
Street-Porter, Tim, 87, 93
Style Trial, 86

Suchet, David, 80
Summers, Anne, 174
Sun, 86, 119
Sunday Express, xiii, 96, 97, 100, 120, 123, 125, 131–6, 140
Sunday Mirror, xiii, 96, 118, 131, 134
Sunday People, 134
Sunday Telegraph, 117
Sunday Times, 115, 117, 121, 129, 135, 139, 141–2, 144, 148–9
Sweeny, John, 137–8

Tabac, Maxine, 195–6
Tatler, 156, 161, 165
Taverne, Suzanna, 154–5
Taylor, Alex, 180
Taylor, Jane, 111
TBWA, 214
TBWA HKR, 183
television, 1–94
television advertising, 169, 170, 174–8, 179–80, 192, 209, 223–4, 239
Tennant, Neil, 89
Thames Television, 31–3, 76–7
Thatcher, Margaret, 26, 202, 203, 225
Theatre Upstairs, 59
Thomas, David, 158
Thorn EMI Screen Entertainment, 33–4
Time Out, 93
Time to Dance, A, 11, 13
Times, The, 70, 98, 100, 111, 112, 114, 115, 117, 140, 162–3, 241–2
Today, 119
tokenism, 111

Toksvig, Sandy, 15–16, 17
Toscani, Oliviero, 158
Toynbee, Polly, 66
Trood, Kennith, 29
Trusthouse Forte, 204
TV-AM, 134, 137, 224
Tweedie, Jill, 66, 104, 105, 110
20/20 Vision, 69
Tyne Tees Television, 21

Ulster Television, 21
Used People, 39, 41

Vampyr, The, 86, 87, 91
Vanity Fair, 121, 123, 126, 129, 161
Vine, Barbara, 16, 50
Vogue, 156, 161
voiceovers, television advertising, 176–7

Wadley, Veronica, 95, 97–8, 115
Walker, Christine, xv, 221–9, 249
Wallace, Marjorie, 54
Walsh, Noelle, 154
Walter, Harriet, 11, 62, 63
Warner Brothers, 75, 76
Waterhouse, Keith, 31
Waterman, Dennis, 34
Wax, Ruby, 3

Wearing, Michael, 51, 52
Weldon, Fay, 135
Wesley, Mary, 11
Westcountry Television, 21
Whilley, Chris, 8
Whiston, Liz, 183
Whitehouse, Mary, 10–11
Widows, 73, 77–8
William Morris Agency, 75, 76
Wilson, A.N., 127
Winterson, Jeanette, 15, 16, 41, 42
Woman's Hour, 238–9
Woman's Journal, 152
Women in Film and Television, 17–19
Women's Advertising Club of London (WACL), 189, 239
women's magazines, 151–66
Women's Weekly, 152
Wood, Victoria, 50
Woods, Vicki, 165
Wroe, Martin, 233, 237

Yentob, Alan, 51, 87, 90–1, 93
Yorkshire Television, 21
You magazine, 134, 148
Young & Rubicam (Y&R), 184–8, 199

Zenith, 221–5, 226–9
Zest, 162